CEMETERY PROTECTIONS IN URBAN ENVIRONMENTS

Cemetery Protections in Urban Environments

Archaeology, Preservation, and the Law

Ryan M. Seidemann

UNIVERSITY OF FLORIDA PRESS
Gainesville

Cover: Painting by Elizabeth Seidemann.

Published in the United States of America

30 29 28 27 26 25 6 5 4 3 2 1

A record of cataloging-in-publication information is available from the Library of Congress.
ISBN: 978-1-68340-510-8
DOI: https://doi.org/10.5744/9781683405108

UF PRESS
UNIVERSITY OF FLORIDA

University of Florida Press
2046 NE Waldo Road
Suite 2100
Gainesville, FL 32609
http://upress.ufl.edu

GPSR EU Authorized Representative: Mare Nostrum Group B.V., Mauritskade 21D, 1091 GC Amsterdam, The Netherlands, gpsr@mare-nostrum.co.uk

For Ericka, Elizabeth, and Michael

In memory of Michael F. Seidemann, PhD, and Glen H. Doran, PhD

CONTENTS

FIGURES

TABLES

PREFACE

Many parts of this book were not easy for me to write. As someone who was trained and educated in many ways by the intellectual descendants of the physical anthropology of generations ago, I have increasingly found myself at odds with my own education and training. This problem seems to be increasingly common in anthropology (e.g., Clancy 2023:8–9). However, as someone fascinated by the intellectual tradition of anthropology, I also recognize that history as no longer tenable.

As many other anthropologists have done in recent years, I take aim at the giants of our profession. I critique the lasting legacy of those individuals through the lens of modern anthropology and modern morals and ethics. I recognize the hypocrisy of this analysis. These people worked and lived by different morals and standards than we do today. Moreover, it is unquestionable that these people sowed the seeds of what would become a holistic understanding of our shared past and present and a recognition and embracing of the things that make us different and diverse.

However, it is through just such a lens, from the point of view of the descendants of those who were mistreated by our profession and contemporary norms of decorum, that we have to view the founders of anthropology today. Simply, many of the things that were done in the name of anthropology were and are hurtful. This is a past that we have inherited and with which we must now reckon.

I take no delight in these critiques and, if control of the world and people's feelings were left to me, everyone would share in my continuous wonder at the things that can be learned about the past and present, especially from the study of human skeletal remains. I know that the world does not, on the whole, view this research in this way anymore, nor should it. In fact, as readers will learn in the pages of this book, this critical, modern examination of historic anthropological practices has actually resulted in many valuable changes that affect both descendant communities and anthropologists.

In my professional position, I sit at the nexus between a hurtful history and a hopeful future when dealing with descendants of enslaved and Indigenous peoples whose ancestors' remains I and those critiqued in this book have analyzed. The outgrowth of this hurtful history and this difficult intellectual past with which we now reckon has resulted in great strides toward both the preservation of archaeological and historic sites and the creation of present-day agency for those minority groups who have long been oppressed. This manuscript twists and turns through often shocking case studies, accounts of historic treatment of both underprivileged and privileged groups' mortal remains, and legal and archaeological analyses of where this history has led us today and how we can use what we have learned as a means for collaboration and site protection in the future. Thus, while difficult to write and difficult to admit to myself, I am fully convinced of the moral and methodological correctness of the ongoing changes in anthropology to which I hope this volume contributes.

While it pains me to harshly critique many of the past practices of my chosen profession, it is a lens that continuously needs to be reapplied to the profession. My observations regarding those among the profession today who would place science and scientific inquiry above human rights go to the crux of the difficulty that I find here. While I never advocate the elevation of religion over science, I absolutely advocate the elevation of human rights over science. As anthropologists, we cannot be the heirs to the legacies of those scientists who in the nineteenth and twentieth centuries would ignore human rights and cause human suffering as reasonable means to the ends of advancing scientific inquiry.

I share in the shock and horror of the descendant communities whose ancestors' remains have been shown to have been treated as pawns in these inquiries. It is a matter of simple human rights. Human rights cannot be factored out of any equation involving scientific inquiry, lest we repeat the Nazi experiments on the Jews (my ancestors), the American experiments on the African American community of Tuskegee, Alabama, or the scientific misuse of the Havasupai people's blood samples in Arizona. As professional anthropologists, we must be better than that and I believe that we are.

This volume recounts terrible historical events. It also challenges modern arguments that advance scientific inquiry above human rights. More than that, though, this volume examines the disparate treatment of the remains and final resting places of the underprivileged. Although news reports inform us that these hurtful actions still occur, I hope that the reader takes from this volume a sense of hope for the future regarding respect for the preservation of historic and prehistoric sites and for the ethical treatment of human remains. More importantly, I hope that this volume helps, in some small part, to educate readers about the harms of these past and present actions for the descendants of people whose human remains have been subjected to scientific inquiry and to the destruction of their final resting places. In many ways, as vague and tenuous as they may be, the connections that these descendants feel to these remains and sites are all that remains of much of their history, and we, as anthropologists, owe these living people a commitment to ethical treatment and site protection.

ACKNOWLEDGMENTS

Thanks are due to all my former and present research partners, mentors, and colleagues who have, whether intentionally or not, facilitated the research that is the subject matter of this book or have helped me to hone my research and writing skills over the years, as well as to those who have endured my endless discussions of cemetery-related matters. Specifically, I would like to extend my gratitude to my doctoral committee members D. Ryan Gray, David Gladstone, and Charles Chamberlain III. Thanks are also due to the following (in no particular order) who have influenced my thinking and research over the years and who have provided moral support through this process: Christopher Stojanowski, Glen Doran, James Wilkins, Christine Halling, Kenneth Kleinpeter, Lucy McCann, Chip McGimsey, and Arbie Goings. My gratitude is also due to Mary Puckett and the staff of the University Press of Florida for seeing this book through to conclusion and to Lauren Sieg and an anonymous peer reviewer. This book also would not have been possible without the interaction with and information from countless people whose stories are told in the vignettes of this volume and who, for reasons of privacy and sensitivity, are not directly identified here. I acknowledge the high threshold of intellectual and educational standards set (and, at least for my early degrees, financial support provided) by my parents, Michael F. and Diane M. Seidemann, as well as the emotional support of my sister, Erin. Finally, and most importantly, this book, and indeed, everything in my life is made possible through the love and support of my wife, Ericka, and my children, Elizabeth and Michael. I have done this work for them, and they have allowed me to do it by extending patience, warmth, and love for the entire process. Thanks to you all.

1

Introduction

In 2010, the Louisiana Department of Justice (LDOJ) received frantic calls alleging that a white male had destroyed an African American cemetery in Bossier Parish, Louisiana. Bossier Parish, one of the suburban areas of Shreveport, and indeed, all of Louisiana, has historically suffered racial violence of some kind (Fairclough 1999; Wilkerson 2010). However, much of this violence—whether direct in the form of Jim Crow (Wilkerson 2010) or indirect/structural (Bullard 2000)—has, or at least is thought so, avoided desecration of minority dead. Thus, these allegations seemed suspect at first. In addition, the alleged location of the cemetery was not reflected on official documents or maps. Nonetheless, especially with African American cemeteries that originated as the burial places of the enslaved, this lack of documentation is all too common. The complainants and their extended families revealed, through numerous interviews, that the site, despite its absence on any official documents, had once been the location of the Palestine Baptist Church and its associated churchyard cemetery (Seidemann and Halling 2023). The congregation had relocated sometime in the early 1990s, leaving the church to be inhabited by a congregant and her daughter.

The alleged church and cemetery site, located in the hamlet of Haughton, is now situated in a residential, predominantly white neighborhood. Interviews with the cemetery's neighbors supported the oral histories collected from the descendants, with at least one resident recounting playing hide-and-seek with friends among the tombstones as a child.

Through subsequent cooperation with the Bossier Parish Sheriff's Office, a suspect, Sidney Jetton, was brought in for questioning. During this questioning, Jetton told police that he wanted to own land that was near the Haynesville Shale active natural gas production field in north Louisiana. He had identified some property that he figured no one would ever complain about if he acquired it through squatter's rights: an abandoned African American church. Throughout all police interviews and later questioning during civil disputes, Jetton readily admitted to occupying the church property, but vehemently denied destroying or desecrating any graves. Indeed, he continuously maintained that he was never aware of a cemetery at the location. Nonetheless, the weight of the circumstantial evidence from descendant and neighbor testimony, along with the appearance of anomalies suspiciously resembling grave markers on historical photographs taken for the nearby construction of Interstate 20, undermined Jetton's credibility.

In the late 1990s, the church had burned down. According to the descendants, the cemetery located around the original church remained after the structure burned. The descendants initiated their complaint against Mr. Jetton, when, on a series of successive trips to the cemetery to visit the graves of relatives, they noticed the landscape changes and the missing grave markers. Although Mr. Jetton denied the existence of the cemetery and claimed never to have seen grave markers when he was clearing the land, he did admit to bulldozing the entire area formerly occupied by some trees and the church (figure 1.1) and its environs in order to level the land for his future occupation.

If the neighbors and descendants were to be believed, all of the aboveground evidence of the cemetery, mostly tombstones, was wiped from its original location never to be found again. There is no evidence that Mr. Jetton ever impacted subsurface burials during these efforts. However, he admitted to having some 300 dump truck loads of dirt deposited on the site to level the ground and to cover any existing surface obstructions.

After being accused of desecration and being brought to police headquarters for questioning, Mr. Jetton became enraged. When neighbors to the land contradicted Jetton's statements to law enforcement about the cemetery and his knowledge of it, he threatened them against testifying, leading to his arrest for threatening witnesses. The district attorney never brought charges for witness tampering in a criminal investigation. Indeed, Jetton never faced any criminal charges for his actions, presumably due to disinterest by the district attorney and a lack of definitive evidence of the alleged desecration.

In Louisiana, as in most U.S. jurisdictions, district attorneys hold primary criminal jurisdiction, and the state attorneys general cannot unilaterally supersede these local politicians to prosecute criminal cases. Although Louisiana's attorney general, as with others around the United States, does possess secondary criminal jurisdiction, the exercise of this jurisdiction occurs only at the invitation or recusal of the local district attorney. Neither occurred here. Thus, in this matter, the role of the Attorney General's Office was in the capacity of counsel to the Louisiana Division of Archaeology for enforcement of civil rights and penalties for violations of the state's unmarked burials act.[1]

Figure 1.1. Standing in the approximate location of the former church and cemetery, facing westward toward adjacent property during the initial site visit. Photograph by the author.

During subsequent efforts by LDOJ to build a civil case under the Louisiana Unmarked Human Burial Sites Preservation Act ("Unmarked Burials Act"), archaeological probing and coring revealed evidence of the presence of a burned structure on the property. This finding supported the oral history obtained from the descendant community, but the cemetery's presence proved elusive. None of the archaeological testing, historical records research, or aerial photography could definitively verify the cemetery's existence on the property around the known burned structure. Nonetheless, oral testimony from the descendant community vividly reconstructed the presence of graves—including even the names of many of those buried at the site—around the former church structure (Seidemann and Halling 2023).

Ultimately, the State of Louisiana filed a civil action that resulted in Mr. Jetton being evicted from the property. However, due to evidentiary shortcomings and procedural difficulties with the court, little else was able to be proven to the necessary legal standards to make a meaningful case against Mr. Jetton.[2] Moreover, the laws intended to prevent cemetery damage proved to still place burdens on the state and on the descendant community that were insurmountable to effectively accomplish any sort of restitution or restoration when presented in a litigious setting. This lack of restitution or restoration meant that the descendants could never be made whole in this matter. Their cemetery, though the bodies likely were sealed in place, had been erased from the landscape. Nothing short of a full archaeological excavation of the entire impacted area would ever be able to locate the covered graves, and no funding existed for this sort of work. Discovery revealed that the accused had no money to fund those excavations. Because this property is private land, constitutional prohibitions restricted the use of public funds to restore the cemetery.

Through discussions with the families and the descendants of those buried at this cemetery, the disparate treatment of marginalized peoples, in this case African Americans, clearly underscored Mr. Jetton's use of this location for his land acquisition plans—a disenfranchised group lacked the agency to oppose his actions and he thought that he could proceed without fear of recourse. The occurrence of such a situation in the recent past—during a time in which substantial legal protections ostensibly exist to stop such actions from occurring—was both surprising and disturbing. Although well-intentioned, these laws fell far short of their intended purpose. Their purported purpose is to protect all peoples from having the graves of their loved ones destroyed by disproportionate treatment, by unknowing development, or by simple desecration.

Today the Palestine Church and cemetery site is protected as an archaeological site, and the rough boundaries of the cemetery are recorded for future protection. Hearteningly, these efforts by the descendants, LDOJ, and the Bossier Parish Sheriff's Office have led to the protection of this site. Several years after the institution of legal action against Mr. Jetton, state and local officials planning the widening of a nearby road specifically altered their designs to provide a wide berth for the boundaries of the suspected cemetery. Disappointingly, the only permanent memorialization that now exists for this cemetery is a minimal cenotaph (figure 1.2) to those who are buried at this site as recollected by the descendants.

This story is all too common—not just in Louisiana, but around the United States and likely the world. Since the close of this case, Louisiana legislators have enacted multiple additional laws, not necessarily as a result of the failures of this case, but simply to mitigate and avoid the possibility of such problems occurring again. The Palestine Church case illustrates a historic (and to some extent, modern) problem or contradiction: that cemeteries are spaces set apart from other landscape features in a de jure sense, yet those de jure aspirations are often inadequate to protect those sites. While cemetery site

Figure 1.2. Cenotaph at the location of the cemetery allegedly damaged by Mr. Jetton. This memorial was paid for and erected by Mr. Jetton as a term of the settlement of the civil lawsuit against him. Photograph by the author.

damage and destruction will always occur, the Palestine Church case is emblematic of a need to critically examine the existing protections for these sites to evaluate what is and what is not working to protect them.

The Palestine Church Cemetery situation is emblematic of a nationwide (and perhaps worldwide) situation in which threats of and the actual destruction of cemeteries occur with regularity. "As a field that studies the materiality of past behaviors, archaeology has an important role to play in preserving the sepulchral artifacts associated with burial grounds" (Rainville 2009:197). While, as Rainville (2009:197) notes, archaeology has a crucial role to play in the preservation of sites that she describes as "sacred sites . . . that document the struggles and successes of . . . communit[ies]," archaeology cannot solve all the problems that threaten these sites. Indeed, though archaeology has evolved into a much more activist field that advocates for social and environmental justice, this activism and advocacy cannot occur in a vacuum. Archaeologists can only protect what the law allows us to protect. Activists are similarly limited by legal strictures. While lawyers and lawmakers are also limited, they can provide both archaeologists and activists with guidance regarding common and antiquated preservation mechanisms and they (particularly lawmakers) can also work to change the law. Thus, for the protection of cemetery sites, all three of these fields are interrelated: archaeology informs the legal and activist world about the presence of threatened sites and the impacts to those sites under certain circumstances; activists provide archaeologists and legal actors the optical visibility of such threats and often collaborate with and provide agency to the descendant communities necessary to affect change; lawyers and lawmakers provide archaeologists and activists with the standing to protect cemeteries (lawmakers) and the muscle to accomplish that protection (lawyers). The symbiosis of these three fields cannot be understated in the preservation of our cultural heritage, especially for the protection of "deathscapes." This book reviews the interactions of archaeology, law, and activism to create a synthesis of action, research, fieldwork, and legal theory and action to provide a roadmap for the protection of cemeteries under existing legal regimes as well as proposals for future protections.

What Is a Cemetery?

To fully appreciate the focus of this book, understanding what constitutes a cemetery is crucial. Differing definitions of a cemetery exist both among various scholarly fields (e.g., Rugg 2000; cf. Nance 1999:41) and among various legal jurisdictions (e.g., La. R.S. 8:1[7]; cf. Ala. St. § 27–17[A]-2[12]).[3] On balance, Louisiana's definition of "cemetery" is among the most inclusive legal definitions in the United States and is the one used here. Louisiana defines, in La. R.S. 8:1(7), a cemetery as

> a place used or intended to be used for the interment of the human dead. It includes a burial park, for earth interments; or a mausoleum, for vault or crypt interments; or a columbarium, or scattering garden, for cinerary interments; or a combination of one or more of these.

While this definition appears only to apply to modern burial practices as evidenced by the nonexclusive list of examples, a concise reading demonstrates the flexibility of the law to encompass modern elite burial practices, country churchyards, enslaved peoples' burial grounds, and the myriad of Indigenous disposition methods from around the world. The key to interpreting the definition is by understanding that the actual description of a cemetery is only the first sentence: "a place used or intended to be used for the interment of the human dead" [La. R.S. 8:1(7)]. This sentence indicates several things: (1) intent is a component of defining property as a cemetery, thus excluding disaster, massacre, and homicide sites from the definition;[4] (2) land need not be actually used as a cemetery to be classified as a cemetery;[5] and (3) that cemeteries afforded legal protection are only those in which human remains are interred.[6] The second sentence of the above definition is merely an illustrative list. It does not exclude the spaces of air or sky burials practiced by certain Native American, Buddhist, or Zoroastrian groups (Iserson 1993). The definition does not exclude mound burials such as those in Crooks Mound in Louisiana (Weinstein et al. 2004), in which various types of inhumation occurred (entombing, interring, and temporary or partial burials), or the mortuary pond at the Windover site in Florida (Doran 2002), in which bodies were staked to the bottom of a peat bog. The definition does not exclude intentional ossuaries such as those used by the Iroquois for the interment of entire communities (E. Seidemann 1999); secondary burials of the Plains Indians (Snortland 1994); or burials by the Maya below the floors of their habitations (R. Seidemann 1999). In other words, the broadness of the first sentence of the Louisiana definition of a cemetery is flexible enough to include every permutation of the postmortem treatment of human remains with the exception of mass fatalities, disasters, homicides, and body donations.

This definition contemplates the intentional interment, inurnment, or placement of human remains for the purposes of final disposition. Louisiana Revised Statute 8:1(2), defines "burial" as "the *placement* of human remains in a grave" (emphasis added). The use of the term "placement" connotes an intentional act and not a disastrous or malicious cause. Moreover, the definition of "interment," a key component of the definition of "cemetery," which is "the disposition of human remains by inurnment, scattering, entombment, or burial in a place used or intended to be used, and dedicated, for cemetery purposes" [La. R.S. 8:1(26)], is also exclusive of such actions as the discard of the remains of crime victims and the death situs of disaster victims. Thus, for the purposes of this book, and also for the purposes of ensuring that laws expansively protect human burial sites, the Louisiana law quoted above constitutes the operative definition of a cemetery.

As noted by Miller and Rivera (2006:334), "whether the bodies of the deceased are placed in the ground, within elaborate tombs, or simply in the presence of ancient or contemporary monuments, their location holds symbolic meaning as well as practical historical meaning for the surrounding living community." It is difficult to deny the unique nature of cemeteries (Foucault 1986; Sheppard-Simms 2016; Sloane 2018), and, because of their connections to the grieving process and the historical nature of a particular place (Silverman 2002), impacts to these spaces that erase them from the landscape clearly have an effect on the descendant community.

Cemeteries under the Law

Throughout history, various cultures have afforded a special status for the resting places of the dead and have mandated the protection of such sites through the law. However, archaeological evidence has recently demonstrated substantial deviations in practice (de facto) from these legal ideals (de jure) that often appear to occur along class and racial lines (Godzinski et al. 2008; Hahn and McCarthy 2012; Hahn et al. 2017; Smith and Stone 2014).

Moreover, cemeteries, both in urban and rural settings, are constantly under threat of damage and destruction from multiple causes (Seidemann 2013; Joiner and Seidemann 2019a, 2019b; Lemke 2020). Individual impacts such as desecration of graves occur regularly, and they are often hurtful to the living family of those whose graves are affected (Seidemann and Halling 2019). However, beyond anecdotal evidence of individual desecration events, little understanding exists of the dynamics of what causes and who authorizes such destruction that results in an entire cemetery's erasure from the landscape. In many cases, such complete erasure of cemeteries is an institutionally sanctioned occurrence. Occasionally, such erasures are not just institutionally sanctioned or a result of institutional ambivalence; rather, they are overt efforts to attack memory and culture (Amanat 2012; Dasgupta 2015:194–195). New Orleans presents a unique laboratory for analyzing cemetery destruction, as recent archaeological excavations in the city have revealed both sanctioned and unsanctioned examples of cemetery destruction. Although much of the focus of this volume is on Louisiana, as is discussed throughout, the lessons learned in that area are often applicable elsewhere.

Recent years have seen sweeping changes to the way in which human remains and burial places are treated under the law, at least in the United States. No debate exists that, historically, human remains and cemetery sites, especially those of the underprivileged, were relegated to the status of curiosities (human remains) (Harrison 2014; Murray and Brucker 1982) and nuisances (cemeteries) (Johnson 2006). The curiosity aspect of human remains later, in some cases, morphed, in the mid- to late nineteenth century, into scientific inquiry that formed the basis of the area of study known as physical anthropology.[7] Nonetheless, many such remains continued (as they do today) to be mere curios for the public (Jarus 2020). The cemeteries, especially in urban areas, began as nuisances because, as they filled and were poorly tended, they often stank and leaked offensive fumes into their environs (Ariès 1981; Johnson 2006; Legacey 2019). Although cemeteries in rural areas may have been less aesthetically offensive, they often eventually stood in the way of agriculture and development, thus becoming planning and development problems for future generations (Kay 1998; Pitts 2015; Klaufus 2014).

Over the course of this period, the law, at least in its written form, recognized that the mortal remains of human beings should not be reduced to property and commodified (e.g., Yiannopoulos 1992). Moreover, during the twentieth century, local and state jurisdictions increasingly recognized cemeteries as sacred spaces (Sloane 2018; Vanderstraeten 2014) to be accorded unique treatment that ostensibly protected such sites from most future reuse or destruction (Seidemann 2018a, 2018b). Historical accounts from around Europe and the United States demonstrate that, though such protective laws existed, they were seldom enforced, as human remains were regularly sold and possessed (e.g., Quigley 2001) and as the cemeteries that contained those remains were converted to myriad other uses (e.g., Curl 2001; Nance 1999), either destroyed by new constructions situated directly atop the burials or with the remains removed as refuse.

Archaeological research has confirmed many such instances of cemetery damage or desecration and an emerging area of inquiry—bioarchaeological structural violence and necroviolence research—has also begun to elucidate acts of postmortem treatment of human remains that, in many cases, are more severe on the remains of various underprivileged groups (e.g., Klaus 2013; Nystrom 2014, 2017; Garcia-Putnam et al. 2021, 2023). As set forth below, the theory of structural violence (Galtung 1969), as it has been adapted to the landscapes of death (Seidemann and Halling 2019) and the dead themselves (Klaus 2013; Nystrom 2014, 2017), helps scholars to understand and analyze the systemic and institutionalized disproportionate treatment of certain cemeteries. Although exceptions exist today (Graham and Huffer 2020; Halling and Seidemann 2016a; Huffer and Chappell 2014; Huffer and Graham 2018; Huffer et al. 2019; Huxley and Finnegan 2004; Jarus 2020; Seidemann et al. 2009; Wellons et al. 2024), human remains, at least in the United States, are being accorded the treatment that the law intended: they are not subject to ownership without the express consent of the deceased.[8]

Taking a cue from Claude Lévi-Strauss's (1968:17) observation in his inaugural lecture (1958) as the chair of Social Anthropology at the Collège de France, that "anthropology can do nothing useful without collaborating closely with [other] social sciences," this book examines the law, history, archaeology, biological anthropology, and urban studies to trace and examine historic practices and recent changes in advocacy, policy, culture, and the law regarding how the dead and the spaces of the dead are treated in the United States and in Louisiana particularly. As part of this study, how cemeteries are treated during the land use and planning process is also considered to provide another perspective on whether changes in the living's interactions with the dead in recent history—or at least since the enactment of substantial laws to force behavioral changes in these interactions—have any impact on such treatment.

Are Some Cemeteries Treated Differently from Others?

Recent anthropological scholarship has examined differential treatment of peoples and their remains as an indicator of institutionalized oppression against disenfranchised groups (Farmer 2004; Nystrom 2014). The experience recounted above certainly raises the question (and seemingly provides the answer in the affirmative) of whether the Palestine Church Cemetery allegedly destroyed by Mr. Jetton occurred because of the identity of those interred therein and their descendants (i.e., disenfranchised African Americans) and because of Mr. Jetton's own racial identity as a white man. In other words, was Mr. Jetton able to destroy this cemetery because the people interred therein were disempowered and the cultural structure of the American South instructs that the empowered class can continue to oppress African Americans through the control of their property and their sacred spaces? While the case of the Palestine Church Cemetery certainly suggests an affirmative answer to this question, the research presented here reveals much more nuanced treatment of the dead and their places of repose. This treatment, whether good or bad, is not as black and white as all that. Rather, numerous forces that would damage a cemetery or destroy human remains—urban development, institutional racism, or others—are often not operating on specific racial or ethnic lines when deciding how to treat these items or spaces. Instead, much (though not all) of the treatment of these spaces in the United States depends in large part on the enfranchisement of the descendant communities.

In chapter 2, the question of disproportionate treatment of the dead and their burial spaces is examined through the growing literature on structural violence. It is important to note that not all disproportionate treatment occurs along ethnic or racial lines. Ample literature that extends beyond the scope of this book has considered such disproportionate treatment from racial/ethnic perspectives (e.g., Gosden 2006), gendered perspectives (e.g., Stone 2020; Zuckerman 2021), and class and poverty perspectives (e.g., Muller et al. 2020), among others (e.g., Tremblay and Reedy 2020). Indeed, as is set forth in chapter 2, much of the disproportionate treatment in the cemeteries reviewed here is attributable to class and socioeconomic status rather than to race or ethnicity.

First introduced in the social science literature in the 1960s, the theory of structural violence argues that certain people are oppressed through existing cultural and institutional structures (Galtung 1969; González-Tennant 2018; Tremblay and Reedy 2020:3). As is discussed more fully in chapter 2, this notion of oppression at the institutional level has been expanded in recent years to examine and to conclude that ingrained cultural prejudices have led to the marginalization of oppressed people not just in life (Farmer 2004) but also in death (Nystrom 2014, 2017; Tremblay and Reedy 2020). Part of this expansion of structural violence inquiries has more recently been extended into the cemetery, with examinations of whether this oppression extends to the landscapes of death (Seidemann and Halling 2019). Chapter 2 situates several Louisiana cemeteries within this theoretical inquiry for the purpose of examining where such violence occurs and to establish a basis to analyze, in subsequent chapters, whether legislation can and has been used to combat this violence both in Louisiana and elsewhere.

Intersections of the law and structural violence are not new, though they have only recently been identified as such. Indeed, such famous U.S. Supreme Court cases as *Plessy v. Ferguson*, 16 S.Ct. 1138 (1896), highlight the critical role of the law in the imposition of structural limitations on growth—precisely the type of violence that, as is more fully discussed in chapter 2, Johan Galtung revealed in his early works on peace and violence. In *Plessy*, the court established a separate-but-equal mandate for racial segregation in America that was anything but equal. This decision imposed a segregated system on the country that, though reversed in the 1954 decision in *Brown v. Board of Education of Topeka*, 74 S.Ct. 686 (1954), resounds today in disparate opportunities between white people and people of color in the United States. Even at the time (1896), the structurally violent nature of segregation legislation was recognized by the dissenting justice John Harlan when he characterized the court's decision as a judgment that, "[i]n my opinion, . . . will, in time, prove to be quite as pernicious as the decision made by this tribunal in the Dred Scott case." *Plessy*, 16 S.Ct. at 1146 (Harlan, J., dissenting). Harlan observed of the Louisiana law in dispute that "such legislation . . . is inconsistent not only with that equality of rights which pertains to citizenship, National and State, but with the personal liberty enjoyed by every one within the United States." *Plessy* 16 S.Ct. at 1145 (Harlan, J., dissenting). Homer Plessy, though buried today in the renowned and integrated St. Louis No. 1 Cemetery, in New Orleans, was a light-skinned man of color whose attempt to integrate New Orleans's passenger rail cars in the 1890s is now emblematic of the power of the courts to impose structural violence on a people. Because the law wields such power, its understanding and context within dialogues of racial-, sexual-, ethnic-, gendered-, and class-differential treatment is crucial for a wholistic anthropological understanding of the past and present (see, e.g., González-Tennant 2018). It is through this lens that this review of the protection of deathscapes is undertaken.

The Law on the Books: Legislative Attempts to Protect the Spaces of the Dead

Chapter 3 contains a review and a critical examination of the de jure protections of the dead and the spaces of the dead in the law and how they have been used or unused in Louisiana and elsewhere. The review and analysis of chapter 3 examines both federal and Louisiana efforts in the recent past to protect the dead and cemeteries. Included in this examination is a historical analysis of the development of those laws as instructive of their use and utility to protect such sites now and in the future. Necessarily encompassed within this review and analysis is the genesis of modern human remains and cemetery protection laws with the passage of the Native American Graves Protection and Repatriation Act (NAGPRA) by the U.S. Congress in 1990. The decades-long struggle to pass this legislation—which arose in part from a growing sense of self-empowerment among Indigenous Americans during the civil rights movement (Bray 2001; Stutz 2013)[9] as well as from the shameful treatment of these peoples, both living and dead, by early anthropologists in their efforts to better understand New World prehistory (Thomas 2000)[10]—began a movement at the state level to provide, at least in theory, for greater protection of such people and places (Seidemann 2010a). These local efforts represent a patchwork of mostly restrictive and penal laws across the United States that, like their federal counterpart (i.e., NAGPRA), have considerable room for improvement and leave substantial gaps in the protection of the dead and their places of rest. Indeed, the late adoption of such laws by some states (e.g., Texas in 2017) have left many cemetery sites arguably underprotected (Seidemann 2012), a topic returned to in chapter 7. Conversely, as reviewed in chapter 2, states like Louisiana have been proactive in legislating protections for human remains and cemetery sites (Seidemann 2014a; Seidemann and Halling 2020), though, as the Palestine Church Cemetery matter reviewed above demonstrates, such efforts have not always been successful in providing meaningful de facto site protections.

Older Laws as Untapped Cemetery Site Protections

In addition to the laws of relatively recent vintage (i.e., post-NAGPRA) that have been created to protect human remains and cemetery sites from damage and destruction, certain restrictive covenants on land containing human burials that have existed in Western legal traditions for centuries are emerging as strong and largely unused cemetery site protections. Chapter 4 examines these laws—commonly referred to as cemetery dedication laws—with specific focus on the evolution and use of these laws in Louisiana.

An amicus curiae (i.e., friend of the court) brief submitted to the U.S. Supreme Court in 2018 (Marsh and Seidemann 2018) displayed the utility of these laws in other parts of the United States. In the matter of *Knick v. Township of Scott, Pennsylvania,* 139 S.Ct. 2162 (2019), a private landowner challenged as unconstitutional an ordinance that authorized regulatory examinations of private property to determine the location of cemeteries. In this case, the plaintiff argued that such governmental intrusions on to private property are prohibited by the Fourth Amendment to the U.S. Constitution's prohibition on warrantless search and seizure. Specifically in this case, government actors in Pennsylvania alleged that an "ancient burial ground" existed on Ms. Knick's property (Seidemann 2018b). Pursuant to the above-noted ordinance, a county official entered Ms. Knick's property without permission and without a warrant to verify the existence of the alleged cemetery. Both the federal court for the Middle District of Pennsylvania and the federal Third Circuit Court of Appeals found no constitutional violation by the challenged ordinance either as a warrantless search or as a taking of private property (Seidemann 2018b). The taking in this case allegedly occurred when a cemetery was found on Ms. Knick's land, and it was recorded by the county. Ms. Knick alleged that such a public recordation devalued her land and represented a violation of her Fifth Amendment right to protection from governmental takings of private property. Ms. Knick sought and was granted review of a part of her case by the U.S. Supreme Court.

In their amicus brief to the United States Supreme Court in support of the Township of Scott, Pennsylvania, in the *Knick* matter, Marsh and Seidemann (2018) argue for the application of the cemetery dedication laws to the property that was the subject of the lawsuit. Such an outcome would have resulted in a finding by the Supreme Court that, because Ms. Knick's land had been burdened with restrictions due to its use as a cemetery long before she or her ancestors-in-title acquired any vested constitutional rights in the land, the challenged classification of the property as a cemetery could not constitute a taking of private property under the U.S. Constitution. Unfortunately, the Supreme Court, departing from the rulings of the lower courts, refused to reach the merits of this case regarding the constitutional implications of classifying land as a cemetery and, instead, remanded the matter to the Pennsylvania district court for additional litigation on largely procedural issues. Justice Elena Kagan bemoaned this sidestepping of the critical legal issues at the heart of the case (i.e., the cemetery access and takings issues) when, citing in part

Marsh and Seidemann (2018), she observed that the underlying state law protecting a right of access to cemeteries seems to do nothing more than codify the common law of land ownership long recognizing that such governmental actions are not unconstitutional.[11]

The *Knick* case is relevant to cemetery site protection because it illustrates the precariousness of modern protective laws such as NAGPRA. If these laws' application to private property can be found to be a compensable taking under the U.S. Constitution, then the cost of cemetery site protection increases exponentially. Not only will actual costs of documentation, repair, and preservation be a part of the management of these spaces of the dead, but private landowners often will have to be compensated for the reduction in the merchantable value of their land as a result of the presence of a cemetery. With the use of the dedication laws reviewed in chapter 4, such untenable costs are eliminated because the ancient nature of such restrictions as predating the formation of the United States and the drafting of its Constitution means that any property devaluation that occurs as a result of a cemetery's presence on a tract of land is not a governmental taking, but rather is an incident of land ownership (Seidemann 2018b).

Also woven into chapter 4 is a review of the archaeological and urban studies literature related to cemeteries and their significance in both those fields of inquiry. This review rounds out the consideration of existing protections for cemetery sites and situates those protections within a modern literature base in archaeology as a possible driver for enhanced protections. In other words, the evolution of archaeological practice and theory—from a largely colonialist and destructive to a more multivocal and preservationist milieu—appears, in some ways, to parallel and perhaps even to influence or inform the need for such site protections. Within the urban studies literature, chapter 4 contains an analysis of a relatively recent awakening in that field of inquiry to the awareness of the significance of and limitations related to cemeteries, especially in a planning context.

Importantly, cemetery dedication laws would not have protected the site allegedly destroyed by Mr. Jetton. These laws, like so many other environmental and historic preservation laws, are intended to act proactively as a deterrent to site destruction (e.g., Callahan 1993). In Mr. Jetton's case, only after he had allegedly bulldozed the grave markers was law enforcement notified of the threats to that site. The dedication laws are not penal in nature, and they do not provide for reconstruction, rehabilitation, or restitution. They are intended to act as a deterrent to such action as Mr. Jetton's alleged destruction, and, because no historical evidence existed other than oral tradition regarding the presence of a cemetery on the site damaged by Mr. Jetton, the dedication laws were useless to help build a case against him.

De Facto and De Jure Experiences with Cemetery Impacts

Chapter 5 is a review and analysis informed by archival and archaeological field research on several cemetery sites to assess the de facto application of these laws. This chapter begins with a review of the Louisiana Supreme Court records of historic cases regarding an oil and gas company's destruction of a cemetery in Acadia Parish (the *Humphreys* case), as well as cases preparing for the removal of remains from a Jewish and a Protestant cemetery in New Orleans (the *Touro Synagogue* and *Christ Church* cases, respectively). These records provide insight into both the psychological and physical toll taken on descendants when their loved ones' graves are destroyed (*Humphreys*) and on the interaction of cemetery spaces with urban planning (*Touro Synagogue* and *Christ Church*). These records are particularly insightful for the purposes of examining whether existing laws aimed at the contemporary protection of cemeteries were actually used for their stated purpose and to what extent the descendant community exercised any agency over the decisions to essentially decommission their cemeteries.

Chapter 5 also includes a review of original archaeological research into the efficacy of de jure cemetery protections. Archaeological field research since the 1980s has provided a unique perspective into the treatment of the spaces of the dead and, as with the archival sources, whether and how the laws intended to protect those sites actually functioned. For this review, archaeological work undertaken in the wake of Hurricane Katrina on the cemetery that was the subject of the *Touro Synagogue* case indicates that the authorities moving this cemetery in the 1950s followed de jure protections only minimally, at best. Additional evidence for this conclusion comes from a review of the archaeological reconnaissance at the site of the *Christ Church* case's cemetery and more substantial excavations at the sites of the Charity Hospital Cemetery No. 2 and Historic Highland Cemetery in Baton Rouge. Rounding out this chapter is an examination of the de facto realities of cemetery protection (or the lack thereof, as the case may be) from an archaeological perspective, considering what information and assistance to the combating of structural violence at and the preservation of these sites modern archaeology can bring to bear.

Isolated and Clandestine Burial Site Protection

Chapter 6 reviews the literature on violent deaths and whether and how such occurrences influence future uses of the land on which they occur. Taking a broad view, this chapter begins with a story of how two executions in early nineteenth-century Iceland can change the nature of land from the situs of violence to protected cemetery land. This single event resonates around the world to provide insight into the protections available for the places of such violent events as lynchings and race massacres in the United States juxtaposed against sites of mass disaster and murder.

Inherent in the discovery of human remains on the landscape is the involvement of law enforcement to ensure that the found remains are not evidence of a modern (i.e., prosecutable) crime. This chapter examines how the cemetery and human remains protection laws discussed in previous chapters navigate the possibility that the discovery of human remains may represent evidence of a modern crime. This chapter also analyzes archaeological and archival evidence for the treatment of isolated and clandestine burials and examines whether the excavation of such bodies as those of King Richard III near Bosworth Field in Leicester, England, and the victims of institutional violence at the Dozier School in Marianna, Florida, evidences a postmortem dichotomy in the treatment of such people and spaces. This chapter concludes by examining how the presence of human burials may be used to trigger protections for spaces of violence from reuse and what can be done with those spaces to commemorate those who suffered through violence and to educate future generations about these painful historical events.

Cemetery Site Protection: Lessons Learned

As is reviewed and analyzed in this book, Louisiana has substantially legislated on topics regarding human remains and cemetery sites before and since the passage of NAGPRA in 1990. Chapter 7 examines the applicability of lessons learned in Louisiana to sites in other states. Particularly, and especially because Texas was late to the game in its enactment of NAGPRA-like legislation (Seidemann 2012), the North Dallas Freedman's Town Cemetery site and its treatment is reviewed through the lens of Louisiana's laws in an effort to determine whether such comprehensive protections as exist in Louisiana may have avoided the well-documented disproportionate treatment of this African American burial site (Davidson 2007; Lemke 2020) compared with the then-extant Texas laws. Comparison is also made to the more well-known African Burial Ground site in New York City for the same purpose.

Chapter 7 also contains a review of emerging legislation, both in Louisiana and at the federal level, to determine the utility of such laws to the protection of cemetery sites. Also examined in chapter 7 is a discussion of the reality that, though expansive, Louisiana's laws are not comprehensive protections for cemetery sites against intentional or unintentional damage and destruction. Among the issues reviewed is whether increased agency is possible for marginalized groups in dialogues regarding cemetery protection.

Also, somewhat contrary to general notions regarding archaeological site preservation, chapter 7 contains a discussion of the merits of cemetery site recordation in public records as an added means for the protection of these sites. In this regard, the cemetery dedication laws, at least in Louisiana, counsel a contrary approach to preservation than exists in much of archaeology. In archaeology, precise site locations are commonly redacted from publicly available sources to minimize the risk of site looting (La. R.S. 41:1609). However, because Louisiana operates under a concept known as the Public Records Doctrine (Mengis 1990), the public recordation of cemeteries' existence can serve as precisely as the greatest protector from unintended (or in Mr. Jetton's case, maybe even intended) impacts. The significance of such enhanced protections through recordation was evidenced after Mr. Jetton was evicted from the cemetery property when the state and local governments sought to expand a road passing the cemetery. At that point, because of the cemetery's recorded existence in the public records, the government had to alter its road widening plans in order to avoid any remaining portions of the cemetery that might be affected by development.

While this study is situated primarily within a review of Louisiana's existing law relating to land use when human remains are interred thereon or entombed therein, comparing de jure mandates for the protection of such sites with the de facto realities of several sites in New Orleans and Baton Rouge, its intent is both to inspire similar inquires into other jurisdictions as well as to bring to the fore underused cemetery site protections that are present in one form or another in many Western legal traditions. Some of the measures reviewed and proposed in this book could have helped to prevent the alleged Palestine Church Cemetery damage, and they may be useful for other sites in the future. These measures are aimed at providing agency among both marginalized and nonmarginalized groups in the process of modern interactions with the dead.

2

Cemeteries as Windows into Structural Violence on a Landscape Scale

"All those men who were killed were given decent burials" (Colbert 2021:160). This was the official government position regarding the treatment of the dead after the Tulsa Race Massacre of 1921. Recollections of survivors and recent archaeological investigations of this shameful chapter in American history cast doubt on this official position. These recollections have legal and archaeological implications today.

The story of the Tulsa Massacre has been ably told by many (e.g., Madigan 2003; Colbert 2021). The massacre of hundreds of African Americans in Tulsa, Oklahoma, over a three-day period from May 30, 1921, to June 1, 1921, was touched off when an African American man, Dick Rowland, was wrongly accused of assaulting a white woman in an elevator at a local store. Rowland was arrested, and Ku Klux Klan–affiliated yellow journalists soon put out a call for his lynching.

At this time, the African American community in Tulsa was an unusually prosperous one for a southwestern state in the postwar 1920s. Despite this prosperity, the African American community still existed within a Jim Crow environment and the members of this community were substantial second-class citizens who were subject to severe punishment for even the most trivial of slights to white people.

Thus, unlike in many other American locales where a call to lynch an African American man who had allegedly assaulted a white woman may have been internalized by the African American population as an incident of life in the Jim Crow South, Tulsa's African Americans decided to take a stand. The community rallied to the jail and confronted the sheriff, demanding security for Rowland. Assured by the sheriff that Rowland would be safe and would stand before a fair tribunal for the accusation, the African American protesters dispersed.

However, this insistence by a large contingent of the African American community was used as a pretext by KKK-backed white Tulsans to instigate a riot. Under false accusations that roving bands of African Americans had mobbed the jail and threatened white interests, the call went out to area white people to arm themselves for a preemptive storming of Greenwood, Tulsa's African American quarter. This call to action largely instigated by local media, resembled many southern lynch mobs of the first half of the twentieth century. In Tulsa, the accused perpetrator of the insult to what King (2013:104) characterizes as the "flower that was 'Southern white womanhood'" was of less interest to the mob. Instead, the Tulsa white community turned its rage against the entirety of the African American section of the town in what is today recognized as an all-out war against the African American residents.

At daybreak on June 1, 1921, white people, armed with weaponry stolen from shops and the national guard armory began an unprecedented and unprovoked attack on Greenwood. Eyewitness accounts liken the assault to Nazi ethnic cleansings in Europe two decades later. The use of national guard weaponry with local law enforcement support substantially resembled later European pogroms. African Americans were run from their houses; any suspected to be armed were shot; any resisting were shot; and Greenwood was put to the torch. More than a generation of African American success and accomplishment was erased in a matter of hours. Those who did not resist the white aggression were rounded up into makeshift internment camps. Those who did resist were killed. The death toll for the day ranges from just over 100 to around 400, mostly African Americans.

African American and white survivors of the massacre, after decades of silence, began to relate stories of bodies being hauled out of Greenwood by the truckload. Many African American victims were interred in mass graves in the local Oaklawn Cemetery, as modern archaeology is now showing (Razek and Wolfe 2022). However, many bodies were simply made to disappear. Reports of where the rest of the victims' bodies ended up vary widely, but there is no particular reason to doubt the probable veracity of any of these reports. Some witnessed bodies being dumped into the Arkansas River; some saw truckloads of bodies being unceremoniously dumped off ravines into gullies. Others are said to have been trucked out of town to mass burial trenches in undisclosed rural areas. Among the most horrifying stories of these truckloads of bodies are reports of moans of pain from the still-living among the dead who were presumably buried alive in the mass graves. All of this is in addition to the burning of piles of African American victims' bodies in the Greenwood area—the whereabouts of those incinerated remains are still unknown.

The terrible events of the Tulsa Massacre can never be righted and should never be forgotten. However, in efforts shortly following the end of hostilities, Tulsa's white boosters tried to do just that—force the world to forget. Although there were minimal efforts to investigate the massacre after it ended, most are accepted today to have been shams intended to whitewash a horrific event that could cause economic hardship for this burgeoning white oil community. The continued fear of Jim Crow–era treatments kept many of the victims silent, as the white people who took part had a lack of statutes of limitations on murder to fear for their actions. Thus, over the ensuing decades, the memory of the riots faded from white Tulsa's collective consciousness and was repressed within the African American community. Most importantly for this book, burial sites were lost as a result of this repression.

Modern Tulsa now faces a reckoning with this brutal past. In addition to modern scholarship and investigative reporting bringing details of the atrocities of June 1921 to light, the practical realities of missing burial places of up to 400 people on the Tulsa landscape should cast a pall over future development in the region. The Tulsa Massacre is an extreme example of what has come to be known as structural violence—violent acts meted out on marginalized or disenfranchised peoples with the tacit support all or part of the predominant or ruling regime.

A review of the de jure cemetery protections should lead the casual observer to the conclusion that cemeteries in that state are sacrosanct in all instances of their interactions with development or other conflicting uses. However, examining the de facto treatment of both spaces of the dead and human remains leads to a different conclusion.

In 1987, Oklahoma passed its state-level equivalent of NAGPRA (21 Okl. St.Ann. § 1168, et seq.). This law is not limited by ethnicity. Thus, many of the Tulsa Massacre burial sites should be protected by the law. However, is it enough that a law is passed in 1987 that prohibits certain activity when human remains are inadvertently discovered to keep the burial sites of the Tulsa Massacre victims from being uprooted by future development? As discussed below, such laws are likely insufficient.

Although there have been a few legal tests of various unmarked burials protection laws over the decades since their passage, there has been no definitive answer to this question provided by the U.S. judicial system. This unanswered question is significant, as the recent enactment of unmarked burials law protections could raise allegations that these laws are subservient to the protection of private property protections present in the U.S. Constitution and many state constitutional counterparts. Basically, the legal scenario runs like this: if someone has vested property rights in a tract of land and the government later makes a rule to control how—or if at all—that land is used, then there is an argument that such regulation constitutes a taking of private property rights in a manner for which the government is liable.

Hints of this concern were voiced during the enactment of NAGPRA, perhaps explaining why that law is limited to burial site protections on federal and tribal property—areas on which the federal government has plenary regulatory authority. The practical reality of an outcome in which each attempt to protect a burial site on private land results in a compensable taking by a state or local government is as fiscally untenable as it is morally repugnant. Essentially such a situation would have governments paying landowners for the ability to protect the dignity of graves on their land. If such laws were found to be takings of private property, cemetery site preservation (in situ) and the archaeological excavation of such sites that cannot be preserved in situ would grind to a halt. If a burial location for Tulsa Massacre victims were found on private land, the focus of such a discovery would not be protecting and memorializing such a sacred site of violence, but rather would be a strictly economic inquiry of the costs and benefits of any such protections. This reality is especially problematic in the Tulsa Massacre scenario, as survivor reports talk of mass graves on rural farms in the area. The discovery and preservation of these sites, which are tantamount to war graves, would stand on tenuous legal and fiscal ground were it not for the ancient nature of cemetery site protections discussed later in this book.

This problem would not be the case at the Louisiana site of the Colfax Massacre in 1873. That massacre, in which approximately 150 African Americans were killed as they tried to defend themselves inside the Colfax courthouse from a marauding band of white people in the years following Reconstruction (Keith 2008), is different from Tulsa's. Many of the burial sites for the African American victims of this massacre are thought to be in defensive trenches dug at the time on the courthouse grounds (i.e., public land). Thus, the application of the Louisiana Unmarked Human Burial Sites Preservation Act to protect this site infringes on no private rights. With financial backing and proper permits, the descendant community could use archaeology to tell the story of this dark event in Louisiana's history without running afoul of private property rights. Not so on the farms surrounding Tulsa where many Tulsa Massacre victims are thought to be buried. Thus, the evidence of 100-year-old structural violence in Tulsa—the actual graves of the victims—is crucially important to unfolding the narratives of these dark events.

The criticality of connecting place to reports of structural violence cannot be understated. Places such as Whitney Plantation in Wallace, Louisiana, are actively working to reclaim the narrative of white American atrocities against

African Americans. At this site, visitors are not treated to the veranda-sitting and mint julep–sipping of the majority of Louisiana's antebellum plantations. Whitney's curators have embraced the story of the enslaved. Visitors are confronted with stark images, stories, and places of torture and death. Nothing about Whitney Plantation is salacious. Rather, it places Louisiana's plantation system within a more balanced context than other plantation sites in the region, which serves to educate visitors about the realities of daily life at such sites and the true legacies left in and by these spaces. Whitney juxtaposes well with the remainder of the plantations on the Mississippi River between Baton Rouge and New Orleans, pitting harsh reality against the gentile, utopic alternative narrative that southern boosters and Lost Cause sympathizers have long contended is the nature of such sites. The story that Whitney has to tell is compelling. However, it is infinitely more powerful for its relationship to a place. The same connection between place and memory exists in cemeteries—especially those of the victims of violence. The protection of these sites is critical to a complete, unvarnished understanding of our past.

This chapter examines the de facto treatment of cemeteries and human remains in Louisiana—especially in New Orleans—by employing the theory of landscape structural violence. As is set forth throughout this chapter, landscape structural violence is a theory proposed by Seidemann and Halling (2019) that holds that institutionalized or sanctioned violence against certain sacred spaces, especially cemeteries, constitutes a vestige of ingrained cultural biases and prejudices used, whether intentionally or unintentionally, by enfranchised peoples and institutions to inhibit the personal growth of marginalized and disenfranchised groups. Although the concept of structural violence long predates Seidemann and Halling's (2019) work, this source first clearly articulated a theory through which to examine differential treatment of spaces of the dead for clues to broader cultural relationships and to tease out possible explanations for past actions taken against certain cemetery sites.

Landscape Structural Violence and Cemeteries

Whitehead (2010:1) describes the idea of a landscape as occupying both physical and cultural spheres in the human consciousness: "the notion of 'landscape' . . . signifies not just material geo-forms and structures but also the way in which the cultural imagination occupies and signifies spatial and biological processes and relationships within discreet limits . . . a landscape is created not just through the presence of human artifact but also through the way in which narration invests meaning in apparently 'natural' earth-forms." In this regard, cemeteries are particularly poignant, as both the physical places where humans house their dead and as the metaphysical and psychological storing places of the hopes, fears, and lore of a people (Moen 2020; O'Gorman et al. 2020; Strangstad 1995). As described by Bowring (2011:252) cemeteries are "memory-filled and melancholy places that provide a dark counterpoint to the relentlessly new world of capitalism and consumption." Such locations make for an important focal point in which to study interactions of the persistence of significance in such spaces and the treatment of those spaces by the establishment. While scholars such as Whitehead (2010:3) are interested in the manifestation of violence in the landscape (e.g., "the notorious gates of Dachau . . . [and the] aesthetic terror in the making of this monstrous landscape of death"), this chapter focuses on the violence wrought against the landscapes of memory themselves and not the violence that may have occurred in those spaces and its present collective memory. Thus, both the Louisiana examples discussed here and the locations of the Tulsa Massacre victims' burials provide perfect examples of treatment of these sacred spaces by those in power. This review is less applicable to the Massacre victims' unmarked burials found in Tulsa's Oaklawn Cemetery than it is to the later treatment of the burial places of those not laid to rest in a recognized cemetery. For the Louisiana cemeteries discussed in this chapter, that narrative is largely known. For the Tulsa burial places, that narrative is only beginning to unfold in ways that archaeology is uniquely situated to interrogate.

Classifications of the cemetery as a unique cultural landscape are not new. Indeed, as Pritsolas and Acheson (2017:49) note, cemeteries are landscapes that, "provide a window into the changing economic fortunes and cultural values of a community." Moreover, archaeologists have long valued these unique spaces as cultural microcosms for the study of trends in material culture (Dethlefsen and Deetz 1966; Veit and Brooks 2011). Kniffen (1967), partially reviewing the work of Dethlefsen and Deetz (1966), challenged scholars to look to diverse "necrogeographic" landscapes as sources of cultural data not available from archaeological sites and archival sources. Stewart (2007) recognized the special nature of cemeteries as repositories of communal mourning for those lost at sea, and Seidemann (2014b) has utilized these unique spaces for insight into modern expressions of popular culture (see also Hobbs 2005). Smith (2009) and Downer (2015) have used cemeteries as microcosms of cultural expression and memorialization for marginalized peoples (see also Lemke 2020). The idea of cemeteries as microcosms of particular cultures was heralded by Francaviglia (1971) in the early 1970s, but these sites have remained, in some respects, understudied in the anthropological literature, especially as windows into past prejudices.

What has occurred more recently is some amount of confluence in the literature of the concepts of cemeteries as special cultural landscapes and landscape violence (Duncan 2004; Seidemann and Halling 2019). As Duncan (2004:207) indicates, such violence, "includes denying the deceased a resting place or destroying the soul of the deceased." Seidemann and Halling (2019) extend this notion to the physical destruction of these spaces and to the denial of living communities' ability to commemorate and venerate their dead through the destruction of such spaces.

The notion that cemeteries are marginalized on the landscape is similarly not new (see, e.g., Sheppard-Simms 2016), as these spaces are often located out of view of the living in the first instance (Nance 1999; Smith 2017). However, it is the interaction between these already marginalized spaces and expanding land development that creates potentially violent encounters. New Orleans presents a unique laboratory for analyzing cemetery damage and destruction, as recent archaeological excavations in the city have revealed both sanctioned and unsanctioned examples of such actions. These actions are examined here through the lens of the theory of structural violence, a theory of differential treatment of human groups by governmental institutions or social structures, in an effort to answer the question of whether institutional violence can be exerted toward a landscape such that it reinforces preexisting social prejudices.

The theory of structural violence was introduced by Johan Galtung in the peace and violence literature in 1969. In his seminal work on this topic, Galtung (1969:170) defined structural violence by juxtaposing it against standard violence thus: "the type of violence where there is an actor that commits the violence [is] personal or direct, and [the] violence where there is no such actor [is] structural or indirect." Galtung (1969:170–171) further explained that,

> whereas in the [the case of personal or direct violence,] consequences can be traced back to concrete persons as actors, in the [case of structural violence,] this is no longer meaningful. There may not be any person who directly harms another person in the structure. The violence is built into the structure and shows up as unequal power and consequently as unequal life chances.

Farmer (2004:307) explains Galtung's concept of structural violence from an anthropological perspective as "violence exerted systematically—that is, indirectly—by everyone who belongs to a certain social order." Galtung (1980) later clarified the concept of structural violence when he stated that the theory applies to "anything avoidable that impedes [the] personal growth" of marginalized and disenfranchised groups.

Structural violence is, as currently discussed in the social sciences literature, a concept of unequal treatment—usually unintentionally and unwittingly—of minorities, the poor, and the otherwise disenfranchised by the established order (often a government or industrial complex) (Parsons 2007). Much of the literature stemming from Galtung's (1969) introduction of structural violence has related to differential treatment of living peoples (e.g., Scheper-Hughes 1992; Farmer 2004). As set forth below, the concept of structural violence has recently been applied to the postmortem treatment of human remains as an extension of the differential treatment of the disenfranchised beyond the grave (e.g., Littleton and Frolich 2012).

To date, scholars of structural violence have only applied the idea minimally to the landscape. Certainly, authors have discussed the psychological implications of significant and violent landscapes on living people (e.g., Whitehead 2010), and even Galtung (1969) postulated that violence could be effected on a landscape as "object violence" or as psychological violence (rather than structural violence). However, whether the differential treatment of certain peoples experienced in life (Galtung 1969) and in death (Fowler and Powers 2012; Nystrom 2014; Halling and Seidemann 2017; Garcia-Putnam et al. 2021) can be extended to the postmortem landscape through selective violence directed at the final resting places of the disenfranchised, is only lightly considered in the literature (e.g., Seidemann and Halling 2019). Scholars such as Blakey (2010:61) have indicated the importance of understanding this differential treatment among disenfranchised communities, when commenting on descendants' reactions to the contested potential outcomes for responding to the discovery of the African Burial Ground in New York City, he observed that the community wanted "assurance that 'we' have human dignity in death." The dignity referred to by Blakey (2010) is directed not just at the protection of human remains, but also at the preservation of the integrity of the mortuary landscape.

Galtung's (1969) concept of structural violence was tailored for analyzing violence effected by the establishment against living people. However, in recent years, anthropologists and historians have begun to extend the notion of structural violence from actions affecting living minorities or less-privileged individuals to the treatment of these peoples' remains after death (Nystrom 2014, 2017; Tremblay and Reedy 2020). In these studies, the effects of structural violence are observed directly on skeletal remains as evidencing differential treatment of human remains among or between groups in a population. Such differential treatments include subjecting such individuals to postmortem experimentation and the maiming or destruction of their mortal remains.

Also sometimes referred to as "necroviolence" (Garcia-Putnam et al. 2021), this area of anthropological inquiry focuses specifically on the treatment of the mortal remains of those who were disenfranchised during life.

Structural violence is often discerned with relative ease when visited upon the living (e.g., Farmer 2004). Indeed, Halling and Seidemann (2017) recount evidence in the historical record of New Orleans of the specter of such violence in a context that could manifest in the postmortem record. In this regard, these authors document the fear in the nineteenth-century African American community that medical professionals were intentionally killing patients to use their bodies for experimentation.[1]

Identifying evidence of structural violence inflicted on the dead is more difficult. In the absence of historical records of this violence (which are often nonexistent), evidence of this violence must often be inferred from the skeletal record. Certainly, as Ruth Richardson (1988) and Suzanne Shultz (2005) ably document in the historical records of the United Kingdom and the United States (respectively), the bodies of the poor and minorities were used in postmortem medical training and research. However, with a few infamous exceptions (e.g., Burke and Hare in Edinburgh and the skeletal remains excavated from the Medical College of Georgia basement) (Richardson 1988; Blakely and Harrington 1997), little direct evidence definitively links such violence to the postmortem violent treatment of human remains. Oblique references to disparate treatment of white and African American remains in anatomical contexts exist in various places but are not catalogued in any compendium. One noteworthy example of such references is the mention by Horwitz (2011) who, recounting the aftermath of John Brown's raid on Harper's Ferry in 1859, noted that the white insurrectionists' remains were allowed to be properly buried, while their African American comrades' remains were given over for anatomization.

Thus, when researchers such as Douglas Owsley and colleagues began writing about postmortem evidence of medical experimentation on human remains from Charity Hospital in New Orleans in the 1990s (Owsley et al. 1990), they were treading new ground. Nonetheless, this relatively recent area of inquiry has produced a respectable body of literature (e.g., Nystrom 2017; Tremblay and Reedy 2020) and researchers have succeeded in demonstrating that structural violence can and does extend beyond life through the violent and sometimes demeaning treatment of the remains of the disenfranchised after their deaths (e.g., Davidson 2007; Lans 2020).

In addition to inquiries into the postmortem treatment of human remains, bioarchaeologists have developed a considerable amount of literature in recent years examining structural violence visited on people during life. For example, research such as that reported by Harrod et al. (2012) examines skeletal evidence for institutional violence against Chinese immigrants in Nevada in the late nineteenth and early twentieth centuries. Harrod et al. (2012:92) reports on findings of substantial antemortem trauma on the skeletal remains of a sample from Carlin, Nevada, suggesting that such immigrants were an "'at-risk' population" as targets of violence by the white majority. In addition, Harrod et al. (2012) identified substantial skeletal evidence of hard work on these people's remains that is consistent with the menial labor of the lower socioeconomic classes of the time. This notion of being an "at-risk" population loudly echoes the concept of minorities and others being legally classified as "suspect classes" of people worthy of closer scrutiny by the judicial system in allegations of equal protection violations beginning in the 1960s. Indeed, from an anthropological perspective, minorities and other traditionally disenfranchised people should be subject to "strict scrutiny" for evidence of structural violence either during or after life. Not looking closely for this evidence is tantamount to perpetuating the structural violence narrative in modern social science research.

While questions regarding whether a particular cut mark on a bone is a result of taphonomic processes, careless excavation techniques, or actual postmortem violence are often difficult to answer, the complete disappearance of a cemetery from the landscape is (generally) a bit more noticeable. Despite the general obviousness of the absence of a cemetery from the landscape, the cause of such disappearances is often somewhat more complex. For example, in New Orleans, the Jewish Gates of Mercy Cemetery disappeared from its original location in the mid-twentieth century. Even though Jews are often disenfranchised and would constitute a suspect class of individuals for disparate treatment under the theory of structural violence, a review of the historical record indicates that this cemetery disappeared intentionally, as discussed fully in chapter 5, at the behest of its descendant community (Seidemann 2018a, 2018b). As such, with the involvement of the minority group in the decision-making process for the landscape alteration that is the removal of a cemetery, the disappearance of the Gates of Mercy Cemetery cannot confidently be considered as some variant of structural or landscape violence against that community.

The recent history of the African Burial Ground site in New York City represents perhaps one of the more flagrant examples of institutional action threatening violence to a cemetery (Frohne 2015; Lemke 2020). In that case, federal authorities identified a burying ground for enslaved Africans on the proposed construction site of a U.S. General Services Administration building in Manhattan. Although the discovery of this site immediately postdated the passage of federal legislation directed at protecting certain graves, that law was inapplicable to this site, and, even today, New York has yet to pass meaningful state legislation to protect unmarked burial sites.[2] Because no federal equivalent exists of non-Native American human remains protection like Louisiana's Unmarked Human Burial Sites Preservation Act, no legal structure existed within which the African American descendant community of New York City had legal standing to protect the African Burial Ground site. Further, though New York jurisprudence protects dedicated cemetery property (see, e.g., *St. Agnes Cemetery v. State*),[3] such protections are underused for unmarked cemeteries. Ultimately, whether a federal government agency would protect this disenfranchised peoples' burial site when most laws did not mandate that protection became the subject of protests. As Blakey (2010:62) observes, the preservation of the burial site is due only to the involvement of activists and the "agency's bureaucratic arrogance [that] led it to violate both the legal requirements of public input and careful archaeological resource management."

The descendant community's response to the plans to develop the African Burial Ground site with little or no consultation or respect for the memory of those interred at the site is emblematic of both the sensitivity of such sites and the real effects that such violence can have (if carried to completion) on the memories of the dead and the psyches of the living (see also Hong 2017). The handling of this interaction of development with the dead is a prime example of violence meted out by an institution (i.e., the federal government) on a disenfranchised people (i.e., enslaved African dead and their descendants) through the structure of the institution. The African Burial Ground debacle is structural violence on a landscape scale. Activism, as is now omnipresent in many U.S. locales when the cemeteries of the disenfranchised are threatened by development (e.g., Jones 2019; Petrella 2019), was a partial solution to ensuring the protection of the African Burial Ground. Although the activism protected part of the African Burial Ground and forced the U.S. government to reckon with its questionable land use decisions through redeveloping its construction plans, creating a National Park Service site and interpretive center, and supporting research efforts by anthropologists from the disenfranchised community, it did not save the entire African Burial Ground site. The planned building still sits atop some burials in Lower Manhattan, thus continuing the violence against this landscape and these people in ways that, as described below, are likely illegal even without the assistance of specific, non-Indigenous burial legislation.

Importantly, two types of landscape structural violence are at play in some of the cemetery examples related in this book. The most common type of such violence is the initial erasure from the landscape of any evidence of the cemetery and that site's reuse as something other than a cemetery. This sort of violence is on display in the Palestine Church Cemetery situation recounted in chapter 1. The second type of violence, though less common, is the later excavation of such sites without consent from or consultation with the descendant community. This disturbance, as is set forth in the following chapters, is, in part, a problem that several recent laws have sought (with varying degrees of success) to avoid. The lack of consent from descendant communities regarding the treatment of their lost and then refound spaces of death can constitute a separate act of landscape violence against these people discussed in chapter 7 in the context of recommendations for increased descendant agency in cemetery-related decision-making.

Returning to New Orleans, the above-noted example of Gates of Mercy Cemetery enables an inquiry into the negative disappearance of cemeteries from the landscape. Indeed, much like what could have happened with the African Burial Ground had the public been complacent or ambivalent, recent archaeological work in New Orleans has identified cemeteries that were erased from the landscape with seemingly no participation by or acquiescence of the descendant community (e.g., Gray 2017). Further, though the erasures of certain cemeteries (e.g., Charity Cemetery No. 2, the St. Peter Street Cemetery, and others), are generally prohibited by law (Seidemann 2014a, 2018a, 2018b), the disappearance of such sites often had the imprimatur of authorization or the tacit acquiescence of the government.[4] In other words, the government either sanctioned, permitted, or did not restrict the destruction of these cemeteries—thus adding structure to the violent landscape change.

New Orleans is certainly not alone in this regard in Louisiana. Archaeological evidence reviewed in chapter 5 suggests that even the "blue-blood" Highland Cemetery in Baton Rouge suffered damage as a result of such governmental complacency (Seidemann and Kleinpeter 2014). Examples of deliberate destruction or desecration of cemeteries across the United States are legion and are more common than deliberate relocations of such sites (e.g., Hoffer 2020; Sanders 2020; Shahzad 2020). Accordingly, structural violence occurs on a landscape scale through the erasure of certain peoples' memories by a destruction of the final locales where a trace of their mortality exists.

Indeed, Galtung (1969:170) hinted at such a notion as landscape violence when he spoke of "object violence":

> Is destruction of things violence? Again, it would not be violence according to the complete definition above, but possibly some "degenerate" form. But in at least two senses it can be seen as psychological

> violence: the destruction of things as a foreboding or threat of possible destruction of persons, and the destruction of things as destruction of something very dear to persons referred to as consumers or owners.

In this regard, Galtung (1969:170) speaks of "the destruction of things . . . [that] are something very dear" to people. Galtung's above quotation fails to clarify whether he had in mind the destruction of landscapes or mere corporeal movable items. Certainly, destruction of either of these substantially affects anyone to whom those things are important, but cemeteries, as the final resting places of a people, seem something apart from the items referred to by Galtung (1969:170) as things held by an oppressed people as "consumers or owners." Applying Galtung's suggestion that psychological violence may represent "the destruction of things as a foreboding or threat of the possible destruction of persons" substantially describes the violence meted out in Rosewood, Florida, and Tulsa, Oklahoma, when the white community destroyed the homes and businesses of African Americans with either direct or indirect support from the government or established institutions. Such destructions, while coupled with interpersonal violence through the killings of minority people, rise to a level, through the destruction of immoveable property, of sending a clear message that such people are not welcome and that either they have nothing to return to after the interpersonal violence event or that they can expect further loss of people and property should they return. Violence exerted against mortuary landscapes is something not contemplated by Galtung and moves a step beyond interpersonal violence, psychological violence, and object violence. It is a unique type of structural violence against a landscape associated with those who often cannot defend against such action. Thus, the destruction of cemeteries should be treated as part of a broader landscape violence that is not damage to mere corporeal immoveables or movables. Moreover, because cemetery site destruction is often carried out in full view (or with the tacit approval) of those with institutional authority to prevent such damage, this type of object violence appears to be much more related to structural violence when it is visited upon the minority and marginalized dead.

The above discussion leads necessarily to the question of whether violence can be inflicted on the landscape or is such activity merely a form of psychological violence? Undoubtedly, a loved-one's final resting place occupies a significant psychological place for people (e.g., Bates 2020; Ellis 2003; Russell 2003; Sloane 2018). Axiomatically, then, the loss of such a place represents a violent psychological event. Indeed, such a notion constitutes a considerable underlying factor to NAGPRA's passage (McKeown 2012). Contempo-

Figure 2.1. Historic cemetery eroding and subsiding into Bayou Lafourche in South Louisiana. Visible today are only the tops of several traditional above-ground crypts. The remaining mortuary structures are already underwater and create a navigation hazard for this busy waterway.

rary media presents more recent examples when intentional or accidental acts disrupt grave spaces (see, e.g., Reever 2018a). No doubt, psychological violence is a problem in the disparate treatment of minorities. For reasons discussed below, such a descriptor seems insufficient to capture both the psychological impacts of burial disturbances and the physical alteration of the landscape through cemetery destruction (Bates 2020). In this regard, Galtung (1969:169) distinguishes psychological violence, which he describes as "violence that works on the soul [which includes] lies, brainwashing, indoctrination of various kinds, threats, etc. that serve to decrease mental potentialities," from actual physical violence. Admittedly, Galtung's concept of physical violence is that directed at humans and not things, but the above description of psychological violence is insufficient to cover the physical activities inherent in landscape alteration that concomitantly influence people's psychological well-being. For this reason, landscape violence is a separate type of physical violence that has tangential psychological implications.

Threats to cemeteries from development and desecration are nothing new in the literature (e.g., Seidemann 2013, 2014a; Joiner and Seidemann 2019a, 2019b). In a recent variation on this topic, Schexnayder and Manhein (2017) review threats to South Louisiana's historic cemeteries not from traditional desecration or physical violence sources but from the loss of Louisiana's coastline and the cultural heritage that is lost along with the land. Each of these types of landscape alteration—development, desecration, and anthropogenically enhanced land loss—could be caused by some institutional (development and land loss) or personal (desecration) violence. As yet, the land loss causation for cemetery disappearance is not evident in New Orleans, and, though desecration does occur in the city (Mustian 2016), it is not the focus of this research. It is important to note that anthropogenically exacerbated sea-level rise is contributing to the loss of minority cemeteries below the rising waters. In the case of the Isle de Jean Charles community evacuation caused by rising waters in Louisiana, this Native American community's cemetery was left behind when the living were moved farther inland. Such cemetery losses also evidenced along Bayou Lafourche in Jefferson Parish, Louisiana (figure 2.1), are likely to continue with the effects of climate change.

The cemeteries reviewed below (see figure 2.2 and figure 2.3) have been affected by development, and the brief history of their disappearances is presented for the purposes of analyzing whether such events constitute violent acts perpetrated on the landscape.

Charity Hospital Cemetery No. 2

Charity Hospital Cemetery No. 2 (also known to as Cypress Grove No. 2) now lies beneath Canal Boulevard at the intersection with City Park Avenue in the Lakeview area of New Orleans (Jumonville 2016). This cemetery served, from the mid-nineteenth century through the early twentieth century, as an overflow cemetery for the indigent dead of New Orleans who died at Charity Hospital and were unclaimed or whose families were unwilling or unable to pay for their burial (Halling and Seidemann 2017). The cemetery also contains considerable medical waste from Charity Hospital. Like the still-visible Charity Hospital Cemetery No. 1 on Canal Street (figure 2.4), all the burials in Charity Hospital Cemetery No. 2 were inhumations, and there is no surviving evidence to suggest that any above-ground crypts existed on the site.

According to Jumonville (2016), in the 1920s, this burial space was converted from a cemetery to a major thoroughfare in New Orleans. According to Douglas Owsley (pers. comm. 2020), then an anthropology professor at Louisiana State University, in the 1980s during reconstruction work on Canal Boulevard, excavations were permitted on one side of the street and burials on the other side were bulldozed. What several archaeological examinations have demonstrated is that, though any surface evidence of the cemetery was eliminated, some subsurface interments were left when the road construction occurred (e.g., Owsley et al. 1990; Smith and Stone 2014; Garcia-Putnam et al. 2021). Although there were disturbances and desecrations to some graves when Canal Boulevard was built, many of the burials remain intact and undisturbed beneath the current roadway. A portion of this cemetery, as shown

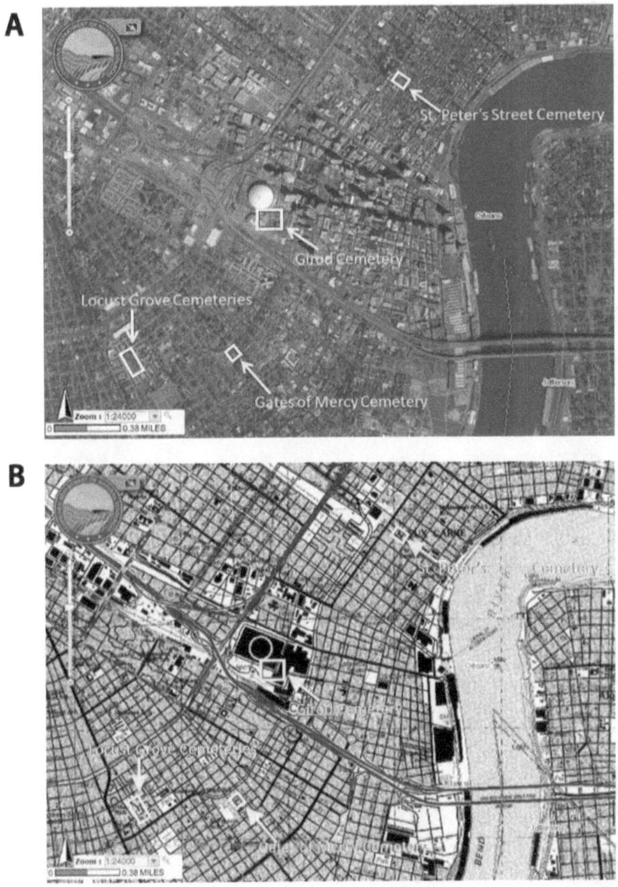

Figure 2.2. Maps adapted using the Louisiana Department of Natural Resources' SONRIS GIS system with 2016 aerial background and current USGS quadrangle map mosaics with four of the five cemeteries discussed in this chapter (St. Peter Street, Girod, Locust Grove, and Gates of Mercy) identified.

in the historic map of the area, also extended beyond the modern roadbed in an eastward direction (figure 2.5).

What is not known today is the integrity of the burials that extend beyond the modern roadbed. This site was once the location of a gas station (presumably complete with large subsurface tanks) that likely disrupted many of the burials to substantial depths. Today, the same site (figure 2.6) is the location of a coffee shop and a popular local eatery.

For reasons unknown, this site was permitted and developed with no requirement to beware of any remaining human burials. No known archaeological testing occurred as part of this 2020 construction, thus it is unknown whether the earlier gas station obliterated any evidence of the cemetery on this site, whether the current construction did additional damage to the graves of these once-marginalized people, or whether the graves are still pres-

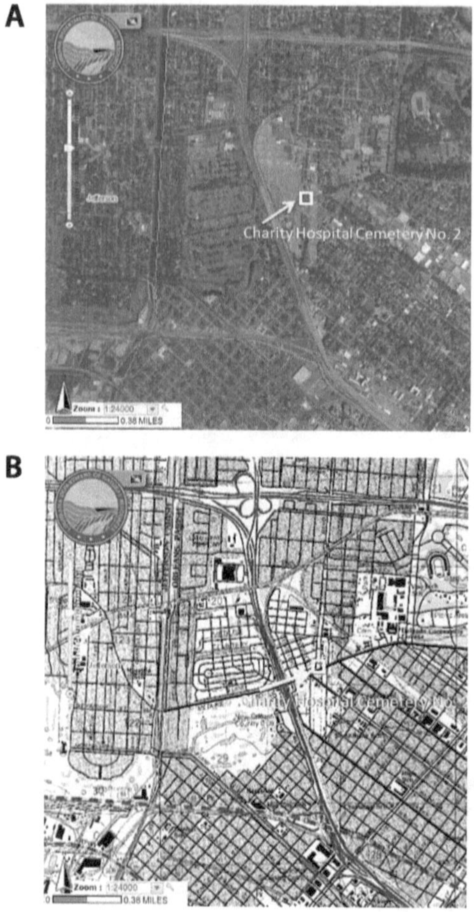

Figure 2.3. Maps adapted using the Louisiana Department of Natural Resources' SONRIS GIS system with 2016 aerial background and current USGS quadrangle map mosaics with the fifth cemetery discussed in this chapter (Charity Hospital Cemetery No. 2) identified.

ent, sealed in place for later discovery. Only when repairs and improvements to the road and adjacent property are undertaken do further disturbances of these burials occur. Effectively, the portion of Charity Hospital Cemetery No. 2 underlying Canal Boulevard is a sealed burial site of New Orleans paupers from the 1850s through the early 1920s. The status of the portion to the east of the roadbed is unknown. No surface evidence of this cemetery remains, and most New Orleanians are unaware of its presence.

The St. Peter Street Cemetery

The St. Peter Street Cemetery was one of the earliest colonial cemeteries of New Orleans (Dedek 2017). Roughly in operation from ca. 1725 through the 1790s, this in-ground burial site was located along the literal ramparts of early

Figure 2.4. The gates of Charity Hospital Cemetery No. 1 on Canal Street in New Orleans. This site is now also the home of the Hurricane Katrina Memorial, which is a series of above-ground mausoleum structures containing the remains of those who perished in the storm but who remain unidentified and unclaimed.

New Orleans (modern-day Rampart Street) (Gray 2017). The city officially closed the cemetery in 1789, though burials likely occurred for some time after its official closure. The colonial government allowed the site to be filled with structures. The city quickly subsumed the cemetery site, which was not preserved intact in contrast to its later neighbor, St. Louis Cemetery No. 1.[5] In fact, as Gray (2017:23) notes, "a Royal Decree . . . approved . . . the use of

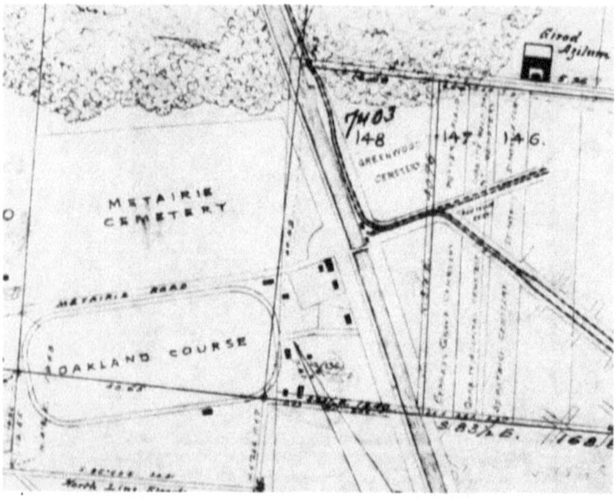

Figure 2.5. An excerpt from an 1884 plat of the area that would eventually become Canal Boulevard in New Orleans. Canal Boulevard now traverses the land in Parcel 147 notated on the map as "Charity Hospital Cemetery" and "Potters Field."

Figure 2.6. The modern situs of Charity Hospital No. 2 Cemetery at the intersection of City Park Avenue and Canal Boulevard in New Orleans (looking north). The cemetery lies partially underneath the roadbed and partially underneath the structures in this image.

the old [cemetery] for the construction of residences" (figure 2.7).[6] Further, Gray (2017:23) correctly observes that, "this latter point is significant, as it makes clear that the old cemetery had been intended for re-use for non-burial purposes almost from the moment that it was closed," a reality that contradicts Spanish law on such property uses at the time (Seidemann 2018a).[7] As with Charity Hospital Cemetery No. 2, the St. Peter Street Cemetery has left no trace of its existence above ground, and the cemetery is now located beneath various structures along the south side of Rampart Street. Archaeological excavations at this site revealed a varied suite of permanent inhabitants, from recently arrived enslaved Africans to free colonial inhabitants of the city (Gray 2017). As with Charity Hospital Cemetery No. 2, the interments in St. Peter Street Cemetery have effectively been sealed in place by overlying construction that intermittently affected the site by new construction activities over the centuries.

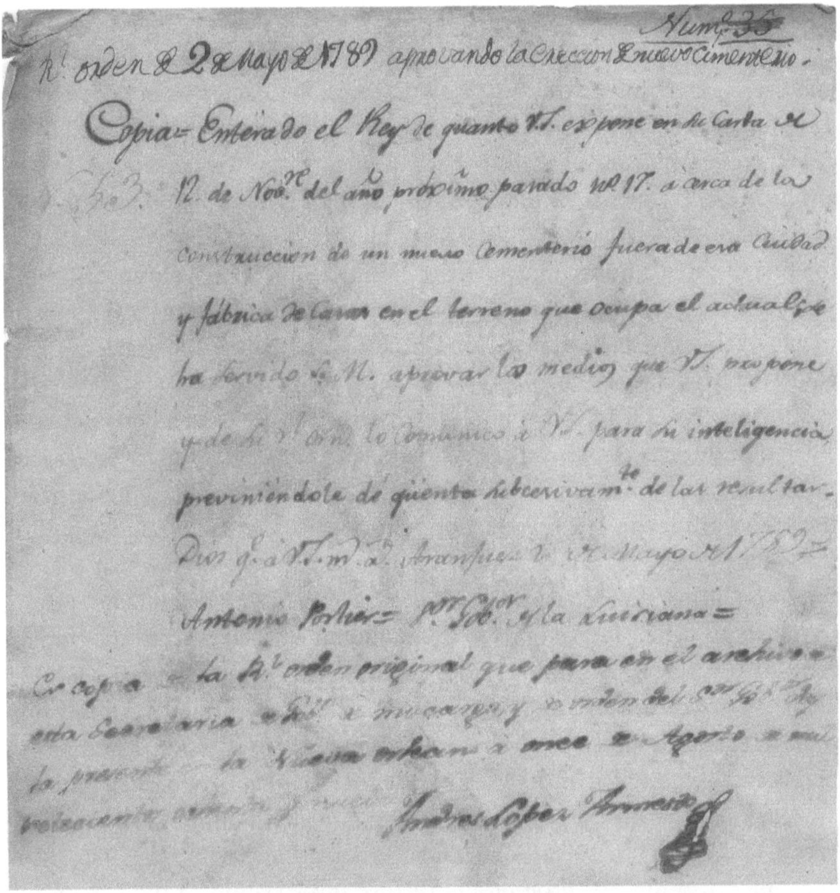

Num.o 35

Rl. orden de 2 de Mayo de 1789 aprovando la ereccion de nuevo cementerio.

Copia= Enterado el Rey de quanto V.S. expone en su Carta de 12 de Nov.re del año proximo pasado No. 17. a cerca de la construccion de un nuevo cementerio fuera de esa Ciudad y fábrica de casas en el terreno que ocupa el actual se ha servido S.M. aprovar los medios que V.S. propone y de su Rl. orn. lo comunico á V.S. para su inteligencia previniendole dé quenta sucesivamte. de las resultas.

Dios gue. á V.S. m. a. Aranjuez 2 de Mayo de 1789

Antonio Porlier= Sr. Gobor. de la Luisiana=

Andres Lopez Armesto

Figure 2.7. A copy of the royal decree for the repurposing of the St. Peter Street Cemetery in the collections of the Records of the Diocese of Louisiana and the Floridas, 1576–1803, Archives of Notre Dame: IV-4-e A.L.S. 5 pp., 8 vo. A very rough translation of this incomplete (due to illegible handwriting) transcription indicates that the document is a copy of the royal decree of May 2, 1789, in which King Charles IV authorized "construction of a new cemetery outside of the city and the construction of houses on the land occupied by the current" cemetery: "Orden de 2 de Mayo de 1789 aprovando la ereccion de Nuevo cementerío. Copia-Enterado el Rey de cuanto V.S. expone en su carta 12 de Nov. del año proxĩmo parado nuestra 17 a cerca de la construccíon de un nuevo cementerío fuera de era ciudad y fábríca de casas en el terreno que ocupa el actual de ha servido __ M. aprovar los medios que V.S. propone y de si V.S. orn. lo comunico á M. para V.S. para su inteligencia previniendole de quenta la __ cerivamente de las resultar."

Locust Grove Cemeteries No. 1 and 2

Located in an area bounded by Magnolia Street, Sixth Street, Seventh Street, and Freret Street in Central City, New Orleans, the Locust Grove cemeteries were among the city's nineteenth-century potter's fields (Jumonville 2016). Documentary evidence suggests that interments in these cemeteries ceased around 1879 (Branyon 1998). The surrounding neighborhoods used the site as a dump (Gray 2020), and, by 1889, the sites constituted the location of the first of three schools known as the Thomy Lafon School (Branyon 1998). According to Branyon (1998), these cemeteries consisted of in-ground interments likely only memorialized on the surface by perishable grave markers (most likely wooden).

The impacts of placing a school atop a cemetery were apparently not considered in the late nineteenth century. and later archaeological investigations suggest that most, if not all, of the interments were left in place underneath the school (Branyon 1998; Pope 1985; Anon. 1952). In fact, the first indication that the general public was made aware of the possibility that a long-forgotten historic cemetery was located near the Thomy Lafon School came in the 1950s, when renovations to the school unearthed caskets and human remains (Landry 2009; Anon. 1952). However, this knowledge and whatever attention it received due to a newspaper report on the findings did not stop the use of the property as a school. Indeed, in 1986, additional human remains and cemetery artifacts were recovered by University of New Orleans archaeologists when they were encountered during plumbing work in the schoolyard (Branyon 1998; Pope 1985; Anderson and Belanger 1985). This encounter also did not prompt any further investigation of the site or any dialogue regarding the proper memorialization of the former cemetery on the school property. In fact, officials only recognized that the law had long mandated meaningful consideration of the property's original (and continuing) status as a cemetery (Seidemann 2010b, 2010c) when Hurricane Katrina decimated the Thomy Lafon School and the Federal Emergency Management Agency began work with the Orleans Parish and Recovery School Districts for the possible rehabilitation of the school. In the wake of Hurricane Katrina, the burden of remediating a massive nineteenth-century cemetery on the school site led city, state, and federal officials to convert the Thomy Lafon School to a greenspace that commemorated not just the historic cemetery and those still interred at the site, but also the significance of the Lafon schools as important locations in the burgeoning twentieth-century civil rights movement in New Orleans (Hahn and McCarthy 2012). Today, this site is a park. The decision for this site to be used as a park was in keeping with historical overlap between cemetery spaces and parks (e.g., Bender 1974; Brown 2013; Evensen et al. 2017).

Unknown to government actors during the immediate post-Katrina efforts to reuse the Thomy Lafon property, New Orleans mayor Martin Behrman issued a directive in 1905 with regard to the Locust Grove Cemeteries (Hahn and McCarthy 2012; Seidemann and Halling 2019), much like the royal decree that lifted the cemetery dedication from St. Peter Street Cemetery. After a city attorney opined that it was permissible to reuse cemetery space, an ordinance issued in 1905 by the City of New Orleans removed the cemetery dedication from Locust Grove Cemetery Nos. 1 and 2 and authorized the construction of the Thomy Lafon School on top of them (Hahn and McCarthy 2012). Although a concurrent ordinance directed the city's contractor to "remove with due respect any remains found in Locust Grove Cemetery No. 1 to Locust Grove Cemetery No. 2" (New Orleans City Ordinance No. 2945, March 15, 1905), the above-noted archaeological investigations suggest that, though superficially well-intentioned, the city apparently did not follow through on its own directive to move the cemetery. Interestingly, though, because Mayor Behrman passed the ordinance removing the dedication in 1905, this property is no longer subject to the cloud on its title that the cemetery dedication represents. Accordingly, the reuse of this site may be accomplished without removing all remains from an area of potential impact, but rather by mitigating any potential impacts pursuant to the Louisiana Unmarked Human Burial Sites Preservation Act and otherwise sealing the rest of the site for posterity.

Gates of Mercy Cemetery

Located in the Central City area of New Orleans along Jackson Avenue, the Gates of Mercy Cemetery was in use from 1828 until 1872 by the Touro Synagogue Jewish congregation (Dedek 2017). After the congregation's establishment of a new cemetery location in the early twentieth century, the Gates of Mercy Cemetery began to fall into disrepair and by the 1950s was characterized by the Louisiana Supreme Court in the matter of *Touro Synagogue v. Goodwill Industries of New Orleans Assn, Inc.*, as having "fallen into ruin."[8] Because of the dilapidated state of the cemetery, the Touro Synagogue community decided to sell the property and move the remains of those interred on the site to a new location. This move became the subject of a court dispute between an attorney appointed to represent the interests of the dead in the cemetery and the synagogue and prospective purchaser—Goodwill Industries, Inc. (*Touro Synagogue* 1957). Unlike the other cemeteries discussed above, the reuse of the Gates of Mercy property was an action that was con-

Figure 2.8. A memorial in Hebrew Rest Cemetery No. 1 in New Orleans to those whose remains were removed from the Gates of Mercy Cemetery. Though the reburials of these people occurred in Hebrew Rest, it is unknown today whether this memorial marks an actual reburial location or whether the remains are located elsewhere in the cemetery.

templated and supported by the descendant community. Also unlike the cemeteries discussed above, the mortal remains of those interred in this cemetery space were removed (to Hebrew Rest Cemetery No. 1) pursuant to law before the area once occupied by the cemetery was put to an alternative use (*Touro Synagogue* 1957) (figure 2.8). Although it is questionable whether all human remains were actually properly recovered from the site, an attempt was made to move the burials (Seidemann 2010c). In addition, post-Katrina archaeological investigations on the cemetery site found only nonhuman bone fragments and broken grave markers (Hahn et al. 2017). A subsequent review of these materials by LDOJ personnel confirmed the absence of human remains in the archaeologically recovered materials. LDOJ, through consultation with Touro Synagogue, has facilitated the repatriation of this recovered material culture. Because the burials at this site were all inhumations and because the removal of those remains to Hebrew Rest Cemetery No. 1 was not accomplished under the direction of trained archaeologists and bioarchaeologists,

Figure 2.9. Historic image of Girod Cemetery from the Hogan Jazz Archive, Special Collections, Howard-Tilton Memorial Library, Tulane University, photographed by William Russell in 1956.

it is still probable that human remains are present on this site today. Similar problems with nonarchaeological exhumations in Louisiana have been observed before (Servello et al. 2003). This reality is not an impugnment of the post-Katrina archaeology at the site. Rather, that work appears to support the proper removal of human remains in the 1950s. However, that project was limited in size and scope, and later work on this site in other areas may yet reveal human remains that were missed in the 1950s exhumations. This cemetery was ultimately put to alternative uses following the court challenges.

Girod Street Cemetery

Perhaps one of the more storied cemetery reuse examples in New Orleans is the Girod Street Cemetery, formerly located on the site now occupied by parking garages, Champions Square, and (partially) by the Superdome in downtown New Orleans (Dedek 2017). This cemetery was a Protestant burial ground in use from the 1820s until perhaps the 1930s. Similar to the Gates of Mercy Cemetery, the Girod Street Cemetery, by the time of its reuse, was, according to the Louisiana Supreme Court, in a state of dilapidation and disrepair (*City of New Orleans v. Christ Church Corp.*).[9] Unlike the rest of the cemeteries discussed above, this site was an above-ground burial space, characterized by the stereotypical New Orleans wall vaults and above-ground tombs (figure 2.9).

Also like the Gates of Mercy situation, the Girod Street Cemetery's descendant population consented to the planning and reuse of the site (*Christ Church* 1955). Ostensibly, the remains from this site were removed pursuant to law and developers used the property for alternative uses. At the time of the de-dedication of the Girod Street Cemetery, it was not intended to be used for commercial development. Rather, city engineers wanted the site to be used as roadways to minimize traffic problems and potential accidents. However, despite the alleged clearance of all such material pursuant to the relevant court orders, later opportunities to conduct limited archaeological reconnaissance within the footprint of the former Girod Street Cemetery revealed human remains in at least one locale (Owsley, pers. comm. 2020).

Structural Violence and Cemeteries

As alluded to above, impacts to cemeteries that erase their existence from the landscape appear to fall under the classification of violence proposed by Galtung in 1969. Although not a perfect fit for the types of violence that Galtung (1969) proposed, as the reuse of cemeteries for noncemetery purposes likely falls somewhere between structural violence and object/psychological violence, the effect, in many cases, on the descendant community is some form of violence.

As noted above, structural violence is recognized as actions or inactions by an institutional or organizational entity that impede the personal growth of a minority or disenfranchised person or group. To fully understand whether impacts to a landscape, cemeteries in particular, can constitute some form of violence, it is crucial to understand whether their damage or destruction can cause problems that impede a person's or group's growth.

Certainly, anecdotal evidence supports the idea that damage to someone's grave or to a cemetery has crippling psychological effects on people. Indeed, in the wake of recent grave space disruptions in a Eunice, Louisiana, cemetery, family and attorneys for a mother whose child's grave was damaged now claim that the grief occasioned by that damage was the proximate cause of the mother's untimely death (Reever 2018b). Beyond the anecdotal evidence of this case as well as the legion of other news reports around the world that recount people's feelings of anger and grief when graves are damaged (e.g., Masters 2020; Shahzad 2020), the adverse impacts of grief to an individual's personal growth are also well documented in the academic literature (e.g., Anderson and Gaugler 2006; Hogan and Schmidt 2002).[10] Even as early as the 1920s, Alfred Kroeber (1927:308–309), observed "the powerful affects released by death and the fact that affects are not expressed spontaneously in culture," indicating the significance of burial places and their long-lasting relevance for people (see also Cannon 2002).

At least during the period that most of the cemeteries discussed here were in operation and decline (i.e., the nineteenth and early twentieth centuries), scholars documented that the grieving process included regular visits to the cemetery as a place to commune with the dead (e.g., Walls 2011). Although there exists some debate regarding the continuance of these grieving practices into the twentieth century (Walls 2011), clearly sites of actual violence or death (as opposed to cemeteries) are becoming more significant locales for visitation and commemoration in the mourning process (Jacobs 2004; Aronson 2016). Thus, little doubt exists that cemeteries continue to figure largely in various individuals' grieving practices (see, e.g., Woodthorpe 2011).

These spaces are thus important from both a mourning and a historical perspective (Pelley 2022), and removing them from the landscape has significant impacts on both aspects of cemeteries' common uses (Wyndham and Read 2011; Maples and East 2013). As poignantly noted by Miller and Rivera (2006:334), "whether the bodies of the deceased are placed in the ground, within elaborate tombs, or simply in the presence of ancient or contemporary monuments, their location holds symbolic meaning as well as practical historical meaning for the surrounding living community." Accordingly, denying the unique nature of cemeteries is difficult (Sheppard-Simms 2016), and, because of their connections to the grieving process and the historical nature of a particular place, impacts to these spaces that erase them from the landscape clearly affect the descendant community. Indeed, Leshem (2015:35) recently observed that "particularly in colonial and postcolonial contexts, burial grounds have played a pivotal role in Indigenous assertion of history and communal identity, resistance to land dispossession and the use of subversive practices in the face of colonial urban policies." In the United States, such assertions are often made by Indigenous peoples, but also the same notion applies to descendants of enslaved peoples. In this regard, Blakey (1996:xiii) observes with regard to African American cemeteries that "cemeteries are shown to resonate with a people's sense of self. African American identities are entombed, marked, fought for, preserved, celebrated, symbolized, mourned, and incorporated in the cemeteries they describe."

As a practical matter, the removal of a cemetery from a landscape may sever from the descendant community the ability to continue the grieving process or to have a place within which to commune with a direct link to its history. In other words, in cases where a decision to remove a cemetery from the landscape is made not by the descendant community but rather by or with the consent of the government, this action directly results in an erasure of the collective memory of those interred in the cemetery from the landscape. Such an action, whether intentional or not, represents the final act to eliminate the existence of a community from the landscape.

An important reality to bear in mind with such erasures is that they are not all illicit. In this regard, a cemetery may be lawfully removed from the landscape contrary to the wishes of the descendant community as long as the landowner follows the mandates of the cemetery dedication laws and the terms of the applicable burial removal permit. While such removals may still represent landscape structural violence, they are not unlawful. Such a reality, while greatly disfavored by the courts, is the paramount right of private landowners in the United States (see, e.g., cases discussed in Seidemann 2013; Joiner and Seidemann 2019a, 2019b).

Although the disappearance of many cemeteries from the landscape can be classified as violent acts, not all landscape changes qualify as violent. The cemeteries reviewed here present examples of both violent and nonviolent landscape changes.

Charity Hospital Cemetery No. 2

In the case of Charity Hospital Cemetery No. 2, little doubt exists that the historic decisions that led to the erasure of this site from the landscape, and in many ways from the collective memory, were acts of violence perpetrated by a powerful structure on a powerless descendant community. With this cemetery, the historic record contains no evidence of efforts made by the City of New Orleans or developers to make contact with the descendant community before removing the surface evidence of the cemetery's existence and converting that space to a roadway. Indeed, this act not only constituted violence against the largely destitute New Orleans population of the nineteenth and early twentieth centuries, but the perpetrators also violated the law in carrying out these acts.

In this regard, such acts violate the long-standing existence of restrictions against using cemetery property for anything other than the interment of the dead as discussed in chapter 4. Despite the knowledge that these violent acts occurred, it is impossible to directly understand the impacts of this landscape alteration on the descendant community. Although the historical record is silent, such violent acts likely represented a loss of identity for the dead and a stripping of agency from the descendant community that perhaps kept them from reaching their full potential. However, through inference from current scholarship, it is possible to deduce that, because such spaces are important to the grieving process and because disruption of that process can have significant adverse impacts on the living, violence was wrought upon the descendant communities as a result of the destruction of these cemeteries (Maples and East 2013). Thus, the development activities that led to the disappearance of at least Charity Hospital Cemetery No. 2 meet the qualifications to represent violence carried out against the landscape with effects on the descendant communities.

Indeed, as Trouillot (2015) insightfully observes, such silences in the historical record can represent evidence of structural violence. In this regard, Trouillot (2015:48) states that "[i]nequalities experienced by [people] lead to uneven historical power in the inscription of those traces." Moreover, "[s]ources are thus instances of inclusion, the other face of which, of course, what is excluded" (Trouillot 2015:48) demonstrates the ability for disenfranchised peoples to be further erased from history (Rainville 2009), not just from a violent physical act against their person or significant landscapes, but also through the recordation of only the history of the enfranchised. Such a reality is crucially important in understanding the often-anemic historical record associated with the cemeteries of the disenfranchised (Rainville 2009). Furthermore, Trouillot (2015) essentially makes the case for archaeology's utility in providing information about those powerless past peoples whose histories were not recorded—a use that is employed in this book. Such an approach is supported by Sloane's (2018:2) argument that "[i]n Western society today, we have come to believe that everyone deserves to be remembered, no matter how famous or obscure, young or old, rich or poor." Thus, where the historic record provides little or no information regarding the existence or destruction of cemeteries, archaeology can be used to partially fill that void and to give voice to those lost in the historical silences (see also González-Tennant 2018).

Charity Hospital Cemetery No. 2's troubled history continues to the present day with the 2020 constructions atop portions of the cemetery not already violently affected by road construction in the early twentieth century. The twenty-first-century constructions of two eateries on the graves of these disenfranchised dead without compliance with any modicum of the laws protecting cemeteries further condemns the histories and memories of these people to oblivion.

Locust Grove Cemetery Nos. 1 and 2

The Locust Grove cemeteries, once thought to have been subjected to analogous violence to that visited on Charity Hospital Cemetery No. 2 (Seidemann 2010b, 2010e), is now known, through the work of Hahn and McCarthy (2012), to be somewhat different. When New Orleans mayor Martin Behrman issued the 1905 ordinances directing the closure of the cemeteries (figure 2.10), the relocation of the remains interred therein, and the construction of a school on the property, he technically complied with the centuries-old customary legal process of removing the cemetery dedication on that land. Importantly, because there was in 1905 no statewide statute mandating the removal of the cemetery dedication through a court proceeding as there is today, the city's enactment of an ordinance (a law) to put the property to an alternative use and to remove the remains constituted a valid dedication removal at the time. Thus, Mayor Behrman followed jurisprudential and customary cemetery law with those ordinances and properly lifted the title cloud of the cemetery dedication on the subject tracts of land. With the passage of those ordinances, the land could be put to alternative uses and the subsequent series of schools were lawfully built. However, the failure of the city to follow through on the legal mandate to remove the remains from that site can be interpreted as nothing less than violence against the descendant community of the Locust Grove cemeteries.

This inaction is eerily similar to the recently reported landscape structural violence against African American cemeteries in Clearwater, Florida (Pelley 2022). In this latter case, until the construction of various noncemetery uses, orders were given to remove African American dead from their final resting place. Modern archaeology has demonstrated that the burials were, in most if not all cases, simply built over (Moates and O'Sullivan 2020a, 2020b), erasing their existence from the landscape and, over time, from the collective consciousness of even much of the area's descendant community (Pelley 2022). Virtually identical activity was reported in Bossier Parish, Louisiana, with the expropriation in the 1950s of African American land—including a cemetery—and many remains were simply built over by the U.S. government when it expanded Barksdale Air Force Base (Servello et al. 2003). This de facto treatment of the burial places of the disenfranchised—often (but not always) the cemeteries of African Americans (at least in the United States)—clearly demonstrates mere lip service paid to de jure cemetery protections by the establishment at least historically and highlights the need to be vigilant today and in the future when such sites may be affected.

Regarding the Locust Grove situation, it is impossible to conceive of a scenario in which either city employees or school contractors for the original Thomy Lafon School were unaware that the remains had not been removed from the former cemetery cites. Perhaps Mayor Behrman and the New Orleans City Council—those who passed the 1905 ordinances—had clean hands in this matter through their directive to remove the remains, but later subsurface disturbances and archaeology that demonstrated that the Locust Grove

A

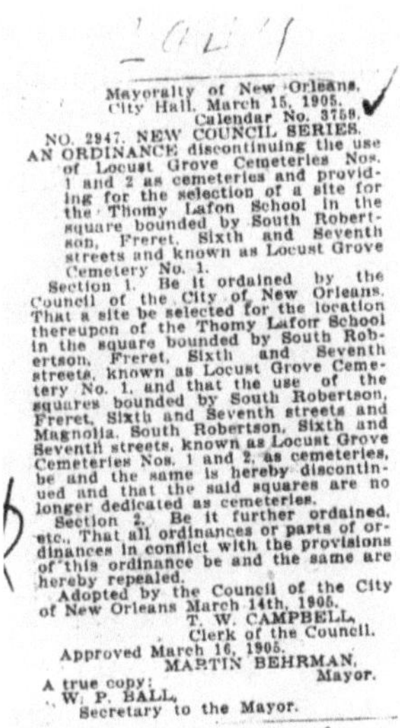

Mayoralty of New Orleans,
City Hall, March 15, 1905.
Calendar No. 3759.

NO. 2947. NEW COUNCIL SERIES.

AN ORDINANCE discontinuing the use of Locust Grove Cemeteries Nos. 1 and 2 as cemeteries and providing for the selection of a site for the Thomy Lafon School in the square bounded by South Robertson, Freret, Sixth and Seventh streets and known as Locust Grove Cemetery No. 1.

Section 1. Be it ordained by the Council of the City of New Orleans, That a site be selected for the location thereupon of the Thomy Lafon School in the square bounded by South Robertson, Freret, Sixth and Seventh streets, known as Locust Grove Cemetery No. 1, and that the use of the squares bounded by South Robertson, Freret, Sixth and Seventh streets and Magnolia, South Robertson, Sixth and Seventh streets, known as Locust Grove Cemeteries Nos. 1 and 2, as cemeteries, be and the same is hereby discontinued and that the said squares are no longer dedicated as cemeteries.

Section 2. Be it further ordained, etc., That all ordinances or parts of ordinances in conflict with the provisions of this ordinance be and the same are hereby repealed.

Adopted by the Council of the City of New Orleans March 14th, 1905.

T. W. CAMPBELL,
Clerk of the Council.

Approved March 16, 1905.

MARTIN BEHRMAN,
Mayor.

A true copy:
W. P. BALL,
Secretary to the Mayor.

B

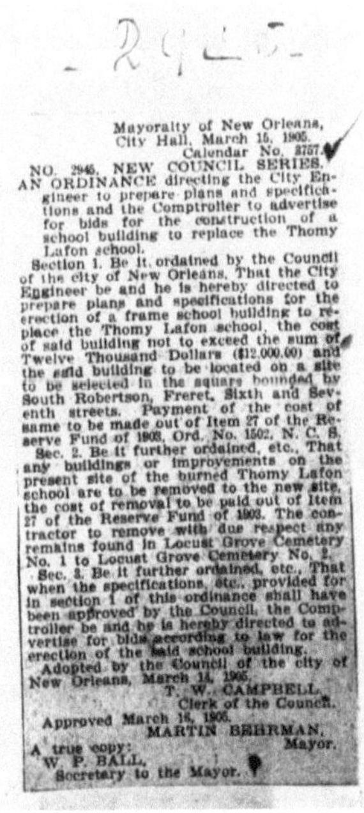

Mayoralty of New Orleans,
City Hall, March 15, 1905.
Calendar No. 3757.

NO. 2945. NEW COUNCIL SERIES.

AN ORDINANCE directing the City Engineer to prepare plans and specifications and the Comptroller to advertise for bids for the construction of a school building to replace the Thomy Lafon school.

Section 1. Be it ordained by the Council of the city of New Orleans, That the City Engineer be and he is hereby directed to prepare plans and specifications for the erection of a frame school building to replace the Thomy Lafon school, the cost of said building not to exceed the sum of Twelve Thousand Dollars ($12,000.00) and the said building to be located on a site to be selected in the square bounded by South Robertson, Freret, Sixth and Seventh streets. Payment of the cost of same to be made out of Item 27 of the Reserve Fund of 1903, Ord. No. 1502, N. C. S.

Sec. 2. Be it further ordained, etc., That any buildings or improvements on the present site of the burned Thomy Lafon school are to be removed to the new site, the cost of removal to be paid out of Item 27 of the Reserve Fund of 1903. The contractor to remove with due respect any remains found in Locust Grove Cemetery No. 1 to Locust Grove Cemetery No. 2.

Sec. 3. Be it further ordained, etc., That when the specifications, etc., provided for in section 1 of this ordinance shall have been approved by the Council, the Comptroller be and he is hereby directed to advertise for bids according to law for the erection of the said school building.

Adopted by the Council of the city of New Orleans, March 14, 1905.

T. W. CAMPBELL,
Clerk of the Council.

Approved March 16, 1905.

MARTIN BEHRMAN,
Mayor.

A true copy:
W. P. BALL,
Secretary to the Mayor.

Figure 2.10. New Orleans City Ordinance Nos. 2945 and 3759, March 15, 1905, held in the City Archives at New Orleans Public Library.

property is choked with human remains lying just below the surface leaves no doubt that those working on the site knew of the failure to move the remains.

In 1952, the extent of the remains left interred on the school site was reported in the local newspaper, which observed (Anon. 1952:13) that, during the construction of a later iteration of the Thomy Lafon School,

> A few bones were turned up first thing on Friday by workmen putting in the pilings in the playground at the rear of the present Thomy Lafon school at Seventh and Magnolia. However, no one guessed the bones were those of humans until Tuesday when several caskets, skulls and other bones unmistakably human were uncovered.

The problem of rediscovering Locust Grove Cemetery was contextualized by the school's supervising architect when he stated, "[f]inding those bones nearly scared the pants off us, for we've got a half a million dollars tied up in construction" (Anon. 1952:13). After some title research that revealed the source of the remains, the City of New Orleans agreed to reinter the disturbed remains elsewhere and that "[e]fforts will be made not to disturb any more burial locations than are necessary to the construction of the school." Rather than making plans for the relocation of the Locust Grove dead nearly a half a century after they should have been moved, a representative of the school board further observed that, "the discovery of . . . the bones fired the imagination of his staff who hoped a cache of gold might be uncovered to pay for the construction of the new school" (Anon. 1952:13). No efforts were made to reckon with the burials at the site.

Although this act of violence—constituting a failure to move the remains of the Locust Grove cemeteries' permanent inhabitants—was not perpetrated at the highest levels of New Orleans government, it still meets the definition of structural violence, because those with superior positions and status (i.e., city bureaucrats and building contractors) perpetrated violence against those in inferior positions (i.e., the descendants of the city's poor) and, as with the structural violence at Charity Hospital Cemetery No. 2, these acts deprived the descendant community of their ability to visit an important site of grieving and wiped that site from the community's collective consciousness. The later (1950s) explicit acknowledgment that the "half million dollars" used to fully reconstruct the school atop the cemeteries with direct knowledge of the cemetery's presence and nature clearly represents a knowing act of landscape structural violence by the architects and school board. This violence only reached an end with the school's complete destruction following Hurricane Katrina in 2005, when the site was converted to green space. However, the risk of additional landscape structural violence at this site is pernicious, as subsequent city administrations since Hurricane Katrina have at least scoped the idea of repurposing the property again. These acts have been stopped only by regulatory diligence at the state level.

Another example that highlights the violent treatment of cemetery sites occurred several years ago in New Orleans. Sometime around 6:00 a.m. on a

January morning, my colleague, Christine Halling, and I were released by our security detail to assist investigators in a high-profile desecration case. As we approached the raised shotgun-style house in the Mid-City neighborhood of New Orleans, four people were kneeling and handcuffed on the porch. We walked past those people who were under guard by members of the New Orleans Police Department (NOPD) and the Louisiana Bureau of Investigation (LBI) and entered the house to begin a search for human remains and to interview the person who had been pilfering human bones from Holt Cemetery in New Orleans.

Holt Cemetery is a city-owned cemetery with in-ground burials that is situated next door to Delgado Community College and is mere blocks away from the storied Metairie Cemetery as well as many other famous New Orleans cemeteries. Holt's history is different from these opulent spaces of death. Originally used as a burial ground in the 1870s when epidemics had filled the city's other existing pauper cemeteries, Holt lies on low ground at the intersection of the Lakeview and Mid-City neighborhoods (Branyon 1998; Moore 2018). This site began as yet another of the city's burial grounds for the poor, akin to Charity Hospital Cemetery Nos. 1 and 2. Over time, the cemetery shifted from a burial place of the city's poor to a public, predominantly African American cemetery. Long ignored by regulators, descendants and friends could employ whatever means they wanted to commemorate their dead (Seidemann and Seidemann 2005). In this regard, along with the largely African American, city-owned portion of Carrolton Cemetery in Uptown New Orleans, Holt represents a space of unfettered commemoration and mourning. It is an anthropologist's dream as a site where unregulated culture of families of the interred have decorated graves with markers made of wood, stolen (and painted over) street signs, and cardboard beer boxes. According to Donald Marquis, there had been as many as nine distinct burial epochs in Holt at the time of his writing about one of Holt's famous residents, Buddy Bolden, in 1978.

Born Charles Bolden in 1877 in what is now New Orleans's Central Business District, Buddy Bolden was a coronet player who plied his trade in New Orleans' Storyville District—an enclave of legalized prostitution just north of the French Quarter—at the turn of the twentieth century. Bolden was described by "Jelly Roll" Morton, another jazz/ragtime legend from the early twentieth century, as "the blowingest man since Gabriel" (Marquis 1978:102). Although no recordings and few photos survive of Buddy Bolden, his ragtime coronetting was legendary. Indeed, a young Louis Armstrong is reputed to have sneaked out of his childhood home to go listen at the brothel windows in Storyville to Buddy Bolden and his band as they entertained the clientele into the late evenings and early mornings. Bolden's stardom burned bright and was snuffed fast. Within a few years, his drug and alcohol problems landed him in a sanatorium. He died penniless in a state facility in Jackson, Louisiana, in 1931. Upon his death, his sister paid for his remains to be returned to New Orleans, where he was laid to rest along with other paupers in Holt Cemetery. Although two commemorations of Bolden now stand in Holt, these are cenotaphs, as his actual burial place was not recorded and has since been lost.

Because this cemetery is composed entirely of shallow underground burials and it is in a constant state of reuse with, until recently, little to no government oversight, grave diggers constantly churn up bones from earlier burials whenever new interments are made. These grave diggers, generally a handful of men who operate by word of mouth and for cash payments (they are not city employees), are neither trained morticians nor skeletal biologists. When my wife and I, in the early 2000s, asked a Holt grave digger whether he or his colleagues encountered human remains while prepping new graves, we were told that all that they ever found was roots and (rangia) shells. Because a walk across Holt's grounds is a veritable study in human osteology to those with a trained eye, we pointed out long bone fragments to the grave digger and asked what they were. The answers were variously that they were sticks or trash. That these grave diggers regularly encounter and disturb human remains during new burials is unsurprising. Many of the dead in Holt were indigent, and because Louisiana law does not prohibit grave reuses under certain conditions nor does it mandate burial in caskets or concrete vaults, these dead are often laid to rest in shrouds, body bags, and, according to a retired police officer whose beat once included Holt once told us, refrigerator boxes. In the hot and wet soil in New Orleans, those bodies quickly break down, with even the bone becoming saturated, friable, and fragmented.

Until recently, Holt was only partially fenced, unlit, and had no other improvements to its grounds. Families could purchase burial spaces from the city for a pittance or, more commonly, simply either find a long-untended grave to claim and reuse or reuse spaces occupied by their own family members for years. An additional cash payment to the grave diggers would buy a wooden "box" for placement around the grave. These rough space delineators were often made of 2×4s nailed into a rectangular shape and placed over a recent burial for boundary and beautification purposes. Further complicating the integrity of burials in Holt is the reality that, during storms, these boxes often float from their original spaces to elsewhere in the cemetery, making keeping track of discrete burial spaces complex at best.

Holt Cemetery is one example of how institutional neglect can, at times, create structurally violent situations in cemeteries. In this case, the structure is provided by governmental ownership and lax regulation as well as the de jure versus de facto application of laws that should keep places like Holt both safe as well as orderly. However, more than a century of the city's ambivalence to the space and blasé regulation of interments has created a violent assault on Holt's landscape of death—one that, by the early twentieth century, had an impact on the city's African American population. Admittedly, in a city legendary for its decaying, gothic spaces of death, New Orleans has seldom had a good reputation for maintaining any of its public cemeteries. Places such as the Valence and Lafayette cemeteries are good examples of poor maintenance. However, these predominantly above-ground cemeteries suffer from the unchecked ravages of time and much less from the active and constant burial disturbances seen at Holt. In fairness, now under the watchful eye of a trained historic preservationist, all the city's public cemeteries are poised for a renaissance of sorts. Even Holt has recently received nice fencing, security with locking gates, paved roads, and streetlights. This revelation in a long-ignored space came to be through the work of committed volunteers, a reenergized city cemetery office, private donations, and academic support from the University of New Orleans's Dr. D. Ryan Gray. Nonetheless, Holt is still a troubled place.

It was within this history and just as Holt was turning a corner toward active city management that a "self-styled witch" whose online avatar was "Ender Darling" began to steal bone fragments from Holt Cemetery for use in their own "spell work" and for sale in a private Facebook group to others around the country and world for similar purposes (Halling and Seidemann 2016a). Ender Darling's illicit Holt activities leaked from their private Facebook group and whipped the press and the public into a frenzy in the waning days of 2015. Deemed "the last great meme of 2015," Ender Darling's action became hotly debated online (Feldman 2016), but also burned out about as quickly as Buddy Bolden's fame.

It is unknown how many human bones Ender Darling sold or gave away online before an anonymous tip led to a Louisiana Department of Justice (LDOJ) investigation. This investigation was complex. Tens of thousands of pages of subpoenaed Facebook and other documents and photographs had to be reviewed to support probable cause for search-and-seizure and arrest warrants. Once complete, surveillance of Ender Darling revealed that they lived in a house with at least four other adults, one child, and pets. Although these people did not have known criminal histories, law enforcement took no chances once warrants were signed, which is why the two anthropologists—Christine and me—were held under security several houses away until the house was secured.

This is how, on the early morning of January 28, 2016, Christine and I walked past the four kneeling and handcuffed people and past agents in full-body armor to begin our search for human remains and the interview of the now-internet-famous Ender Darling. Although seemingly heavy-handed, the team, composed of LDOJ anthropologists, LBI agents, NOPD officers, social services, the Orleans Parish Coroner, and representatives from the Louisiana SPCA, ensured that no one was hurt, pets were safe, and especially, that the child was safely and well treated. Ultimately, Ender Darling's housemates were cited for minor drug possession, and the child had such a good time with the LBI agents that she asked if she could be taken to school that day in the police car.

Our search of the house identified an altar in the back room with candles, human remains, and bondage ropes that we had seen used in the private Facebook chat posts. The remains were secured for analysis and ultimate return to Holt. Wholly unrepentant, Ender Darling could not recall from which graves the bones were stolen and was adamant that they were doing a service to these remains because they were using them respectfully compared with their descendants who could not be bothered to visit and clean their graves. The latter is, of course, far from the truth, as Holt is often an active place with families visiting and tending their grave spaces (Krummel 2013), just not in ways always understandable or obvious to outsiders.

Unlike their housemates who promptly dealt with their citations, Ender Darling skipped the state and evaded police and court dates. They were eventually apprehended near Tampa and transported by federal marshals back to New Orleans to stand trial for charges of drug possession and theft in a cemetery. After spending several months in the notorious Orleans Parish Prison, Ender Darling pled guilty and received a sentence of time served and five years of probation.

Ender Darling's actions were direct violence on Holt Cemetery. The city's structural violence was what led to these actions. Despite long-standing legal mandates for cemetery operation, the city left Holt to become an attractive nuisance—one that also happened to be an important place for the local African American community. This ambivalence and structural violence has meant that Ender Darling's story is not exclusive.

At about the same time of Ender Darling's bust, LDOJ also identified a completely unrelated online seller of "cemetery dirt." Although seemingly innocuous and often merely fraudulently created bags of potting soil, real sales of cemetery dirt can and often do contain human bone fragments, and their removal from the burial grounds meets the legal definition of grave desecration (Seidemann and Halling 2022). In this instance, the dirt, which is typically sold online purportedly for use in spells or voodoo rituals—indeed, the anthropologist Wade Davis notes the magical properties of grave dirt in certain Vodun practices in his 1985 book, *The Serpent and the Rainbow*—was claimed to have been taken from the graves of "a murderer," "a soldier," "a mother," and "a child." According to the seller, the dirt had different magical properties and uses based upon from whose grave it was derived. The seller's description of the cemetery of origin sounded suspiciously like Holt Cemetery. Research into the seller identified an address, again, in the Mid-City neighborhood of New Orleans near Holt, Charity Hospital Cemetery No. 1, Greenwood, Cypress Grove, and several other Jewish, Catholic, and fraternal cemeteries. Because of this confluence of information, along with the raging online discussions about Ender Darling's activities, the LDOJ's anthropologists and an LBI agent quietly planned a "knock-and-talk" encounter with the seller on another early morning. When we arrived at the seller's residence, the LBI agent went straight to the seller's door (with us meekly following behind) and used his "cop knock"—a sound created by a simple door knock with a human hand that law enforcement seem to be exclusively able to make, one that made us start—to rouse the residents. A youngish woman opened an upstairs window after several knocks, and we quickly identified ourselves. She just as quickly threw her boyfriend (not there at the time) under the bus, telling us that he had indeed gathered several bags full of dirt from Holt Cemetery to sell online. She then came to the door with several gallon-sized Ziplock bags full of dirt, underbrush, and other odds and ends. She readily admitted that they had made up the classifications such as "a child" when listing the dirt online and that the dirt was indiscriminately picked up around Holt from graves that she could not now remember. She relinquished all bags, the contents of which were later returned to Holt, and promised to stop the desecration and the associated side hustle of dirt sales online. Because this activity was not the intentional removal of human remains from a cemetery and because desecration cases are notoriously difficult to prosecute and fall low on overtaxed district attorneys' dockets, these sellers were left alone with a stern warning. However, this direct violence against Holt Cemetery—like that of Ender Darling—exemplifies the structurally violent result of the city's lax upkeep and protection of these spaces of the marginalized and minority dead. In this city proudly courting the world's thanatology tourists for its real and imagined association with all things goth and dead, New Orleans has created a culture in the local and tourist consciousness that occasionally leads to these violent treatments of African American and other marginalized groups' sacred places.

To suggest that New Orleans is alone in Louisiana in this regard would be a falsehood and a gross oversimplification of the city's relationship with its cemeteries. Acting on another anonymous tip in 2019, LBI agents and LDOJ anthropologist Christine Halling investigated criminal mischief in Baton Rouge's Sweet Olive Cemetery.

Sweet Olive is among Baton Rouge's oldest known African American burial grounds, and its use as a burial place can be traced at least back to the late nineteenth century (Pingitore et al. 2023). Unlike Holt, Sweet Olive is a private cemetery, owned originally by several religious and benevolent entities (Mahoney 2014). Although now disputed by one owner, the cemetery is owned by a church and untold hundreds of descendants of the original incorporators of one of the benevolent associations (Pingitore et al. 2023). The property is now in severe disrepair. The original burials were exclusively in-ground, and the cemetery was deemed full and closed by the city in 1929 (Pingitore et al. 2023). The cemetery's use never actually stopped, and, like Holt, multiple burial events atop one another have led to a confused record of burial locations. Also, because the ground in Baton Rouge does not sink like that in New Orleans, the successive in-ground burials have led to a raised-ground surface as in many English churchyards. After Sweet Olive's ground was full, the community began to place concrete burial vaults atop older in-ground burials, sometimes stacking the vaults two-high. Sweet Olive today is a crumbling cemetery in which falling trees and neglect have led to above-ground burials being broken open and exposing the skeletons inside.

Again, an attractive nuisance, Sweet Olive is occasionally the target of desecration. This most recent situation involved an Instagram user posting videos of himself in the cemetery jumping on tombs and taking bones out of graves. The user played with the bones and added text to his videos such as, "Is this bad luck?" As it turned out for him, it was bad luck. The community was angered and subpoenas to Instagram and Facebook led fairly quickly to an identification and arrest. Caleb Davis was booked on desecration charges and later pled guilty to this misdemeanor instead of facing trial by LDOJ's Criminal Division.

Davis never actually removed the Sweet Olive remains from the site. He would take them out to play with them in his videos and then place them somewhere nearby. Thus, when Christine Halling arrived at the cemetery, she was able to confirm the presence of all the remains seen online. However, because these remains were now internet-famous and left in the open, a new law was used to fully document the location of the remains and then to take them back to LDOJ's anthropology lab for secure retention until such time as the graves could be repaired and the remains safely returned. Although, as of this writing, the Sweet Olive remains have not yet been reinterred, others have been protected and respectfully reinterred under this and similar laws.

Just as with Holt, Sweet Olive's story of decay is a result of the City of Baton Rouge's ambivalence to this African American burial space. Admittedly, there have been recent efforts for the city to acquire Sweet Olive and bring it under its maintenance umbrella like another cemetery down the street. Magnolia Cemetery, a mere two blocks from Sweet Olive, stands in stark contrast to the latter. The site of the Battle of Baton Rouge in 1862, Magnolia is the city's crown jewel cemetery that is predominantly white and is the final resting place of Baton Rouge luminaries and numerous Confederate soldiers. Although some individual graves are in disrepair in Magnolia, the majority of the cemetery looks immaculate compared with Sweet Olive. As with Holt, Sweet Olive's situation and condition is a result of mismanagement and structural (legal) reasons, and that is why it is not subject to the same treatment as Magnolia. This structural treatment has led to the neglect- and desecration-based landscape structural violence that has made Sweet Olive what it is today.

Similar disparate treatment has occurred in other cemeteries in Louisiana, with a recent African American cemetery in Rayne, Louisiana, making news because of desecration (Evans 2023). In that situation, human remains were removed from an exposed grave and were placed in an arrangement on the steps of a nearby Catholic church. These remains are among those recovered by LDOJ under the law and returned for safe reburial. The person who stole the remains is now facing criminal desecration charges and the African American community is shaken by this violation. Again, governmental and structural systems created an environment in which violence was visited on the underprivileged.

St. Peter Street Cemetery

Although later development erased the St. Peter Street Cemetery, like both the Charity and Locust Grove cemeteries, from the landscape, the potential impact upon a disenfranchised descendant community by this action is unclear. Thus, the disappearance of this cemetery from the New Orleans landscape falls into a different category of surface alterations than those discussed above. As noted previously, the St. Peter Street Cemetery contained the remains of both enslaved peoples and free New Orleanians (Gray 2017), representing, at least in part, a clear demographic difference from the impoverished Charity and Locust Grove cemetery populations. However, as with these three cemeteries, there is no historical evidence of consultation with or participation from the descendant community in the decision to put this property to a noncemetery use. In fact, according to Gray (2017), the royal edict issued in Spain initiated the decision to repurpose this land. In the absence of such consultation, had the interred population been anything like that of Charity or the Locust Grove cemeteries, one could conclude that the decision to remove the surface evidence of this cemetery represented an act of violence against a disenfranchised people. Indeed, if future archaeological research on this site reveals that those of a high socioeconomic status or of a particular ethnicity who were buried at the site were removed before the cemetery's reuse for other purposes, then one could conclude that this reuse is likely not an example of violence.

At this time, however, economic expediency assured the conversion of the St. Peter Street Cemetery from a place of burial to commercial uses. In the 1780s, removing surface evidence of a cemetery and reusing the property for commerce was easier than going through the laborious process of removing the remains from the property. King Charles IV (or, more likely, his advisers) likely considered this issue when he issued his 1789 edict, and eventually, as was the case here, people simply forgot that the cemetery existed until it was much later noticed on old maps. In this regard, the treatment of the St. Peter Street Cemetery is substantially similar to that of Highland Cemetery in Baton Rouge. As noted above, this latter cemetery contains the remains of Baton Rouge's elite, but it is clear that, over time, the surrounding neighborhood encroached on the cemetery boundaries (Seidemann and Kleinpeter 2014). Indeed, old maps show burials in the place where single-family residences now stand adjacent to the modern boundaries of Highland. Contrarily, such divergent treatment is on full display a few short miles from Highland Cemetery in Baton Rouge on the property of the former Hollywood Plantation. This land, now part of Louisiana State University's agriculture arm, though substantially decimated by the ravages of time, is protected from impacts by fencing (figure 2.11). In contrast, the nearby cemetery of those once enslaved on the Hollywood Plantation enjoys no such protection. This cemetery now lies within active agricultural fields and exists only on historic maps. It is not protected from any violent reuse as is evidenced by the nearby oil and gas exploration shown in figure 2.12, that had to be monitored by state-employed archaeologists to ensure that no burials were affected.

As with the St. Peter Street Cemetery, the reuse of Highland Cemetery property may or may not constitute a violent act of the ruling class or the bureaucracy against a disenfranchised people. Indeed, such a Marxist perspective of cemetery impacts as violent acts by the elite against the proletariat—the perspective that Galtung (1969) had proposed in his early writings on violence—simply does not fit all scenarios (Parsons 2007). Sometimes greed, expediency, or ignorance simply wins the day and no particularly oppressed people are influenced by the disappearance of all or a portion of a cemetery

Figure 2.11. The remnants of the Hollywood Plantation's planter cemetery. Though in substantially damaged condition due to years of neglect, it is still surrounded by a fence and (minimally) maintained by the landowner (Louisiana State University). Photograph by Elizabeth Seidemann, used with permission.

Figure 2.12. Former Hollywood Plantation land (now owned by Louisiana State University) in Baton Rouge. The left side of the image shows crews preparing to sink an oil well in 2020. This activity was monitored for possible burials, as the plantation's enslaved cemetery is known to be located near the right side of the image in the modern agricultural fields. No burials were encountered during this work.

from the landscape. The Hollywood Plantation enslaved peoples' cemetery is at risk of violence by ignorance.

Gates of Mercy and Girod Street Cemeteries

The final two New Orleans cemeteries considered here fall into the category of those spaces converted from burial places to other uses in which the historical record clearly demonstrates no violence against a disenfranchised community. In both the Gates of Mercy and Girod Street Cemetery examples, the descendant communities, represented by their respective religious institutions and legal representatives, actively participated in the deconsecration of the cemeteries and the movement of the interments to other final resting places. At least, this is the traditional understanding of these events based upon the published court cases. As is demonstrated from archival sources (chapter 5), it is possible that this movement of remains—at least in Girod—was superficial. The reported court cases that recount the transformations of these spaces from sacred ground to other uses certainly indicate that opponents to the conversions existed. However, with both of these cemeteries, the descendant communities approved of their erasure pursuant to law and in full view and with their tacit (if not explicit) approval. Thus, neither of these cemetery destruction events can be said to represent violence in a Galtungian sense. Indeed, even though evidence supports a poor job of retrieving the interred remains from Girod Street Cemetery (Owsley, pers. comm. 2020), this potentially sloppy cemetery move cannot be said to undermine the consent and knowledge of the descendant community granted in the 1950s. Therefore, modern reuses of the Girod site should certainly proceed with caution as, though stripped of its cemetery dedication protections, the identification of human remains at a former cemetery site still triggers the restrictions and permitting mandates of certain modern archaeology laws.

Based upon the above review of New Orleans cemetery repurposing, a picture of a unique form of violence emerges that is ascribable to cemetery destruction, though that violence does not exist each time a cemetery is destroyed or removed from the landscape. For such acts to constitute violence in a Galtungian sense it is not enough that disenfranchised people are on the receiving end of the act (i.e., the impoverished New Orleanians in the case of Charity Hospital Cemetery No. 2 and the Locust Grove cemeteries). Rather, such violence exists in situations where there was a lack of consent from or participation by the descendant community in the decision to move the cemetery. That the latter component is missing from the Gates of Mercy and Girod Street cemeteries and perhaps from the St. Peter Street Cemetery makes suggestions dubious regarding accusations of such violent landscape changes. In this regard, and specifically with respect to the St. Peter Street Cemetery, it is important to consider that many of those interred in this space were enslaved peoples. Because it is a substantial certainty that no consent was sought from the descendants of these people before the repurposing of the cemetery by royal decree, even the adherence to the de jure law of the time (i.e., the removal of the cemetery dedication before the land's reuse) cannot really be said to have been done with the consent of the enslaved people.

This notion of the psychological significance of a link between a group's history and identity and their ability to access the cemetery sites of their presumptive ancestors has been on full display in Louisiana recently as descendant groups of enslaved peoples in St. James Parish have conducted their own archaeological research to ensure the protection of such sites located on land owned by Formosa Plastics and slated for industrial development (Coastal Environments, Inc. 2020a, 2020b). These presumptive descendants have even gone so far as to file legal proceedings in federal and state court to gain access to the sites and to protect them from future disturbance.[11]

These clashes between differing uses of land is a recurring theme in Louisiana. The story of the Revilletown Cemetery is an illustration of these interactions that do not necessarily result directly from structurally violent activities but rather from unintended series of the consequences of various actions.

The Revilletown Cemetery, like many others in the River Parishes region of Louisiana between Baton Rouge and New Orleans, seems to have originated as an enslaved peoples' burial ground on one of the countless antebellum plantations that fronted on the Mississippi River. Around the cemetery following Emancipation was a Freedman's village that grew into a small African American community known as Revilletown. In the latter half of the twentieth century as the descendants of the formerly enslaved moved away from Revilletown to surrounding communities and as the land was converted, through property sales, from agricultural to industrial uses, the town disappeared but the cemetery remained. In the growing industrial area, the Revilletown Cemetery became enveloped by what is now the Axiall chemical plant. This capture of historic cemeteries within the grounds of industrial plants is a common reality in much of South Louisiana, and, as Hochschild (2016) has noted of a white cemetery on the grounds of a Sasol natural gas plant in Westlake, Louisiana, is not exclusively experienced by the African American community. Nonetheless, due to the often-unmarked nature of enslaved peoples' burial grounds and because such sites were present on each plantation, the violent erasure of these African American sites, as was avoided on the Formosa Plastics plant land through proactive community activism (Carrega 2020), is much more common than for white peoples' cemeteries.

The Revilletown Cemetery is a unique exception to the violent ends experienced or faced by other African American cemeteries in the River Parishes. Because it was a continuously operating cemetery through the site's acquisition and enclosure by industrial plants, it was saved. Indeed, many of Revilletown's troubles only began after the turn of the twenty-first century when a church schism led to a years-long (and still unresolved) legal battle by different factions of the descendant community.

Although located within a restricted-access portion of Axiall's plant, Revilletown Cemetery is fenced-off, and reasonable access has been granted over the years for interments, visitation, and cleaning of the burial ground. Thus, because of a seemingly accidental circumstance of history (i.e., the site's continued use and maintenance over time), Revilletown Cemetery has survived the industrialization of the area. Revilletown Cemetery's troubles began when the battling factions sought government sanctioning for the actions of their respective sides in the dispute. Specifically, one faction complained to the Louisiana Cemetery Board (LCB) that a nonowner of the land—the now-fractured church—was unlawfully making burials and sought not only to stop the burials but also to wrest control from the church by obtaining a license to operate the cemetery from the LCB. This complaint led to the LCB's finding that, contrary to the complaining group's claims, title to the burial ground likely did not devolve through the former town's residents' successions, but rather was likely part of the larger grant of land now owned by Axiall.

This ownership dispute, with Axiall caught in the middle, resulted in at least three lawsuits and not much resolution. Based upon appellate decisions, it does now appear that Axiall indeed owns the cemetery land.

Because Louisiana law only allows the state to license a landowner or its designee to operate a cemetery, the continued use of Revilletown Cemetery was now in doubt. No faction of the descendant community had legal control over the cemetery. Although it may be arguable that such a legal outcome in which a multinational corporation obtains control over a minority cemetery represents structural violence by either the company or the legal structure against the minority community, the specific history of this site and its control are much more nuanced and thus circumspect for being a true candidate of structural violence. In many ways, the control problems are a self-inflicted wound of the warring descendants. However, under the acrimonious circumstances, Axiall's attorneys were unable to decipher which faction should have authority over the property. Because of this, Axiall opted not to obtain a cemetery license from the state and would not pick favorites from the descendants and grant one legal authority over the other to operate the cemetery on its (i.e., the landowner's) behalf.

Compounding the ownership and control problems was another finding by the LCB: there was (and never had been) any burial records kept of the cemetery. Although the location of some discrete graves were identifiable by visible inspection, many were unmarked in addition to the reality that older in-ground graves likely filled the remaining space in the cemetery. Without proper documentation, the LCB could not legally issue a license to anyone.[12] Moreover, because Louisiana law mandates permission from existing interment rights owners to reuse a grave space and because most of those owners were unknown, future (lawful) burials in this cemetery became unlikely. Requests by one faction for an expansion of the cemetery on Axiall's grounds were denied. Again, this expansion denial could arguably represent an event of structural violence whereby American notions of private property rights held by a corporation directly conflicted with the wishes and traditions of a minority community. The possibility of this conflict actually representing structural violence is tempered by the internal descendant dispute.

Although largely dying with the leader of the church's breakaway faction in the 2020s (cf. Hawkins 2023), this dispute of control is illustrative of the complexity in determining when actions affecting cemeteries are or are not a result of structural violence. Unlike the clear structural violence examples of the Thomy Lafon School/Locust Grove cemeteries and the Canal Boulevard/Charity No. 2 Cemetery clashes in New Orleans, the Revilletown Cemetery situation is much more nuanced. Certainly, the Revilletown Cemetery situation exhibits and contains some hallmarks of structural violence—legal controls and property ownership affecting minority rights and traditions—the internal descendant schism makes it difficult to conclusively classify the Revilletown Cemetery situation and the heartache experienced by both sides of the schism as a result (certainly not the exclusive result) of the structurally violent application of majority-enacted laws and rules to a minority cemetery. Deep dives into these historical details are essential in such inquiries, and even then the answer of whether something is a result of structural violence may not be apparent or definitive.

Because cemeteries (when compared with other types of land) occupy a unique place in the consciousness and even the subconsciousness of most Western cultures, violent acts directed at these spaces rise above the level of mere violence against an object (Seidemann and Halling 2019). Often grouped with spaces in which great calamities or battles occurred (Walls 2011), cemeteries are indeed special (Maples and East 2013). The effect of violence that erases these spaces from the landscape runs deeper than the demolition of a beloved structure. It functions to erase from the collective consciousness the final vestiges of the actual existence of people (Pelley 2022). When these people have been disenfranchised during life, their resting places in the cemetery are often all that is left of their memory. The demolition of such spaces with no consideration for the descendant community effectively erases whatever tenuous links such disenfranchised people had to immortality. Because the consequences of such violent acts are so grave to the collective consciousness of a people, the violent demolition of cemeteries should be considered a form of structural violence and not, as Galtung (1969:170) might argue, a "'degenerate' form" of violence.

3

The Native American Graves Protection and Repatriation Act and Its Louisiana Progeny

As an undergraduate in anthropology at Florida State University, I had the honor of working on arguably one of the most incredible skeletal samples from the prehistoric Americas and was lucky enough to have a mentor who trusted my respect for the remains and genuinely wanted me to succeed. It was the early 1990s and Glen Doran and others had saved the Windover mortuary pond (8BR246) from destruction and oblivion by a residential development near Cape Canaveral almost a decade earlier. By the time I arrived at FSU—a clueless undergraduate transfer student from New Orleans who registered for Glen's human osteology class on a whim—the department was undertaking the necessary inventories of human remains and burial artifacts as mandated by the Native American Graves Protection and Repatriation Act (NAGPRA). Despite the ongoing processes nationwide to catalogue Indigenous remains for probable repatriation and reburial, I was blissfully ignorant of the dark history of anthropology and Indigenous treatment that led to NAGPRA's 1990 passage. During Glen's class, we students were taught the intricacies of the human skeleton and the analytical techniques to recover from them basic information about the people during life. These lessons largely were undertaken using highly fragmentary remains from such sites as Sowell Mound (8BY3) and others plundered by Clarence B. Moore in the early twentieth century. In fact, Moore's skull and pot recovery efforts resembled nothing like what we would recognize today as acceptable or ethical mortuary archaeology (Milanich 2000).

Moore, a Philadelphia socialite, plied the waters of the southeastern United States in his custom-outfitted steamer, the *Gopher*, searching for Native American mounds. Once identified, Moore would, with crews of seasonal laborers, hack into the mounds to recover intact ceramics and human skulls (Milanich 2000). The broken bits of postcranial skeletons and potsherds were often left behind. Certainly, Moore consulted no Native Americans regarding the propriety of his fieldwork nor obtained any sort of informed consent from descendant groups or the deceased before essentially robbing graves on a massive scale. The skulls and ceramics were typically sent to Philadelphia for analysis and curation. Indeed, much of the skeletal material on which FSU's osteology students were taught by my time were the postcranial "scraps" and "leftovers" from Moore's plunderings later excavated in salvage operations and curated at the university (Dailey and Morse 1984). Having little research value, these remains were used as teaching tools for generations, and similar collections have been used across the country and world to teach generations of skeletal specialists.

When Glen informed the class of mostly graduate students that, not only was the semester's grade based on weekly practical exams on bone analysis and fragmentary identification, but that a major component would also be an original research paper on human skeletal remains and that "good papers approach 60 pages," I began to question my course scheduling decisions. Intent on researching some exciting topic related to skeletal trauma, I was crushed and left without a topic when Glen informed me that the FSU collections did not contain a meaningful sample size of traumatic injuries for me to research. Instead, Glen suggested that I examine what I considered at the time to be the painfully uninteresting femur. Specifically, Glen suggested that I "take a look at the femur neck. I don't think much work has been done on that." Because of the fragmentary nature of the Sowell Mound and other such "teaching" samples, there were not many intact femora for me to examine. For reasons that I will never know, Glen allowed me to use the Windover sample for my term paper.

The humbling nature of this Early Archaic skeletal sample and the honor of being able to work with it as a teenager was life-changing for me. Indeed, now at nearly 50, I recently made a pilgrimage to the Windover archaeological site in Titusville on a family vacation with my wife and children to Cape Canaveral. What began for me as a sophomore term paper ultimately resulted in two peer-reviewed publications on skeletal biology and lifelong friendships and collaborations with both Glen Doran and my erstwhile research partner, Christopher Stojanowski.

When, in 1996, Glen helped Chris and me to obtain funding to undertake femur research on documented skeletal collections at the Smithsonian Institution, I began to gather an idea of the dark intellectual and academic history from which I had benefited (and to a lesser extent, still do). Although Chris and I were at the Smithsonian to obtain femur neck metrics from the anatomical samples of the Terry and Huntington collections, I could not help but be struck by the endless cabinets of Indigenous skeletal remains that lined the walls of the National Museum of Natural History (NMNH).

The Darkness of Physical Anthropology

The Huntington Collection was particularly difficult for us to access, as it was housed in various places throughout the NMNH. At one point, I climbed a ladder to reach the top shelf of the Smithsonian's famously tall collections stacks, and, reading the drawer tags on my way up, noticed that the Indigenous remains stored below me originated from Kodiak Island in Alaska. These samples of remains were undergoing inventory and consultation for their ultimate repatriation to Alaska Native groups (Loring 1995; Pullar 2008). At the time, the return of such remains seemed to me anathema—a disservice to science. Although not being repatriated as part of a NAGPRA process, the Kodiak remains and others like them at the Smithsonian are emblematic of the troubled history of modern biological anthropology and, as I later learned, never should have been acquired in the first place.

From the 1920s until just before his death in 1943, then-Smithsonian curator and physical anthropologist, Aleš Hrdlička, spent several field seasons in Alaska obtaining human remains for the national collections in Washington, D.C. (Cook 2006). However, before his Alaska field days, Hrdlička was party to perhaps one of the most sinister chapters in American anthropological history: the acquisition of the Greenland Inuit for the American Museum of Natural History in New York (AMNH).

Fresh off the successes of exhibiting anthropology and living and dead "specimens" as curiosities at the 1893 World Colombian Exhibition in Chicago (Boas 2016 [1893]), the father of American anthropology, Franz Boas, was working in New York at AMNH. Boas and his then–Columbia University student, Alfred Kroeber, were presented with six living Inuit brought to New York from Greenland by Robert Peary.

Peary, a self-promoting explorer, was in the midst of championing the United States' race for the North Pole in the 1890s. His attempts and later claim to success in attaining the Pole,[1] though disputed even today, originated from base camps in remote portions of Greenland. For numerous attempts at the Pole, Peary employed Indigenous Greenlanders as guides and laborers. After his failed 1897 expedition, Peary persuaded six of these Inuit to accompany him back to the United States in the hopes of raising his own profile (and more expedition money) by exhibiting these living "savages" to the "civilized" masses of New York.[2]

In reality, as Harper (2000) notes in his recounting of the Inuit's deadly journey south, Peary was little, if at all, concerned with the well-being of his living exhibits. Indeed, only his consummate colleague, Matthew Henson, had even bothered to learn the Indigenous language. Not knowing what to do with these six people, Peary presented them to the AMNH upon his return to New York and promptly abandoned them to the care of Boas and Kroeber.

Throngs of New Yorkers crowded the AMNH basement where the Inuit were living to gawk at these "primitives," while Boas and Kroeber attempted to obtain ethnological information from the captives. Like Peary, Boas seemed little concerned about the Inuit as they were kept in cramped quarters and were presented as veritable sideshow attractions to the public. Not surprisingly, all of the Inuit were soon sick from various maladies contracted from their unprepared immune systems' barrage by pathogens from the ogling New York public. Although Kroeber and, to some extent, Henson and the museum staff, tried to alleviate their suffering, the Inuit began to die.

Among the six Inuit were a father and his young son, Qisuk and Minik. Although all of the Inuit became ill, six-year-old Minik somehow survived. He watched his father and fellow countrymen waste away in the museum and later at Bellevue Hospital in Manhattan. Minik was deeply traumatized, and, though the Inuit were promised the ability to return home on a subsequent Peary voyage, most died before they could leave. Only Minik and Uisaakassak, a young man, survived, and only Uisaakassak made the return journey. Minik, as an orphaned minor, was left behind as a ward of the museum.

Upon his father's death, Minik pleaded with his captors to provide Qisuk with a decent in-ground burial. It was too late for this. Boas had already turned Qisuk's remains over to Hrdlička for them to be defleshed and housed in the AMNH collections ostensibly for study. Fearing the public relations nightmare of the truth, Boas, Kroeber, and the museum's staff constructed a fake burial of Qisuk on the AMNH grounds and conducted a memorial service at the site for Minik's (and, by extension, the press's) benefit.

It was not until much later that Minik learned that his father's remains had been defleshed and added to the AMNH anatomical collections. Although he had the press on his side, Minik was never able to secure the release of his father's remains for a proper Greenlandic burial during his lifetime. Minik never psychologically recovered from this ruse and spent the rest of his life plagued with illness (largely attributed to his near-death infections on arriving in New York) and depression. Despite Minik's suffering, Boas and Hrdlička had obtained their scientific samples and went on to bigger and better things—the former training several generations of anthropologists and founding the American school of that field at Columbia University, and the latter as the NMNH's curator of physical anthropology and the founder of American physical anthropology.

Hrdlička's unethical skeletal acquisition practices were far from over. As he moved to the NMNH, he scoured the planet for remains to add to that museum's collections. These efforts ultimately culminated in his excursions to Alaska and the acquisition of the skeletons that I came face to face with more than a half century later. The basis for Hrdlička's bone-collecting wanderings was to support and further inquire into questions of racial typology, though Hrdlička may have disputed such a characterization (Clever 2020:18). Although ardently rejected by the likes of Boas as a means for justifying differential treatment of humans (Armelagos and Van Gerven 2003:55–56), "racial typology was [the] major theoretical and methodological focus" of American physical anthropology during Hrdlička's time (Armelagos and Van Gerven 2003:53). In fairness, Hrdlička was less concerned with racial typology than with a data-driven analysis of "a historical process driven by the forces of human migrations, diffusion, and racial admixture" (Armelagos and Van Gerven 2003:55). The data sought by Hrdlička often lay in the bones of past and current people (though many of his works also include soft tissue and morphological analyses of living people) (Hrdlička 1908; Comas 1960).

According to his own diaries, Aleš Hrdlička, originally trained as a physician, undertook many of his skeletal acquisitions under dubious and clandestine circumstances that did not use anything resembling modern archaeological methods or ethics. In Alaska, Hrdlička would travel—often by boat—from village to village, searching for cemeteries as he went. Although many of the sites he encountered were the resting places of Russian colonists, these were left undisturbed. Hrdlička wanted Indigenous remains and would often go to great lengths to obtain them. One of his diary entries recounts how he began to collect skeletal remains from a relatively recent above-ground tomb when he was accosted by the dead man's wife. She pleaded with Hrdlička not to take her husband's remains and instead directed him to another cemetery nearby as a consolation prize. The exchange, even as recounted by Hrdlička, is shocking by any modern standards of ethics and decency. In this instance, Hrdlička (1943:235) recounted the following story of his 1929 Alaskan bone hunts:

> Find some Russian cross burials and, under a tree, a rotten box with a partially exposed male skeleton. Send word down to people to ask if they have no objection—say, after explanation, "all right, take bones." Call M., and so with a bag begin to gather the remains. But this seems to arouse an old woman who comes and without looking our way talks excitedly and evidently in disapproval of what we are doing. Cannot make out what it all means, so send down Mike to find out and to tell her, if she wants, we will put bones back. Says yes, put back, it was her "long ago" husband—the burial is at least thirty or forty years old, judging by the conditions. As I am anxious not to do anything against

> the native's wishes, put skeleton back and cover as well as possible. The woman, appeased, calls we should go to the "old place," in the direction of which she points, and take bones there. . . . In a short time take out a male and two females from the oldest burials—rest not of much value and left. On returning all passes well and we soon leave, everybody, old granny too, content.

Although seemingly demonstrating some amount of complicity by Alaska Natives in Hrdlička's bone-collecting efforts, the opposite is a more logical interpretation of the above quoted encounter. In the recounted excerpt, it is clear that Hrdlička's efforts were known to many Alaskans. Indeed, other portions of his diary refer to him being denied landing of his boat because the locals knew that he was coming to loot graves. The above excerpt, rather than complicity, appears to represent the Alaska Native's quick decision in a Morton's Fork situation. She was presented with an untenable scenario: a known grave robber was going to dig up her husband's remains. She could either stand by and let her husband's remains be looted or find something else for him to loot. As repugnant as the choice may be viewed today, this woman's lousy choices in the moment demonstrate how resigned these people had become to the violence of grave desecration by white people and the fact that fighting back was not seen as a viable third option. This outcome is hauntingly similar to the actions of many terrorized Jews in Nazi Europe and African Americans during the Jim Crow era in the American South.[3] Other accounts have Hrdlička waiting behind trees and snow piles for funerals to finish so that he could rush over and disinter the recently deceased. The remains were then crated and shipped to Washington, D.C., for addition to the NMNH collections.

The Beginnings of Modern Biological Anthropology

To suggest that the entirety of Indigenous opposition to the scientific inquiry into their past and using their human remains for such inquiry is solely limited to the clandestine activities of the founding generation of American anthropologists and physical anthropologists would be a gross misconception and mistake. However, this early period is particularly important because the activities, like those summarized here, were, by modern standards, outrageous. These outrageous activities formed much of the basis, behind the drafting and creation of National Museum of the American Indian Act (NMAIA), and NAGPRA.

Certainly, as physical anthropology moved into the middle of the twentieth century, methods became more standardized, the field became more professionalized, and ethical codes of practice were implemented. The majority of these changes brought an end to the clandestine excavation, and removal of Indigenous remains in academia, and indeed, any other human remains at least among the anthropological and archaeological community. What did not change was the massive scale by which the mid-twentieth-century excavation, removal, curation, and analysis of these Indigenous and other human remains were carried out. As observed by several scholars of the history of anthropology, the Works Progress Administration (WPA) implemented by President Franklin Roosevelt began a jumping-off point for archaeological excavations on a colossal scale in the United States (Milner and Jacobi 2006).

Because of the massive public works projects that were being undertaken, especially in the southeastern United States during the pre–World War II period, the excavation and removal of Indigenous burial sites in advance of such things as flooding of vast areas by the Tennessee Valley Authority were occurring on a scale not seen by the prior generations. This large-scale excavation of archaeological sites and especially of burial sites across the United States continued from the WPA activities in the 1930s through substantial damming operations in the Midwest and Great Plains into the 1960s and 1970s (Owsley and Jantz 1994). All these works, as observed by Milner and Jacobi (2006), resulted in unknown numbers of human remains pouring into university and museum collections around the country. Thus, while it is impossible to separate the legislation of the 1980s regarding protections against the excavation and curation of Indigenous American human remains from the rather sordid past of anthropology's founding generation, the reality is that the majority of the collections found so offensive by Indigenous Americans that led to the legislation was actually undertaken by a later generation of anthropologists. It simply seems that the stories of these collections were lost in the shuffle of that legislating because, though vast in scope, they did not represent the conscience-shocking activities of men like Hrdlička, Perry, and Boas.

It was these latter stories, coupled with the large numbers of remains in American institutions that led to the legislation of the 1980s. Considering this history, it is small wonder that the Alaska collections were among the first repatriated by the Smithsonian under NAGPRA's sister law, the NMAIA.

What I did not know in the 1990s when I was researching the human femur in the hopes of creating a method to assist in the identification of missing persons was the sordid academic history on whose shoulders I stood and from whose collection practices I had benefited. Thankfully, my beloved

Windover collection was not among these sinister acquisitions. Glen Doran, a trained archaeologist and bioanthropologist, excavated the site in the 1980s in a manner that exceeded best practice standards of the time. Much meaningful research has been generated from those excavations. But even that collection, excavated before the passage of Native American burial protection legislation in the United States or in Florida is now on its way to repatriation. It is not samples like Windover that gave rise to NAGPRA. Rather, it is the history of mistreating the New World's Indigenous peoples and their graves that gave rise to NAGPRA. An understanding of this law and its place in the pantheon of cemetery site and human remains protections is crucial to understanding legal and archaeological developments over the past 30+ years and to understanding how archaeologists can better operate to ensure that the sins of the profession's past are not repeated on both Native Americans and other disenfranchised groups in the future.

The Legal Structure: NAGPRA and Related Laws

Arguably the passage of NAGPRA is, to date, the most visible acknowledgment in United States history of the systemic, indeed structural, violence against the dead. Although the passage of this law in 1990 predates much of the adaptation of Galtung's (1969) concept of structural violence to the dead in scholarly circles, the law clearly demonstrates all the hallmarks of human rights legislation intended to atone for perceived sins of the past and the lack of consultation and agency afforded to such people regarding the treatment of their ancestors' remains occasioned by the systematic treatment of Indigenous American human remains in a manner that, whether intentional or not, "impedes personal growth" (Galtung 1980) in many Indigenous American communities.

Following more than twenty years of lobbying on the part of the Native American community (McKeown 2012), the U.S. Congress passed NAGPRA in 1990,[4] thereby setting in place a mechanism for the return and reburial of certain Native American skeletal remains and sacred objects from museum and university collections across the United States as well as providing for the protection of in situ human remains and burial sites (McManamon 2001).[5] NAGPRA is seen by many, as it was characterized by Senator John McCain during the congressional debates on the law, as

> legislation [that] effectively balances the interest of Native Americans in the rightful and respectful return of their ancestors with the interests of our Nation's museums in maintaining our rich cultural heritage, the

heritage of all American peoples. Above all, . . . this legislation establishes a process that provides the dignity and respect that our Nation's first citizens deserve.[6]

Understanding the significance of NAGPRA's passage and the changes that it wrought on human remains and cemetery site protection is impossible without an understanding of the genesis of the law and the events leading to its passage. Properly conceptualizing the past 30+ years of both human remains and cemetery protection legislating in the United States is also not possible without a complete understanding of NAGPRA and its history.

NAGPRA and the Treatment and Protection of Native American Human Remains and Cemeteries

The tension between Indigenous peoples and the anthropological community over the latter's treatment of the former's skeletal remains, came to a head over certain revelations during the congressional efforts to establish the National Museum of the American Indian. Although such tensions had been simmering for years, they reached a boiling point in the mid-1980s during congressional testimony regarding the size of the Indigenous American skeletal collections housed at the Smithsonian Institution (Harjo 2004; Seidemann 2003; 2004). These revelations led to nationwide inquiries into the treatment of Indigenous American human remains and cemetery sites that, in turn, substantially led to the passage of NAGPRA in 1990. To fully understand NAGPRA's importance it is critical to summarize the prior existing law.

Violence such as that recounted above was rife within American medicine, anthropology, and physical anthropology for much of the nineteenth and twentieth centuries (see, e.g., Harjo 2004). Mercifully, this has begun to change. However, anthropology has by no means been the exclusive source of structural violence meted out to various groups through the treatment of their cemeteries and their ancestors' human remains. Indeed, until the passage of NAGPRA, the American legal system established its own form of structural violence through the silence in prior enactments of cultural resources laws on topics related to the treatment especially of human remains. Cemeteries as archaeological sites were afforded somewhat better protection under these earlier laws. Even NAGPRA, as landmark human rights legislation, represents a continuity of structural violence as against non-Indigenous peoples in the United States by restricting its protection of human remains and cemeteries only to Native Americans and not to other peoples who have historically been subjected to structural violence. Nonetheless, NAGPRA was a significant step forward in combating structural violence. One need only quickly examine the prior laws to understand the paradigm shift that occurred in 1990.

The Antiquities Act

The first such law in the United States was the Antiquities Act of 1906. The Antiquities Act of 1906 occupies only a small amount of space in the United States Code, 16 U.S.C. §§ 431–433, but the impact of this law has been substantial. From its inception in 1906 until the Archaeological Resources Protection Act (ARPA) was passed in 1979, the Antiquities Act was the dominant enforcement law for the protection of archaeological sites on federal lands in the United States (Ades 1995).

Section 431 outlines the president's power under the Antiquities Act. This section grants power to the president to declare "historic landmarks, historic and prehistoric structures, and other objects of historic or scientific interest that are situated upon lands owned or controlled" by the United States as national monuments (16 U.S.C. § 431). The practical implication of section 431 is realized in section 432. Section 432 grants authority to the Secretaries of Interior, Agriculture, and the Army to issue excavation and artifact collection permits to qualified individuals to conduct such activity on Antiquities Act–protected lands (16 U.S.C. § 432). The only restriction on securing such permits, assuming that the qualified individual requirement has been met, is that "the examinations, excavations, or gatherings are undertaken for the benefit of reputable museums, universities, colleges, or other recognized scientific or educational institutions, with a view to increasing the knowledge of such objects, and that the gatherings shall be made for permanent preservation in public museums" (16 U.S.C. § 432). Section 433 provides for criminal and civil sanctions for violations of the Antiquities Act.

The National Historic Preservation Act

The National Historic Preservation Act represented another watershed moment in historic preservation and archaeological site protection when it was passed in 1966. This law provided a legal scheme, largely given power through the enactment of the National Environmental Policy Act of 1970, to assist in the preservation and conservation of historic sites in the United States. Important as it was and is, this law has limited application as it is triggered only by a federal undertaking or for activities occurring on federal or tribal land. Moreover, this law provides no explicit protection of human remains or cemeteries, thus continuing the structurally violent legal framework against such sites as existed before its enactment.

The Archaeological Resources Protection Act

In 1979, things seemed poised to change with regard to human remains protections with the passage of ARPA. The stated purpose of ARPA is to "secure . . . the protection of archaeological resources and sites which are on public lands and Indian lands and to foster increased cooperation and exchange of information between governmental authorities [and] the professional archaeological community" (16 U.S.C. § 470aa[b]). From this stated purpose, it appears that ARPA was intended to protect against one thing: pothunting. This is further bolstered by the congressional findings stated in the act (16 U.S.C. § 470aa[a]). These findings identify the threats to archaeological materials and sites rooted in "their commercial attractiveness" (16 U.S.C. § 470aa[a][2]) combined with inadequate protection from destruction due to "uncontrolled excavations and pillage" (16 U.S.C. § 470aa[a][3]).

It is clear in the congressional materials that ARPA was created for one purpose: to stem the tide of illegal excavation and the sale of artifacts from federal and Native American lands.[7] The purpose of ARPA is carried out by

> providing penalties commensurate with the value of the resource damaged or removed from public lands or Indian lands without a permit. In addition, information concerning the nature and location of any archaeological resource which might create a risk to such resource would be exempt under the Freedom of Information Act.[8]

The legislative history provides a precise explanation of the intent of ARPA: "The bill provides for the protection of archaeological resources on public and Indian lands by prohibiting unauthorized removal or sale of antiquities and outlines a means of assessing penalties to be imposed on violators."[9] Indeed, the author of the Senate version of ARPA, Senator Domenici, commented that the law was intended to address the problem of looters.[10] Much of the realization of this purpose was to be accomplished by shoring up the then-faltering Antiquities Act of 1906. This purpose is also supported in H. Rep. No. 96–311, which cites the Ninth Circuit decision in *United States v. Diaz*, 499 F.2d 113 (9th Cir. 1974), a federal case declaring a portion of the Antiquities Act unconstitutional,[11] "coupled with the dramatic rise in recent years of illegal excavations on public lands and Indian lands for private gain."[12]

Again, though well-intentioned and providing a needed boost to the Antiquities Act as it faltered, ARPA similarly does nothing to stem the structural violence directed at human remains and cemetery sites that had become so commonplace in the United States by this time. Indeed, it could be argued that these laws increased the violent burden on human remains and cemeteries by creating a permitting scheme whereby, among other things, these items and sites could be collected to bolster institutional holdings (human remains) or destroyed through excavation (cemeteries). The latter risk seems minimal, as such permits were used to require a level of competency in the event that cemetery sites needed to be moved that had not yet existed in federal law. However, because this law did not require consultation with descendant communities before excavating a cemetery, the violence carried out through such excavations on descendant communities remained intact and, indeed, sanctioned.

The American Indian Religious Freedom Act

At roughly the same time, Indigenous America again put its faith in Congress to fill the legislative gaps left open that continued to threaten its burial sites and human remains with, in 1978, the passage of the American Indian Religious Freedom Act (AIRFA). As with NAGPRA, AIRFA was civil rights legislation intended "to preserve and protect Native American traditional practices and religious freedom" (Harjo 2004:130). As it relates to human remains and burial sites, as Harjo (2004) and others later observe, AIRFA was expected to both provide Native Americans with a pathway to claiming human remains in institutional collections and to provide protection for burial sites. This law was substantially policy-based and lacked meaningful mechanisms to foster repatriation (Trope 2013). Nonetheless, in some ways, likely politically rather than morally based, some remains were delivered from federal agency collections to claimant tribes as a result of AIRFA and its congressional hearings. Simply, though, whether politically or morally based, AIRFA's aspirational policies were insufficient to resolve the deep divide growing between Indigenous Americans and anthropologists. Something "legally enforceable" was needed (Tsosie 2004:169) and NAGPRA was the ultimate answer to that need.

NAGPRA and the Red Power Movement

NAGPRA represents, at least with respect to the treatment of Indigenous human remains in the United States, a significant development resulting from (though not exclusively) the civil rights movements of the 1960s (Thomas 2000). The laws passed during this period in the United States were aimed directly at providing agency and protection to disenfranchised people. As an outgrowth of such laws, NAGPRA provides direct agency to Native peoples over the control of their deceased ancestors' remains. Human remains, as objects imbued with substantial psychological and metaphysical significance for descendant communities, when treated poorly, disrespectfully, or inconsistently with the wishes of oppressed people, fall within the penumbra of concepts covered by Galtung (1969) when he introduced the concept of structural violence as a theory within which to analyze and combat disproportionate treatment of certain people.

During the civil rights movements, while the more visible African American civil rights protests and demonstrations dominated the news, other minority groups also began to assert their dissidence with Anglo-America. The so-called Red Power movement began in the mid-1960s (Josephy 1971; Harjo 2004). This movement represented a Native American backlash against nearly 500 years of oppression and is recognized by some as the turning point in Native American perspectives regarding the treatment of their dead and their cemeteries (Thomas 2000).

In 1969, Vine Deloria Jr. published his provocative book, *Custer Died for Your Sins: An Indian Manifesto.* In this book Deloria attacks virtually all non-Native American institutions in the United States; one entire chapter is devoted to anthropologists. While making such lighthearted jabs at the anthropological community as "Indians are certain that all societies of the Near East had anthropologists at one time because all those societies are now defunct" (Deloria 1969:83), some of Deloria's observations were acute and have become a sounding board for Native Americans across the United States. Deloria (1969:97) commented that "[a]cademia [including anthropology], and its by-products, continues to become more irrelevant to the needs of the people." Further, Deloria (1969:98) characterized anthropology and Native American[13] relations thus: a "[c]ompilation of useless knowledge 'for knowledge's sake' should be rejected by the Indian people. We should not be objects of observation for those who do nothing to help us." Much of Deloria's tongue-in-cheek ridiculing of anthropologists was "playful" and was not intended to be the focus of his broader criticisms of "Indian policy" (Arndt 2023:468).[14] Nonetheless, over the past 50 years, his perspectives regarding anthropology—and especially archaeology and physical anthropology—and the associated political activity led to increased agency among Native American groups regarding their historic existence in the New World, that often developed into a general distrust of the pronouncements of academic anthropology—especially those on topics related to the peopling of the New World (Mihesuah 1996) and the prehistory interpreted from the analysis of cemeteries and human skeletal remains (Riding In 2000; Zimmerman 2007). A consensus exists among many Native American communities with respect to the researching of skeletal remains and cemeteries for the purpose of understanding past cultures and, indeed, their own cultures: that Native Americans do not need to know such things (see, e.g., Hammil and Zimmerman 1983).

Central to many Native Americans' objections to science, and especially the work of archaeologists and biological anthropologists, is their opposition to the disturbance of the dead for research purposes. As Roger Byrd, a Lakota medicine man, once commented (Hammil and Zimmerman 1983:15), "[w]e don't believe in digging up our own people, nor do we believe in digging up other people. When we bury our dead, we use sacred ceremonies, we do certain sacred rituals. . . . It is one of our laws that we leave our dead alone."

Because of the extreme variation of cultures and perspectives within Native America, concluding that all Native American people are not interested in learning about their past through human remains analysis is impossible. Rather, likely the sole unifying theme among these groups seems to be a desire for increased agency in such endeavors. Indigenous American groups want to participate fully in decisions regarding control of the content and methodology of what is studied (if anything is studied at all). This general position continues to evolve over time. As collaboration between archaeologists and Indigenous Americans increases, levels of comfort and trust allow for more research to be undertaken (e.g., Farris 2003; Simon 2006; White 2014). Moreover, and contrary to one recent publication's allegations (Weiss and Springer 2020), the more agency afforded to Indigenous Americans in the conduct of this research, the more cooperative and meaningful such endeavors become (see, e.g., Hanna 1999). Such cooperation must not be just a passive cooperation, though. Weiss and Springer (2020:159) criticize what they call collaborative research as one-sided, in which passive living Indigenous research subjects can restrict later uses of the data collected by non-Indigenous institutions and researchers. Such later uses—particularly the blood studies on the Havasupai peoples that generated considerable press in the early 2000s (e.g., Shaffer 2004), raises questions about informed consent and smacks of research debacles such as those surrounding the HeLa cell research (Skloot 2011)[15] and the Tuskegee Institute's syphilis research (Thomas and Quinn 1991; Willoughby 2022)[16]—is not the sort of constructive collaboration that is now sought by most anthropologists or Indigenous Americans. Rather, for collaborative research to be meaningful and to allow continued access to human remains for study, it must be truly collaborative—research that provides agency to the studied populations in addition to participation in the research design, data collection, and analysis. Passive collaboration, absent Indigenous or other descendant consent, is, in most cases, no longer tenable as a research model.

The Functional Realities of a Century of Federal Laws

In discussions of the results of repatriation and Indigenous agency, the focus is often on the perceived loss to science (Kakaliouras 2014) of viable research subjects and objects when materials are returned to descendant communities (e.g., Weiss 2008; Weiss and Springer 2020). Such alleged losses are often overstated and are based on isolated examples. That Weiss and Springer's (2020) focus on a handful of ancient human skeletons that were repatriated is one such example.[17] Contrary to Weiss and Springer's (2020) assertions that repatriation represents an us-versus-them fight (i.e., scientists versus Indigenous peoples or descendant communities) over the control of truth—one that is based on the age-old dispute over the establishment of religion by legislation (in their view, NAGPRA)—emerging scholarship suggests that Indigenous religious beliefs play but a minor role in repatriation efforts. For example, Simpson (2008:64) identifies situations in which the return of remains and associated burial objects work to "contribute to the production of living heritage" in Indigenous groups' efforts to "revitalize their cultural heritage." The empowerment of Indigenous and descendant communities that arises from such repatriations is no less important or significant than the data that might be available to scientists from these peoples' remains and cultural patrimony (Killion 2007). Indeed, though the history of NAGPRA's enactment (McKeown 2012; Seidemann 2003, 2004) contains some commentary on Indigenous religious beliefs and practices, the legislation was brought and continues to be human rights focused—aimed at undoing the centuries-long unequal treatment of Native American human remains when compared with the treatment of the remains of their colonizers. Further bolstering the human rights nature of NAGPRA is a similar (as well as disappointingly different) law recently passed by Congress and signed by President Biden: the African American Burial Grounds Preservation Program (Seidemann 2023). This law was passed partially in response to activist and academic calls for the protection of African American remains and cemeteries on par with existing Native American rights (Dunnavant et al. 2021). While not at all identical to NAGPRA and, in many ways disappointing for the preservation of such sites (Seidemann 2023), this law also recognizes—not in any way tied to a First Amendment notion of establishment of religion—the disappointingly poor treatment of African Americans in death much as did NAGPRA for Native Americans (Halcrow et al. 2021). As noted by Watkins (2008), such importance is largely dependent upon the perspective of the individual advocating for or opposing repatriation. Moreover, personal experience has demonstrated that assisting in the provision of descendant agency and supporting repatriation efforts actually can result in more scientific inquiry being collaboratively undertaken. Because of these multifaceted benefits for Indigenous and descendant communities, the importance of collaborative efforts in repatriation scenarios cannot be simply reduced to a science-versus-religion binary. Thus, when Weiss and Springer (2020) go so far as to equate modern repatriation efforts with attempts to muzzle science in the evolution-creation disputes, they fail to consider nuances and nonreligious factors in such discussions, thereby denigrating any argument in support not just of repatriation but also of any anthropology-descendant collaboration.

The pitting of belief systems against science creates a tension where possibly none should exist. It also creates a straw man theory that can be pilloried as anti-intellectual more easily than can the nuanced disputes actually at the heart of the discord. One need look no further than the arguments advanced by William Jennings Bryan during the Scopes evolution trial in 1927. In the Scopes case, boosters of a small Tennessee town forced a "showdown" between religion and science when they put on a sham trial pitting the Darwinian theory of evolution against fundamentalist Christian interpretations of Genesis (Larson 2006). This debate for the ages pitted Bryan, a three-time presidential candidate and ardent Evangelical Christian, against Clarence Darrow, the civil rights lawyer known as "the attorney for the damned" (Farrell 2011).

This sham trial bears many resemblances to the fringe anthropologists still clinging to the notion that NAGPRA is the sponsoring of religion by the U.S. government to the detriment of science. Lacking from the NAGPRA dispute is the boosterism of Dayton, Tennessee, that occurred in the Scopes trial. However, the overblown polarized positions pitting Indigenous religions against common-sense science is a direct replica of the Scopes trial, merely switching Evangelical Christianity with Indigenous religions. In both cases, the proponents of science seek to portray religion in any form as necessarily backward and an impediment to scientific "progress." Sometimes religion does serve this purpose (e.g., *Edwards v. Aguillard,* 482 U.S. 578 [1987]; Quammen 2006:14),[18] but in these two situations the tension is wholly manufactured. In 1927, Christianity could and did exist and function at the same time as the theory of evolution and continuing inquiry into that then-somewhat new scientific idea. Today, the actual basis for NAGPRA—civil rights protection—simply should and does prevail over conflicting scientific inquiry. This lesson has been painfully learned many times over in the last two centuries. As to an establishment of religion, NAGPRA is silent. It neither supports a religious perspective nor does it wholly quash the ability to conduct scientific study of Native American human remains. Such study can be and is continued under NAGPRA through inventorying, permitted excavations and analyses, and collaborations with Indigenous peoples who want answers to the things that their ancestors' remains can tell them. Thus, the alleged clash between science and religion in NAGPRA simply falls flat.

Science lost the Scopes trial both in court and, arguably, in the minds of many Americans. The polarized positions of Bryan and Darrow—positions calculated to entertain rather than to actually resolve a dispute over Tennessee's ban on the teaching of evolution in public schools—has reverberated through popular culture to the present. The polarized and entrenched positions over access to and the use of human remains by Weiss and Springer (2020) and those supporting their arguments on the extreme side of science and Rep. Faleomavaega's extreme antiscience stance in the NAGPRA (and other) debates (discussed below) serve no purpose other than to sow distrust and to perpetuate arguments and disputes whose resolution lies somewhere in between these profoundly diametrically opposed positions. Certainly, the more recent alarmist allegation by Weiss and Springer (2023:34) that "[o]nce research collections are slated for repatriation, tribal activists will come for teaching collections believed to be Native American; then they will come for all human bones" serves no purpose other than to sow discord. The simple reality is that, as a recognition of people's basic human rights, the United States has now provided for Native Americans (and perhaps soon for African Americans) a means to ensure that the right guaranteed to Euro-Americans to control the disposition of their dead is protected—nothing more. All the demands "for all human bones" could be made at any time and by any descendant group. This reality ensures that modern notions of informed consent, scientific ethics, and simple human decency are extended to all U.S. citizens. Certainly, under these laws, skeletal collections will be repatriated and lost to scientific inquiry. As a bioarchaeologist, that reality disappoints me. However, my disappointment does not supersede a people's right to control the remains of their ancestors. Moreover, I have also learned that, in many cases, simple respect and collaboration with descendant communities can overcome many objections and scientific inquiry can continue in a manner beneficial to all. If the Scopes trial is at all instructive of the destructive forces of such disputes, continuing down the path espoused by Weiss and Springer (2020) will certainly lead to entrenchment, a lack of trust, and incentives to hide collections or refuse scientific inquiry for decades or more. Collaboration and respect is the answer.

Collaboration and Mutual Respect

Weiss and Springer's (2020) forced dichotomy is unsustainable in view of the multiple interests of all involved in human remains studies and the multiple truths that can be elicited from such studies and interactions (Halcrow et al. 2021).[19] Rather, as Poirier and Bellantoni (1997:231) suggest, "[i]rrespective of rhetoric, a new philosophy and momentous change has been established, with ancestral rights coming to the forefront of the decision-making process." When the rhetoric is removed, what is left is a collaborative process to researching and managing human remains and burial sites. What may be gained from such collaboration extends beyond skeletal data recovered in a traditional biological anthropology inquiry such as that championed by Weiss and Springer (2020). Rather, from a broader anthropological perspective, these collaborations, even if they may result in repatriation, provide crucial insight into living cultures in a manner reminiscent of the early days of the participant observer in cultural anthropology. From my own experience in consultations and collaborations with African American descendant groups in Louisiana, we learn volumes about modern mortuary rituals, practices, beliefs, and ideals via collaboration that would be lost if we continued past practices of assuming that Euro-American approaches to burial and human remains analysis were the only legitimate approaches and barreling forward without any community participation.

As part of working within this collaborative research process, it is crucial to acknowledge that many Indigenous American religions contain concepts of creation that describe how their people came to their current locations, how they have interacted within and without their groups from the dawn of time, and why they have acted in this way (Rivera 1989; Mihesuah 1996). Under such a worldview, science's divining or discovery of contradictory or even supportive evidence is of no consequence to such peoples' worldviews (Toner 2020). Far from being an "establishment of religion" in a constitutional sense, these histories are built on oral tradition rather than the strictly religious basis that Weiss and Springer (2020) assert. Indeed, many Indigenous Americans consider science as just another of the world's religions, with no greater claim to legitimacy than their own (Thomas 2000). Such a reality could arguably, from an Indigenous perspective, create and "establishment of religion" situation under the U.S. Constitution that could undermine the continued conduct of Western science on Native Americans' or other people's remains. In addition to the general disregard for Western science's methods and questions, many Indigenous American groups have begun to compile their own histories based upon their oral traditions (Thomas 2000). As Jones and Harris (1998:260) observe, the compilation of these histories "often means disputing the scientific version—not necessarily because it is wrong but because it does not contribute to the version of history which the indigenous communities wish to affirm."[20] In other cases, Indigenous Americans have expressed concerns regarding traditional scientific inquiry's inherent importation of colonialist notions and ideals (Tsosie et al. 2020). In such situations, there is not so much of a rejection of scientific inquiry as a cautioning of the means of conducting that inquiry on Indigenous peoples' remains and the importance of decolonizing such inquiries by engaging with Indigenous communities during the conduct of such research. Within this context, collaboration and a general respect for one another's worldviews, methods, and goals is critical to ensuring the future of biological anthropology. History is not monolithic, nor are the various religious or cultural perspectives on history. Rather than championing one Euro-American, scientifically informed history, the scientific community should be telling multiple histories from multiple stakeholder perspectives to decolonize the past and allow for multiple interpretations of the same known information, thus avoiding a whitewashing on the past so endemic to much academia until very recently.

Impacts of Looting and the Concept of the "Other"

In addition to the tension between anthropologists and Native Americans in the 1970s and 1980s, looters acting outside any scientific community and operating under no ethical codes were (and still are) destroying Indigenous American sites—including burial sites—at an alarming rate. This destruction, characterized as to the trafficking in looted remains by Tsosie (2004:170) as "a horrible, horrible problem," was typified by the mass desecration of the Slack Farm site in Kentucky in 1987, an event that figured largely in Congress's decision to enact some legislation that could protect Indigenous American burials and cemeteries (Henderson 2015). At about the same time, Louisiana tribes (particularly the Tunica-Biloxi) were experiencing their own problems over looting and preservation of their material cultural identity with the dispute over the Tunica Treasure. This dispute also figured into the debates over controlling the looting of cultural patrimony and human remains that led to the passage of NAGPRA a few years later (Klopotek 2011).

Considering the complex history between Native Americans and anthropologists over the past century and a half, Congress's passage of NAGPRA should not have been surprising. Modern looting by relic hunters aside, anthropologists' past questionable ethical behavior did much to precipitate Congress's action in 1990. To properly understand the significance of NAGPRA and its progeny, it is essential to briefly review this structurally violent history.

Much of early anthropology began as an imperialistic study of the "other."[21] Often, the situs of each particular researcher's work defined the "other." For example, the Iroquois in his home state of New York exemplified Lewis Henry Morgan's "other" for his kinship research (Morgan 1871). As anthropology began to grow as a field of social-scientific inquiry in the early twentieth century, such founding individuals as Franz Boas, Margaret Mead, Ruth Benedict, and Bronislaw Malinowski focused their research of the "other" on the Indigenous inhabitants of the Northwest Coast (Boas 1909), Samoa (Mead 1928), the southwestern United States (Benedict 1934), and the Trobriand Islands (Malinowski 1922) (Bohannan and Glazer 1988).

In the United States, Native Americans provided the fertile ground for early anthropological research. Thus, in so many American cases, the "other" existed as one group or another of Native Americans. The perceived importance of studying such groups at the time was informed by the notion that Indigenous groups that were largely untouched by European influence and continued to practice traditional lifeways offered windows into our shared past as human beings and that, with enough data on such "primitives,"[22] a picture of humanity's origins could be developed (Bohannan and Glazer 1988). The push to conduct largely ethnographic research among these peoples was driven by the colonial, paternalistic view that such groups were dying off and that research into the then-current push of European colonialism across the globe could provide unique data on our shared past as humans (Mead 1960; Lewis 2023).

Running in a largely parallel track with anthropology (specifically, sociocultural anthropology), and substantially informing its understandings of the interrelatedness (or lack thereof) of living and nonliving groups, was the development of the subfield of physical anthropology. This field was (and to a large extent, still is) characterized by its examination of living and dead humans and closely related nonhuman primates to understand adaptations and changes in human development and structure over time (Barrett 1997). While this field of inquiry did not grow out of Darwin's work in *On the Origin of Species* (1859), his (and Alfred Russell Wallace's) research and writing substantially influenced others' ideas that life adapted slowly to various environments and from other outside or selective pressures. Unfortunately, both early anthropologists and anatomists[23] applied Darwin's basic biological evolution theories in ways not envisioned or intended by Darwin.[24] The result of this unfortunate usage effectively provided scientists and social scientists of the mid-nineteenth century with what they believed justified the treatment of nonwhite peoples—and in the United States, especially Native Americans—as an "other," allowing them to disregard their humanity in life and in death (Halcrow et al. 2021). This improper interpretation led to the rise of social Darwinism among social scientists and a general disrespect for the human remains of the "other" among scientists undertaking studies on the dead. Indeed, early research on human crania by such individuals as Samuel Morton (2009 [1839]), a Philadelphia anatomist, was specifically tailored to justify the existence of race as a biological construct and the differential treatment of these "others" (most of Morton's "others" were Native American and African American) during life (Gould 1981). Such differential treatment is similar to that suggested by Weiss and Springer (2020) for Native American human remains (Halcrow et al. 2021). Morton began his cranial capacity research with at least two general premises in mind: (1) the larger the cranial capacity, the larger the brain, and thus the smarter the individual; and (2) there would be a ranking of intelligence based upon this research with Western European white people at the apex, followed by Asians and Native Americans, with Africans and African Americans at the bottom. Morton set out to prove his preconceived notions, often forcing the data to fit his conclusions (Gould 1981). As evolutionary biologist Steven Jay Gould so ably demonstrated in his book *The Mismeasure of Man* (1981), Morton's methods were flawed and the race-based conclusions that he drew from his data were baseless. Unfortunately, these biased conclusions were accepted as fact during the nineteenth and early twentieth centuries and beyond and continued to serve as the basis for racist theories, structurally violent treatment, a stripping of agency, and a general sense that Native Americans and others are less than human. Within this context and through existing prejudices of the nineteenth century, friction (and worse) existed and continues to exist between the anthropological and Indigenous communities today.

Misappropriation of Indigenous remains during the nineteenth and early twentieth centuries also existed outside the United States. Paul Turnbull (1991) reviewed the acquisition policies of the Australian Museum and found similar, if not more shocking, policies than those in the United States. Edward Ramsay, curator of the Australian Museum during the late nineteenth century, openly encouraged the collection of recently deceased Aborigines by means akin to grave robbing. Anthropologists and anatomists acquired many of these remains after veritable ethnic cleansings in rural parts of the country. Indeed, Ramsay even produced a publication that detailed the methods for removing the skull and brain of a defleshed individual without damaging the "specimen." Ramsay also arranged for the museum's acquisition of skulls of the Moriori, offering Australian Aborigine skulls as an exchange.

Stories of such acquisitions are eerily similar to those of collections of Native American remains by the U.S. Army during the "Indian Wars." Battlefield killings were collected, crated, and shipped to Washington, D.C., for study within hours of the end of battles (Colwell 2017). Such battlefield collections were not always made in the name of medical advancement. As Colwell (2017:84) recounts, on a visit to one such site in 1868, General W. T. Sherman "ordered that all the men search the area and collect anything of value." These "things of value" included "'Indian baby skulls [and] many skulls of men and women'" (Colwell 2017:84). Although these collections of human remains such as those in the Army Medical Museum (AMM) (later transferred to the Smithsonian Institution) originated as samplings of "morbid anatomy" on U.S. Civil War battlefields (Faust 2008), following the war—especially during the so-called Indian Wars period of the 1870s—such collections shifted from soldiers to Native Americans (Colwell 2017; Spatola and Pearlstein 2023; Thomas 2000). This shift provided fodder again for the dark early history of physical anthropology in which not just were collection practices dubious, but research focuses and the use of the collections were also offensive. A prime example of this research is the conclusion drawn by the noted curator of the AMM, George A. Otis—a man lauded for his contributions to the founding generation of physical anthropology (Buikstra 2006a:13–14)—reported on cranial measurement studies that, "the American Indians must be assigned a lower position in the human scale than has been believed heretofore" (Lamb 1917:56). As with other accounts retold here and in other sources, it is unsurprising that anthropology began, in 1990, to have a reckoning with its past that continues—as it should—to affect research on human remains and their burial places today and for the foreseeable future.

Considering this bleak and sordid history,[25] it is also not surprising that, following decades of lobbying by Native American groups, the U.S. Congress passed NAGPRA in 1990. Indeed, many of the stories reviewed here became part of the congressional record during these hearings, leading the congressman from American Samoa, Rep. Eni Faleomavaega, to comment on the record, in an only partially tongue-in-cheek manner, that, "the next anthropologist I catch coming to Samoa, I'm going to shoot him."[26]

Indigenous Americans thus viewed the passage of NAGPRA as a watershed civil rights moment (Thomas 2000).[27] Through this law, Native Americans, Native Hawaiians, and Alaska Natives acquired agency never before realized (Klopotek 2011):[28] they had the ability and authority to participate in the dialogue regarding the return of their ancestors' remains, and they earned a guaranteed seat at the table in discussions over future disturbances of such human remains.

Importantly, many scholars in the bioanthropological and archaeological communities opposed the process that led to the passage of NAGPRA (Thomas 2000; McKeown 2012). However, what some scholars predicted as the end of a profession and field of scientific inquiry ultimately,[29] with some fits and starts, became a basis for Indigenous-scientific collaboration regarding site protection and respect for the remains of the Indigenous dead (McKeown 2012; Boutin et al. 2017; Watkins 2020). Indeed, though NAGPRA had detractors during its congressional debates and even in its early years, most anthropologists felt that the repatriation of culturally affiliated human remains to living descendants was the morally correct response. As a result of the efforts to return such remains, the ties and allegiances formed between Indigenous peoples and those in the anthropological and museum communities led to far reaching benefits (Ubelaker and Grant 1989; Bernstein 1991; Dongoske 1996; Ferguson 1996; Monroe 1993). Today, even the most ardent repatriation opponents from the 1970s–1990s (see Buikstra's 2006b review of various scientific organizations' initial responses to repatriation compared to their positions today) largely admits to the success of NAGPRA and similar laws to bringing together otherwise opposed groups of scientists and descendant communities (cf. Weiss and Springer 2020). In an open email to the membership, former Society for American Archaeology president Joe Watkins characterized NAGPRA, on the eve of its thirtieth anniversary, as "a landmark human rights law that formally acknowledges tribal sovereignty . . . [and that] [i]ts passage transformed the practice of archaeology" (Watkins 2020). The mandatory consultation process of these laws has substantially contributed to this goal by forcing anthropologists to interact with descendant communities and to implement, at least in part, their interests and desires with regard to their ancestors' burial sites and remains.

NAGPRA's Functionality

NAGPRA, as it was enacted and as it is now enforced, serves several purposes: (1) it provides Native Americans a means of reclaiming affiliated human remains housed in the nation's museum and university collections;[30] (2) it protects Native American burial sites from disturbance or destruction when they are inadvertently discovered; (3) it promotes collaboration on scientific research undertaken on Native American skeletal collections; (4) it requires an inventory to be made available to Native American groups of all skeletal remains and associated funerary objects curated by federally funded museums and universities; and (5) it restricts the illegal trafficking of Native American remains for profit (Seidemann 2003).

Other scholars have spent their careers analyzing and explaining de jure and de facto aspects of NAGPRA. The entirety of those efforts is not recounted here. However, a brief examination of the law's functionality is warranted to contextualize subsequent efforts to similarly legislate in other jurisdictions.

NAGPRA applies to Native American[31] human remains in two contexts: curated remains housed in museums or other institutional collections that receive federal funding and remains found on federal or tribal lands. Both aspects are relevant to this study and are discussed below.

Under NAGPRA, all federally funded institutions are required to create an inventory of all "Native American human remains and associated funerary objects" (25 U.S.C. § 3003) under their control by November 16, 1995, and have continuing obligations to inventory and update this information from that time forward. If, as a result of a NAGPRA inventory required under 25 U.S.C. § 3003, a modern lineal descendant group can be identified and such a group requests the return of the remains, the request must be granted. NAGPRA provides for civil penalties for failing to comply (25 U.S.C. § 3007). A "Review Committee" created by the Secretary of the Interior and composed of seven members must review these inventories. At the request of an "affected party," the Review Committee must make findings from these inventories of cultural affiliation of curated items as well as arrange for the repatriation of affiliated remains when requested.

Under 25 U.S.C. § 3005, lineal descendants can make claims for remains identified pursuant to the findings of an inventory as affiliated with a Native American group. This also extends, as one of the most complicated parts of NAGPRA, to remains not affiliated in an inventory where the claiming Native American group "can show cultural affiliation by a preponderance of the evidence based upon geographical, kinship, biological, archaeological, anthropological, linguistic, folkloric, oral traditional, historical, or other relevant information or expert opinion" (25 U.S.C. § 3005[a][4]). Remains that are not identifiable through these means may remain in the possession of the holding institution, or they may be (pursuant to regulations drafted nearly three decades after NAGPRA's passage) claimed by other, possibly unaffiliated groups. Certain remains, though they have valid claims for repatriation attached, may also be retained by the holding institution under certain circumstances. This narrow area allows for the retention of claimed remains if "such items are indispensable for completion of a scientific study, the outcome of which would be of major benefit to the United States" (25 U.S.C. § 3005[b]). The funerary artifacts associated or unassociated with burials also are subject to similar repatriation mandates. Although these items are authorized for reclamation and repatriation under NAGPRA as it has been regulatorily expanded,[32] in practice, these items are often not claimed by any Native American group and, as a consequence, simply remain in institutional collections as inventoried items indefinitely.[33]

NAGPRA also applies to Native American remains discovered on federal and tribal lands. If remains are found on such lands after the date of enactment, NAGPRA applies. NAGPRA prioritizes the order of the right of possession of such remains.[34] If lineal descendants can be associated with the remains, those individuals hold the primary position of possession. However, where direct lineal descendants cannot be identified, a three-part scheme of possession determination is employed in 25 U.S.C. § 3002(a)(2) (in the following order of priority):

A. First, ownership shall be "in the Indian tribe . . . on whose tribal land such objects or remains were discovered," and if that does not apply, then;
B. Ownership shall be "in the Indian tribe . . . which has the closest cultural affiliation with such remains or objects and which, upon notice, states a claim for such remains or objects; or"
C. "[I]f cultural affiliation . . . cannot be reasonably ascertained and if the objects were discovered on Federal land that is recognized by a final judgment of the Indian Claims Commission or the United States Court of Claims as the aboriginal land of some Indian tribe," then
    1. The ownership shall be "in the Indian tribe that is recognized as aboriginally occupying the area in which the objects were discovered, if upon notice, such tribe states a claim for such remains or objects, or;"
    2. Ownership shall be "in the Indian tribe that has the strongest demonstrated relationship . . . if it can be shown by a preponderance of the evidence that a different tribe has a stronger cultural relationship with the remains or objects."

Additionally, NAGPRA does not prohibit the excavation of remains after November 16, 1990; it just sets in place a mechanism for determining who ultimately controls the remains. Finally, NAGPRA (the statute itself) provides no mechanism for the disposition of remains that cannot be validly claimed by any person or group whether found before or after November 16, 1990, thus leading to the shaky constitutional basis of the unaffiliated remains regulations.

One of the fundamental requirements of NAGPRA, as noted above, is that federal agencies and other institutions holding Native American human remains must compile an inventory of those remains. In compiling this inventory, each institution must make reasonable efforts to identify the cultural affiliation of the human remains that are part of their collections. Such conclusions are generally drawn from nondestructive bioanthropological analyses. Those human remains for which the institutions are not able to make affiliation conclusions become classified as culturally unidentifiable human remains under NAGPRA.

One estimate of the number of culturally unidentifiable individuals in institutions' collections as of 2007 exceeds 118,000 (Kline 2007).[35] Thus, a large number of the human remains that may be subject to NAGPRA that are currently held in institutions' collections around the United States are classified into the somewhat nebulous category of culturally unidentifiable.

Human remains are classified as culturally unidentifiable for several reasons. As was intimated above, one reason for this classification is that even though their cultural affiliation may be known, the tribe that such remains are affiliated with is not recognized by the Bureau of Indian Affairs. Many other culturally unidentifiable classifications result from the methods of excavation or curation. In other words, either when the remains were removed from the ground or during many years of being held in one or more institutions, the provenience data that would link the remains to either a general region or perhaps a particular group has been lost. In such cases, a general nondestructive analysis of the remains has presumably not led to any better understanding of the cultural affiliation of these individuals.

The final large category of human remains that are classified as culturally unidentifiable are those that are simply too old to reasonably be said to share a cultural link with any currently existing Native American group (the statutory standard under NAGPRA). In most cases, it is probable that no amount of analysis will result in an ultimate determination of cultural affiliation. These remains are simply too old to be able to decipher their cultural connections in any scientifically grounded sense. Kline's report on culturally unidentifiable human remains is telling of this fact. In his study of culturally unidentifiable human remains held in collections in Alabama, Florida, Illinois, Kentucky, Ohio, and Tennessee, Kline (2007:11) noted that, "[e]xamination of the time period when the [culturally unidentifiable remains] were believed to have been alive presents a near even spread of [culturally unidentifiable] between

8000 B.C.E. and 1400 C.E." Twenty-nine percent of Kline's sample came from the Mississippian period (AD 1100–1400). Cultural identification of these remains may be possible through advanced (and possibly destructive) analyses. However, for the 42 percent that are classified as either "no age information," "Prehistoric," or "Archaic," cultural identification will be difficult at best, as it is likely that there are no living cultures that share enough of a link to these peoples to be considered affiliated under NAGPRA.[36] These tenuous links have been regulatorily sanctioned for repatriation by the National Park Service's regulations whether or not affiliation can be determined. Again, this clear extension of the statutory law places these regulations on uncertain constitutional grounds.

NAGPRA's Legacy: Raising Awareness and Fostering More Protective Laws

Perhaps more importantly than what NAGPRA accomplished for the protection of Native American human remains was the domino effect that it began for the protection of the burial sites and human remains of non-Native American marginalized peoples across the United States. As NAGPRA is written, it applies only to Native American burials located on federal and tribal lands and Native American human remains in the collections of institutions that receive federal funding (Seidemann and Moss 2009). With the passage of NAGPRA, many states, Louisiana among them, enacted copycat legislation for the protection of burial sites within their borders (Seidemann 2010a). Importantly, these state efforts have considerably greater legal reach than does NAGPRA. In most cases, state-unmarked burial protection laws apply to burial sites and human remains regardless of ethnic or cultural affiliation, a considerably broader application than the Native American-only focus of NAGPRA. Not all states have enacted such legislation in the 30 years since the passage of NAGPRA, with New York representing the most glaring absence from the litany of states that have passed such human rights legislation. Furthermore, most state-level enactments reach beyond just public property. By way of example, burial site protections enacted in Louisiana in the wake of NAGPRA apply to state, parochial, municipal, and private property (Seidemann 2014a). Thus, between federal and state laws in most jurisdictions in the United States, there now exists a virtual ban on the disturbance of the burial sites of "others." The ban is virtual because such sites may be disturbed subject to a permitting process that requires consultation with descendant communities and archaeological precision to remove burials.

It is important to note that, though most of these laws protect the graves of "others," they also protect the graves of the white majority when such graves are encountered in an unexpected context. One such example occurred in Louisiana in 2020, when a landowner sought to develop property in Ascension Parish along Bayou Manchac into residential lots. During this process, a single grave of an earlier white inhabitant was encountered that presented the landowner with a dilemma: try to develop the land while leaving the burial intact or follow the legal process to move the burial. The landowner chose the latter and collaborated with archaeologists and historians in an effort to locate descendants and to move the burial into an established local cemetery. In addition, under NAGPRA and its state counterparts, it is also unlawful in most jurisdictions to commodify the remains of any such individuals whether they have been obtained before or after the enactment of such laws (Halling and Seidemann 2016b).

Thus, one of the most surprising results of the passage of NAGPRA and similar state laws has been the focus of the police power on the protection of at least certain types of archaeological sites. Because NAGPRA and other laws contain restrictions and permitting provisions for the disturbance of unmarked burial sites, a new wave of site protection has become available in recent years. Under prior regimes of cultural resources protection laws such as the National Historic Preservation Act of 1966 and the Archaeological Resources Protection Act of 1979, virtually no power existed to stop the damage of many archaeological sites, especially those not situated on federal or tribal property. However, under NAGPRA and its ilk, not only does substantial power exist to protect the cultural resources embodied by the spaces of the dead, but some of that power is vested in the descendant community of those dead through mandatory consultations. Thus, as recent site protection laws that deal with human remains have been passed, the ability of marginalized peoples to be actively involved in the protection of their own cultural heritage is becoming a reality. No longer do such peoples have to rely on scientific or bureaucratic assessments of significance and importance to invoke the police power of the government to protect certain sites. This accomplishment in the evolution of anthropology's (often shameful) interactions with the dead of "others" is perhaps the most significant accomplishment of the past 50 years in terms of site and cultural heritage protection. In this regard, the evolution of the spaces of the dead has been substantially affected—in a positive way—by the past injustices visited upon the mortal remains of marginalized peoples by anthropologists and others.

It is also important to bear in mind that many states (e.g., Louisiana) already had laws in existence when NAGPRA was enacted that, theoretically, at least should have provided some protection from outright unmarked burial destruction (Seidemann and Moss 2009). Many such laws were enacted in the late 1960s and early 1970s in the wake of the publication of Jessica Mitford's (1963) funeral-cemetery industry exposé, *An American Way of Death* (Sloane 1991:215). This book was important because it, like Rachel Carson's (1962) environmental exposé, *Silent Spring,* riled the public regarding perceived and actual shady actions by members of the deathcare industry to defraud and upsell the public in times of grief.[37] This public attention spurred legislators to act to attempt to regulate this industry. Although revolutionary, Mitford's (1963) examination of the deathcare industry in the United States was not directed at cemetery protection or preservation. Rather, Mitford set out to expose what she perceived to be a corrupt industry that would regularly overcharge and upsell grieving families during vulnerable times. Although Mitford reviewed cemetery operations in her book, that review revolved around consumer practices. However, the book's wide popularity led to congressional hearings and a nationwide reform (mostly at the state level) in the regulation of funeral directing and cemetery operations (West and McKerns 2009). From these reforms arose, among other things, Louisiana's Cemetery Act in 1974.

Louisiana's Human Remains and Cemetery Protection Laws

Provisions such as Louisiana's cemetery dedication laws were codified in 1974 as part of the Mitfordian nationwide effort to regulate the deathcare industry (Murphy 2007). In a broad sense, these dedication laws provide that once a human body (ethnicity unspecified) is placed in the ground, that piece of property is forever considered to be a cemetery and it cannot be put to any noncemetery use (Seidemann and Moss 2009; Seidemann 2014a, 2018a, 2018b). Unfortunately, as Quetone (1987) notes in a Florida context, despite the existence of these state antidesecration laws, unmarked burials, especially those of Native Americans, were often destroyed or disturbed and the perpetrators were seldom, if ever, held to account (see also Tesar 1986; S.Rep.100–601). Indeed, such laws as the cemetery dedication provisions and grave desecration prohibitions both were and are substantially underused protections in most American jurisdictions (Seidemann 2018a).

Importantly absent from the pre-NAGPRA cemetery protection laws of dedication and desecration are those prohibiting the unauthorized use of human remains. Such laws existed, but, as Halling and Seidemann (2016b) have noted, they were and are underutilized in the protection against and prevention of commodifying human remains of any ethnicity. Laws that regulate the possession, ownership, and transmission of human remains generally appear in the form of various states' iterations of the Uniform Anatomical Gift Act (Bernard 1966). NAGPRA presented a clear procedural mechanism to hold to account those who would commodify Native American human remains and even those holding such remains in institutional collections for research purposes by specifically identifying prohibited actions and providing the descendant community with agency in the form of civil causes of action for certain violations (Seidemann 2003). In fairness, the Uniform Anatomical Gift Act was not designed to stem human remains commodification. Rather, as observed by a commentator in the 1960s, "the Uniform Anatomical Gift Act was drafted specifically with a view to transplant operations" (Anon. 1969:694). NAGPRA thus presented a clear model for legislating prohibitions on illicit cemetery damage and human remains commodification that was copied by many states in the years following its passage (Seidemann 2010a).

Louisiana's enactment of the Louisiana Unmarked Human Burial Sites Preservation Act (Unmarked Burials Act) in 1991 was part of this state-level movement (Seidemann 2010a). No substantive testimony or debate survives related to the passage of the Unmarked Burials Act. Thus, while it is known from anecdotal information that this law was a response to federal legislative movements at the time (i.e., NAGPRA and NMAIA), whether the expansion of this law beyond the federal analogue to cover other groups was a tacit recognition of the structural violence that could disproportionately affect the graves of marginalized peoples is unclear. However, it can be assumed from the illustrative list of other at-risk graves in that law (i.e., "Indian, pioneer, and Civil War and other soldiers' burial sites") that the unequal treatment of certain peoples' graves was not the motivating factor behind this law in 1991. Although the law, by its plain terms, does apply to enslaved peoples' graves, these people are conspicuously absent from the illustrative listing of at-risk graves in the law. Nonetheless, many states, Louisiana included, enacted burial protection laws that were more comprehensive and preservation-oriented than is NAGPRA. The stated legislative purpose in La. R.S. 8:672 suggests that the Unmarked Burials Act should be broadly construed. That provision states:

> The legislature finds that existing state laws do not provide for the adequate protection of unmarked burial sites and of human skeletal remains and burial artifacts in such sites. As a result, there is a real and growing threat to the safety and sanctity of unmarked burial sites, both from economic development of the land and from persons engaged for personal or financial gain in the mining of prehistoric and historic In-

> dian, pioneer, and Civil War and other soldiers' burial sites. Therefore, there is an immediate need for legislation to protect the burial sites of these earlier residents of Louisiana from desecration and to enable the proper archaeological investigation and study when disturbance of a burial site is necessary or desirable. The legislature intends that this Chapter shall assure that all human burial sites shall be accorded equal treatment, protection, and respect for human dignity without reference to ethnic origins, cultural backgrounds, or religious affiliations.

With this statement—one that is common in similar state enactments around the United States—the legislature recognizes the significant threats to cemetery spaces, and it extends its coverage equally, regardless of the ethnic or cultural affiliation of the burials. Equally important is that the legislature distinguished three classes of things in need of protection: human remains, burial artifacts, and burial sites, thus wrapping into one law (as does NAGPRA) the protection of sites, artifacts, and remains.

Under the Unmarked Burials Act, cemeteries that are otherwise exempt from the purview of general cemetery law in Louisiana (also known as "Title 8") (i.e., they are not operating cemeteries) are not subject to the regulatory authority of the Louisiana Cemetery Board (LCB), but rather are under the authority of the Louisiana Division of Archaeology ("the Division") by virtue of the Unmarked Burials Act. As created by Act 704 of 1991, the Unmarked Burials Act was placed under the enforcement authority of the Louisiana Unmarked Burial Sites Board. However, in Act 713 of 2006, the Louisiana legislature rolled this board's duties into the Louisiana Department of Culture, Recreation, and Tourism, with the board's permitting duties now delegated to the Division, led by the state archaeologist.

Regulatory authority over isolated and abandoned cemeteries is grounded in the language of the Unmarked Burials Act. That act specifically defines "unmarked burial site" in La. R.S. 8:673(5) as "the immediate area where one or more human skeletal remains are found in the ground that is not in a recognized and maintained municipal, fraternal, religious, or family cemetery, or a cemetery authorized by the Louisiana Cemetery Board." This definition leads to the following inferences. First, it clearly exempts any cemetery authorized by the LCB (i.e., operating cemeteries) from the regulatory authority of the Division and the purview of the Unmarked Burials Act. Accordingly, this positive statement in the law leads to the conclusion that, if a cemetery holds a current certificate of authority issued by the LCB pursuant to La. R.S. 8:70–8:72, the Division has no jurisdiction over that cemetery, and the Unmarked Burials Act does not apply. Second, clearly exempted from the

Unmarked Burials Act's protection by La. R.S. 8:673(5) are cemeteries classified as "recognized and maintained municipal, fraternal, religious, or family cemeter[ies]." No definition exists in Title 8 for either the words "recognized" or "maintained." However, within the broader context of Title 8, "recognition" appears to refer to the presence of a cemetery on the LCB's register of operating cemeteries that are subject to less stringent governmental regulations but that are also under the LCB's jurisdiction. Importantly, under La. R.S. 8:673(5), both recognition and maintenance are required to avoid a cemetery's classification as abandoned. Thus, the simple fact that a cemetery is registered with the LCB does not exempt that cemetery from coverage by the Unmarked Burials Act. Under this provision, only cemeteries that do not hold a current LCB certificate of authority but are recognized by the LCB and are maintained can claim an exemption from the Unmarked Burials Act.

As with the term "recognition," no definition of the term "maintained" exists in Title 8. Following the requirement of La. C.C. art. 11, which states that "[t]he words of a law must be given their generally prevailing meaning," a dictionary definition of the term "maintain" is required to divine the legislature's intended application of the Unmarked Burials Act. "Maintain" is defined as to "keep (a building, machine, etc.) in good condition by checking or repairing it regularly" (Soanes and Stevenson 2006:860). Although an unmaintained cemetery may be the equivalent of what is colloquially referred to as an abandoned cemetery, the question of abandonment is not determinative of the classification of a cemetery as "unmarked." In other words, if a cemetery is in a poor state of maintenance—a state that evidences years of neglect—though it may not be legally abandoned, it has likely met the requirements for a lack of maintenance sufficient to trigger this prong of the Unmarked Burials Act.

Act 707 of the 2010 Louisiana Legislative Session, known as the Louisiana Historic Cemetery Preservation Act ("Historic Cemetery Act"), was originally introduced and failed to pass the legislature in 2008 as House Bill 1092 of the 2008 Regular Louisiana Legislative Session. The Historic Cemetery Act is more detailed and more specific to abandoned cemeteries and isolated graves than is the Unmarked Burials Act. However, a review of Act 707 reveals that the newer law is largely superfluous, and it does not change the preexisting protections of the Unmarked Burials Act. The purpose of the Historic Cemetery Act is similar in nature to that of the Unmarked Burials Act. As noted in La. R.S. 25:933, that purpose is described as follows:

> [t]he legislature hereby finds the demolition, destruction, and damage of historic cemeteries and isolated graves a disrespectful practice. The legislature further finds that existing state laws do not provide for the

> adequate protection of historic cemeteries that are not under the jurisdiction of the LCB, are not on state lands, and are not solely comprised of unmarked graves. Cemeteries are considered by most cultures to be sacred spaces. In addition to being resting places for our dead, many of Louisiana's cemeteries are repositories of significant examples of art, architecture, and archaeology as well as containing the history of their respective communities. The importance of cemeteries should not be taken lightly, as these significant elements represent a substantial tourist attraction for the state of Louisiana, and also present an endless source of data for historians, taphologists, anthropologists, archaeologists, and genealogists that collectively lead us to a better understanding of our own culture.

In addition to a recognition of a reverence for the space of death and a removal of any ethnically exclusive examples, the Historic Cemetery Act also evidences the importance of such cemeteries as repositories of history for a community and, at least for Louisiana, as a potential tourist draw (e.g., Hotard 2003). These are merely additional reasons for the preservation of these sites that were not noted in the Unmarked Burials Act.

To fully understand why the Historic Cemetery Act does not change the existing protections for cemeteries under the Unmarked Burials Act, it is necessary to review the scope of several portions of those laws in tandem. In several ways, the Historic Cemetery Act clarifies the extent to which certain cemeteries are protected. This is not an actual change in the law, but the act certainly provides substantial clarity over the previous law. The jurisdictional scope of the pre-2010 law and that of the Historic Cemetery Act is best set forth in the definitions of the various cemeteries and activities subject to the later law. Under the Unmarked Burials Act, "unmarked burial site" is defined as "the immediate area where one or more human skeletal remains are found in the ground that is not in a recognized and maintained municipal, fraternal, religious, or family cemetery, or a cemetery authorized by the Louisiana Cemetery Board." The legislature did not intend to confine the Unmarked Burials Act's protections to cemeteries and graves lacking markers (i.e., a literal definition of "unmarked"), but rather intended for protections to be applied to threatened areas in which human remains were interred, though not to those areas that are cemeteries authorized by the LCB. The Historic Cemetery Act provides concise definitions for "abandoned cemetery," "historic cemetery," and "isolated grave" that clarify that the scope of cemetery protections under Louisiana law extend beyond a narrow reading of the term "unmarked" in the Unmarked Burials Act. Those relevant definitions, in La. R.S. 25:933, are:

> (1) "Abandoned cemetery" shall mean any cemetery which is no longer being used for interments, is not being maintained in good condition, and has fallen into a state of disrepair, including tombs and headstones that have collapsed or been destroyed, walls and fences that have fallen apart, and trees and bushes that have grown amongst and within grave spaces.
>
> * * *
>
> (10) "Historic cemetery" shall mean any abandoned cemetery located in the state that is more than fifty years old and is not subject to the laws, rules, and regulations of the [LCB] or Chapter 10-A of Title 8 of the Louisiana Revised Statutes of 1950.
>
> * * *
>
> (12) "Isolated grave" shall mean any marked grave site that is not part of a larger cemetery and is not subject to the laws, rules, and regulations of the [LCB] or Chapter 10-A of Title 8 of the Louisiana Revised Statutes of 1950. The term shall also include groupings of multiple graves that are not part of a larger cemetery.

Because the enforcement jurisdiction of the Historic Cemetery Act and the Unmarked Burials Act both rest with the Division of Archaeology, the scope of protections from both of these laws vests the permitting authority over cemeteries not authorized by the LCB in one state entity. Further, because the prohibited acts under these laws are convergent, their application is seamless under the Division's oversight. Under the Unmarked Burials Act, covered human remains are protected against "disturbance" (La. R.S. 8:678). "Disturb" is defined in La. R.S. 8:673(2) as including "excavating, removing, exposing, defacing, mutilating, destroying, molesting, or desecrating in any way any unmarked burial sites or any human skeletal remains, burial artifacts, or burial markers on or in an unmarked burial site without a permit." The Historic Cemetery Act encompasses the prohibition against disturbance from the Unmarked Burials Act within its definitions of "damage," "destruction," and "modification." Those definitions provide:

> (5) "Damage" shall mean the intentional or inadvertent hurt, harm, or injury to a component of a historic cemetery or to an isolated grave so as to lessen or destroy its historic, cultural, or scientific value.
>
> * * *
>
> (7) "Destruction" shall mean intentionally or inadvertently destroying components of a historic cemetery by violent disintegration of its fabric so as to reduce the components to ruin.
>
> * * *

(13) "Modification" shall mean the altering of the original substance of a grave space.

These same protections are provided for under the Unmarked Burials Act definition of "disturb," but the Historic Cemetery Act language, by specifically defining these three terms, clarifies the protections available for grave spaces in historic cemeteries or for isolated graves under the Unmarked Burials Act. Further, through the addition of the term "modification," it is clear that the Historic Cemetery Act extends its grave space protections to substantial modifications. Thus, in many cases, even the historic integrity of a grave space in such cemeteries is protectable, giving teeth to architectural and aesthetic provisions of historic preservation laws that does not exist under most federal or state laws. Read together, both the Unmarked Burials Act and the Historic Cemetery Act provide protections for grave spaces against disturbance, damage, destruction, and modification. Louisiana is not alone in the enactment of such laws (see table 3.1).

The above-reviewed laws constitute the current state of Louisiana's burial space protections. Nonetheless, despite the substantial legal protections present in no less than six different legal schemes in Louisiana, cemetery damage and the commodification of human remains continued to persist following the passage of the Historic Cemetery Act in 2010 (e.g., Seidemann and Hawkins 2019). Thus, in 2016, the Louisiana legislature enacted the Louisiana Human Remains Trafficking and Control Act (Act 531 of 2016). This most recent law in Louisiana regarding human remains treatment goes a step further than laws such as NAGPRA and the Louisiana burial site protection laws by incorporating long-standing civil and common law jurisprudence into the statutory law ensuring that human remains cannot be possessed, owned, or trafficked without the express permission of the deceased and providing for the disposition of remains seized in trafficking operations or those held in unauthorized public or private collections. Importantly, this law does not upend any human remains acquisitions made by institutions of higher learning that are curated according to existing laws or the wishes of the deceased or descendant community. As of this writing, this law represents a one-of-a-kind statutory protection for human remains in the United States. It has been used as recently as late 2022 to recover Native American remains that otherwise would not have been covered by NAGPRA or other such laws.

One additional cemetery protection law worthy of mention, and one that exists across the United States, is the criminal code provision that prohibits grave desecration: La. R.S. 14:101. This law explicitly criminalizes the opening of graves or the theft of burial or grave artifacts. Although Louisiana's

Table 3.1. U.S. states and territories with explicit unmarked burials protection laws

State/ territory	Unmarked burials protections?	Citation	Original enactment date
Alabama	No	N/A	N/A
Alaska	No	N/A	N/A
American Samoa	No	N/A	N/A
Arizona	No	N/A	N/A
Arkansas	No	N/A	N/A
California	Yes	Cal.Health & Safety Code § 8010, et seq.	2001
Colorado	Yes	C.R.S.A. § 24-80-1305	1990
Connecticut	No	N/A	N/A
Delaware	Yes	7 Del.C. § 5401, et seq.	1987
District of Columbia	No	N/A	N/A
Florida	Yes	F.S.A. § 872.05	1987
Georgia	Yes	Ga. Code Ann., § 36-72-1	1991
Guam	No	N/A	N/A
Hawaii	Yes	HRS § 6E-72, et seq.	2005
Idaho	No	N/A	N/A
Illinois	Yes	20 ILCS 3440/0.01, et seq.	1989
Indiana	No	N/A	N/A
Iowa	Yes	I.C.A. § 523I.316	2005
Kansas	Yes	K.S.A. 75-2741, et seq.	1989
Kentucky	No	N/A	N/A
Louisiana	Yes	La. R.S. 8:671, et seq.	1991
Maine	Yes	13 M.R.S.A. § 1371, et seq.	1991
Maryland	No	N/A	N/A
Massachusetts	No	N/A	N/A
Michigan	No	N/A	N/A
Minnesota	Yes	M.S.A. § 307.08	1976
Mississippi	No	N/A	N/A
Missouri	Yes	V.A.M.S. 194.400, et seq.	1987
Montana	Yes	MCA 22-3-803	1989
Nebraska	Yes	Neb.R.S. § 12-1204, et seq.	1989
Nevada	No	N/A	N/A
New Hampshire	Yes	N.H. R.S. § 227-C:8-b, et seq.	1986
New Jersey	No	N/A	N/A
New Mexico	Yes	N.M.S.A. 1978, § 18-6-11.2	1989
New York	No	N/A	N/A

State/ territory	Unmarked burials protections?	Citation	Original enactment date
North Carolina	Yes	N.C.G.S.A. § 70-26, et seq.	1981
North Dakota	No	N/A	N/A
Northern Mariana Islands	No	N/A	N/A
Ohio	No	N/A	N/A
Oklahoma	Yes	21 Okl.St.Ann. § 1168, et seq.	1987
Oregon	No	N/A	N/A
Pennsylvania	No	N/A	N/A
Puerto Rico	No	N/A	N/A
Rhode Island	Yes	Gen.Laws 1956, § 23-18-11	1992
South Carolina	No	N/A	N/A
South Dakota	Yes	SDCL § 34-27-21	1990
Tennessee	No	N/A	N/A
Texas	Yes	V.T.C.A., Health & Safety Code § 711.0105	2009
U.S. Virgin Islands	Yes	29 V.I.C. § 960	1998
Utah	No	N/A	N/A
Vermont	Yes	18 V.S.A. § 5212b	2001
Virginia	No	N/A	N/A
Washington	No	N/A	N/A
West Virginia	Yes	W. Va. Code, § 29-1-8a	1991
Wisconsin	No	N/A	N/A
Wyoming	No	N/A	N/A

Note: Many of the states and territories listed as lacking such protection often have laws that can be made to apply to burial protection (e.g., criminal desecration). This table includes only those laws that are roughly analogous to NAGPRA. Not included is a list of state criminal desecration statutes.

desecration law has existed for some time, it appears to have been seldom used. One probable reason for the lack of reported cases under this law is that it applies to individuals and is penal in nature rather than permissive. In other words, though the law contains restrictions, it may only be applied when a violation has occurred. Contrarily, the preservation laws noted above apply to property and both prospectively shape and restrict the uses of that property rather than merely punishing wrongdoing. Another reason that few desecration cases appear in the reported jurisprudence (indeed, there are no true reported criminal desecration cases in Louisiana) is that a violation of this law is a misdemeanor and simply does not warrant prosecutions when a district attorney's docket is clogged with felonies.[38] Indeed, in the recent Ender Darling case discussed in chapter 2, that instance of human remains pilfering from Holt Cemetery in New Orleans was pled as a theft rather than a desecration as the former is a felony (Simerman 2016). Thus, while criminal desecration is a cemetery protection law, its utility apparently is questionable in most circumstances.

Taken together, little doubt exists that, though not so identified, the notions of structural violence as applied to human remains and burial sites underlie motivations to the passage of NAGPRA in 1990 and the Louisiana analogues in 1991 and 2010. Other states' efforts are likely similarly influenced (Seidemann 2010a). Louisiana's own experiences with grave looting through the Tunica Treasure situation undoubtedly informed these legislative efforts to both provide enhanced protection for human remains and burial sites and to provide agency to disenfranchised groups (Klopotek 2011). Although the legal review in this chapter is somewhat tedious, an understanding of where state laws regarding cemeteries and human remains stood before the enactment of NAGPRA and how much those laws have developed since that event is essential to understanding modern interactions with spaces of death. Louisiana is both instructive of how various U.S. jurisdictions have implemented such protections and serves as a model for other jurisdictions for the implementation of more stringent controls than currently exist. In many ways, Louisiana has been the proving ground for cutting-edge human remains and cemetery site protection regimes. The agency provided by such laws to disenfranchised groups is important. As Klopotek (2011:94) noted, though in an event that predated the passage of NAGPRA, the Tunica-Biloxi peoples' acquisition of control over the grave goods and human remains that constituted the Tunica Treasure was, "rank[ed by tribal members] with federal recognition and the opening of the casino in 1994 as among the most important achievements for the tribe in recent memory." Unlike when this hard-fought victory under Louisiana's civil code provisions of treasure and abandoned things was litigated (*Charrier v. Bell*, 496 So.2d 601 [La.App. 1 Cir. 1986]), NAGPRA, the Unmarked Burials Act, and the Historic Cemetery Act now both provide agency for such groups as the Tunica-Biloxi in these crucially important scenarios and represent a substantial step toward atoning for the structural violence of the past with respect to the treatment of the burial spaces and human remains of the disenfranchised.

Importantly, through lessons learned in recent desecration cases (e.g., Simerman 2016) and through the enactment of more stringent laws since 2010, a desecration event like that alleged in the Jetton matter would now possibly be viably prosecutable both civilly and criminally. Certainly, the evidentiary problems of the Jetton matter continue to be problematic for such cases, the law now carries added incentives for prosecution (i.e., the classification of certain such acts as felonies that will be more attractive to district attorneys). In the end, Louisiana's protections substantially outstripped those set forth in NAGPRA and provide agency to descendant communities and site protection not heretofore extant in much of the United States. Moreover, laws such as NAGPRA have provided for the repatriation of the morally repugnant acquisitions from Kodiak Island and of the Greenland Inuit remains discussed earlier in this chapter. Such repatriation efforts and Indigenous agency is crucial to ensuring mutual respect, trust, and the survival of skeletal studies as a viable field of scientific and social-scientific inquiry in the United States and elsewhere.

4

The Cemetery Dedication and Archaeology

Along the fringes of New Orleans' French Quarter on Rampart Street is a forgotten and now-invisible cemetery. The St. Peter Street Cemetery was one of the first cemeteries to serve the colonial city, with its active years running from ca. 1725 through the 1790s. At the time of its creation, as the "Rampart" street name suggests, the St. Peter Street Cemetery[1] was located beyond the outskirts of colonial New Orleans. However, by the time of its closure, the new colony had expanded to within reach (and smelling distance) of this cemetery site. Today, the cemetery, along with most of its postmortem inhabitants, lies underneath the shops and residences on Rampart Street. The reason for this seemingly macabre and disrespectful reuse of a cemetery actually arises more than 200 years and nearly 8,000 km (5,000 mi) away at the Spanish royal court in Madrid.

As discussed in the chapters above, as a general rule, once a piece of land is put to use as a cemetery, at least from a legal perspective, that land is forever a cemetery. From a practical perspective, though, this legal reality does not always hold true. Time after time around the world, cemeteries are unceremoniously converted from sacred sites of mourning to commercial or residential uses, often with the grave markers removed and the remains either left in place or bulldozed out of the way. Examples of these unfortunate cemetery demises are legion, including the African Burial Ground in Manhattan (Frohne 2015), the First Baptist Church of Philadelphia Cemetery (Leader et al. 2022), and the areas of the Milwaukee County Poor Farm Cemetery (Richards et al. 2016). Indeed, New Orleans boasts many of its own shameful examples of this activity—from the construction of Canal Boulevard over Charity Hospital No. 2 Cemetery to the development of the Thomy Lafon School over the nineteenth-century pauper cemeteries of Locust Grove Nos. 1 and 2. The ramifications of these past acts for managing modern landscapes cause complications today for archaeologists and lawyers alike. The St. Peter Street Cemetery stands as a bizarre exception to the illegal nature of reusing a cemetery for other purposes because of a virtually unknown act of the king of Spain in 1789.

According to unsubstantiated legends, burials in early New Orleans occurred haphazardly around the area now known as the French Quarter, with some in the various levees that ringed the city (Dedek 2017). No archaeological evidence has yet appeared to support these legends. What is known is that there were several early city cemeteries throughout the French Quarter that filled and became olfactory and public health nuisances fairly quickly. Although the bodies buried in these cemeteries would rapidly decompose, the runoff was offensive and space was briskly consumed. One of these cemeteries was located at the intersection of St. Peter and Rampart streets, and reports contemporary with its later years in the mid-eighteenth century relate terrible smells and visible human remains protruding from the ground.[2] The city needed a new cemetery, and the St. Peter Street Cemetery needed to be closed to future burials. At the time, city leaders did not have considerable power to undertake such actions. The authority to close the cemetery rested with Spain's King Charles IV.

By all accounts, Charles IV was not particularly interested in governing. Unlike his father, Charles III, the son, who ascended to the Spanish throne in 1788, wanted to spend the majority of his time hunting rather than worry with the intricacies of running a vast world empire. Much of his monarchical duties were tasked out to underlings, including the management of Spain's New World colonies.

Contrary to popular belief, much of New Orleans's formative colonial years—and indeed the development of its civilian system of law—was overseen by agents of Spain rather than by the French. What New Orleans, and indeed the entire Louisiana colony, inherited in the way of cemetery law came to it through Roman and Spanish sources that were enforced at a distance by the Spanish monarchy. Thus, when the question of what to do with the fetid area of the St. Peter Street Cemetery arose in the late eighteenth century, the local Spanish government had to seek answers from a disinterested king in Madrid. At that time, for the reasons examined in this chapter, the decision regarding what to do with the St. Peter Street Cemetery rested solely with Charles IV, as the law vested him with full authority to open and close cemeteries and to manage those spaces' future use in the overseas colony. The legal, archaeological, and land use decision of Charles IV (or more likely his ministers) for the management of this cemetery would ripple into the twenty-first century.

The Cemetery on St. Peter Street

In the early twenty-first century, a landowner and developer of properties in New Orleans along Rampart Street reached out to the Louisiana state archaeologist inquiring into his obligations when redeveloping an area rumored to be a colonial cemetery. The developer's plan was simple: he owned desirable property on the fringes of the French Quarter that he wanted to turn into high-end condominiums that could be sold at a premium. However, contrary to many developers when their interests intersect with cemeteries, he was concerned about his legal and moral obligations when he heard rumors that some of his land might lie atop burials.

In the late twentieth century, archaeologists working in the area had indeed confirmed that the location of the now-planned condominium development was also the lost location of the St. Peter Street Cemetery. The site contained the remains of both the city's early European colonists and enslaved Africans and free people of color who were among the city's early non-Native American inhabitants.

What immediately vexed state regulators about this site was what the legal ramifications would be of its redevelopment. Certainly, the site had been disturbed for centuries. It had been used for warehouses, residences, and shops for a long time. But these uses occurred during a time in which the American people were seemingly less concerned about cemetery protection and the laws associated with such spaces. When the redevelopment inquiry arose in the twenty-first century, not only had an awakening occurred relating to the need to protect cemetery sites (see previous chapter), but modern archaeological techniques were mandated for any such reuses of cemetery property under Louisiana's relatively new Unmarked Burials Act. The real vexing problem was this: could the land even lawfully be reused now, or would it have to sit idle because of the cemetery known to lie underneath?

The developer was more than willing to fund limited archaeological investigations on the property to respectfully and scientifically remove any human remains from the impact area of his planned redevelopment. This alone was seen as a triumph, as most developers are not so willing. However, the real legal question with this property was whether that activity was enough. From an archaeological perspective it was. Removing the remains from the impact area and sealing in place anything else was a more reasonable conservation-minded and cost-effective approach than actually damaging the remains (not an option) and removing absolutely everything in the project area. The legal limitation that once a property is a cemetery it is always a cemetery and cannot be put to alternative uses presented a real problem for this archaeologically sound approach. A strict application of these laws would require the removal of all remains from an impact area and a court's approval before the land's reuse—a requirement that likely once was not so burdensome when a few guys with a shovel could remove the remains quickly and cheaply, but one that was, today, a real logistical and cost burden. Shockingly, the answer to the state's and the developer's dilemma lay in the stroke of a quill by King Charles IV in 1789.

King Charles and New Orleans's Dead

Though Charles IV was not an overly engaged monarch, either he or his ministers (with his approval) executed countless documents relating to the management of Spain's holdings in the New World. Eventually, one of the documents that came before the king was one that questioned how to manage the aging St. Peter Street Cemetery. In one simple act, King Charles IV issued a decree that closed the cemetery, directed the reuse of the land as residential property, and opened the still extant and world-famous St. Louis No. 1 Cemetery in New Orleans. Because the King was vested with complete legal autonomy at the time, there was no need for a judge to review a monarchical directive to repurpose cemetery property. Indeed, there was no need for a removal of the remains from that property. That requirement came later. All that Spanish law at the time required was that cemetery property be treated differently—more reverentially—from other land. And that is exactly what King Charles IV did: He treated it differently and then decided not to.

With his decree in 1789, Charles IV treated the cemetery differently by recognizing that the law required him to pay it special attention. However, he opted to ignore the rest of the law, and, rather than treat the land reverentially by restricting its reuse or mandating the removal of the remains to a new location before its reuse, he simply decreed that the site was no longer a cemetery and could be used for residential purposes. Because Louisiana inherited many of its laws and ancient property restrictions from the prior sovereigns, including France and Spain, this decree was a binding act that allowed for the redevelopment of the cemetery at any time after 1789. It was through this unique legal loophole that the archaeologically driven management of the cemetery's reuse could proceed in the twenty-first century. By de-dedicating the cemetery, Charles IV had eliminated the draconian mandate to remove all remains from the site.

The thought process in late Bourbon Madrid with regard to a small parcel of land in a colony nearly 8,000 km (5,000 mi) away is virtually impossible to divine. Such reasons are particularly difficult to deduce when, during this period in Spain, regal secrecy was prized. Simply, the kings of this time did not explain themselves—primarily because they did not have to. An exemplar of this is Charles III's decree in 1767 expelling Jesuits from the realm. As Maturana (2014:311) observes, the "king refrained from explaining his motives for such a traumatic decision, merely stating that it was a consequence of his 'royal wishes' (real ánimo) and forbidding discussion of the matter." What we do know of this period is that the absolute monarchy of Charles III was in the process of transitioning to one that incorporated some ideas and suggestions from important elites (Maturana 2014). Thus, it is not unreasonable to think that the Spanish Louisiana governor in the 1790s, either Esteban Rodriguez Miró (1785–1791) or Francisco Luis Héctor de Carondelet (1791–1797), had the ear of the king's ministers in Madrid in such a manner that they could request a royal decree that repurposed land in this far-flung colony. Indeed, of particular importance for at least the closure and covering of the St. Peter Street Cemetery, as Maturana (2014) states, trickles of public opinion began to emerge during Charles IV's reign, especially on matters of public health. "At the end of the eighteenth century . . . public announcements, periodicals, medical treatises . . . and sermons were riddled with allusions to the advantages of burying the deceased outside of the cities" (Maturana 2014:39). In light of this breach in the royal court's control of open communication, it is unsurprising that the overflowing stench of the St. Peter Street Cemetery—now squarely within the New Orleans city limits—caught the attention of Charles IV's inner circle such that a decree directing its closure was issued.

That such a decree exists at all on a matter that is arguably a trivial colonial land use is testament to the public's concern with disease spread from cemeteries, the understanding when the reuse of a cemetery was significant, and it is also testament to the centrality of royal power under Charles IV. To the latter point, despite efforts to reform the absolute monarchy, it appears that the Spanish crown was reluctant to share control on even minor colonial matters.

A contemporary Spanish jurist with the St. Peter Street Cemetery decree, Count de la Cañada, observed that "'[t]he laws receive all their worth from the mouth of the Sovereign'" and that "'notoriously inferior'" vassals "'are simply to obey'" (Maturana 2014:26). However, another contemporary jurist, Lázaro Duo, recognized the importance (as now in civilian legal traditions) of custom and practice even in the sovereign's legal pronouncements. The reality of this observation is that, while not bound by precedent or ancient legal concepts (e.g., Roman law), Charles IV can be expected to have considered such prior and customary sources of law in his decrees and legal decisions. Within this political and legal framework, it is easy to understand why Charles IV (or his ministers) gave credence to the ancient cemetery land use limitations and the need to deal with a fetid cemetery in New Orleans when he issued a decree specifically to abrogate those precedents and customs and arguably to protect the public health.

Of course, Louisiana's more recent Unmarked Burials Act also applied to the cemetery, but the removal of the cemetery dedication without the requirement to remove all bodies from the land allowed the well-intentioned developer in the twenty-first century to proceed with his plans for converting the area to condominiums while still respecting the existing legal mandates that applied to the property as a cemetery. Accordingly, following negotiations with the State of Louisiana, a permitted excavation of human remains from the impact area of the planned redevelopment—specifically a substantial ground disturbance that would become a hot tub in the courtyard of the condominium development, was undertaken with full archaeological and bioanthropological analysis of the excavated materials.

In many ways, the act of King Charles IV in 1789 continues to protect the St. Peter Street Cemetery today. It allows for limited archaeological investigations of the site and its former inhabitants, while allowing the state to mandate sealing for posterity the remainder of the site underneath the protective foundations of later developments. What follows is a technical analysis of the development of the restrictions that gave rise to this inquiry with respect to the St. Peter Street Cemetery and how those laws continue to apply today nearly 2,000 years after their first appearance in Christian Rome.

Basic Modern Cemetery Legal Protections

Until the advent of the NAGPRA and similar state laws, little codified guidance existed regarding both how to interact with spaces of the dead when they were encountered archaeologically or during development and what to do in terms of protecting them from development or other threats (e.g., desecration). As discussed in earlier chapters, since 1990, at least at the federal level, one exception to this lack of guidance is with respect to Native American cemeteries, around which a massive compilation of both academic and legal literature has arisen and legislation and regulations have been drafted (see, e.g., Riding In et al. 2004). Contrarily, a dearth of such critical analysis exists related to the protections available to virtually all non-Native American cemeteries. To understand the complex interactions of the spaces of the dead with those of the living and how archaeological practice may be affected by ancient legal mandates, an investigation of the history of the cemetery dedication laws of Louisiana and the application of those laws in the jurisprudence follows. Louisiana's cemetery dedication laws are used here as a proxy for other jurisdictions.

Contrary to popular belief, from a legal perspective, New Orleans, and indeed all of Louisiana, is substantially similar to other U.S. locales. Moreover, threats such as those noted above to New Orleans's cemeteries are not unusual for historic and cultural resources around the United States. For this reason, as noted earlier, various state and federal laws have been enacted since the mid-1960s in an effort to minimize damage to such sites (e.g., the National Historic Preservation Act of 1966, 54 U.S.C. § 300101 et seq. ["NHPA"]; the National Environmental Policy Act of 1970, 16 U.S.C. § 4321 et seq. ["NEPA"]). Such laws often lack substantial and meaningful site protections (Seidemann 2007). However, cemeteries occupy a liminal legal space when it comes to status and protection between continuously used sacred spaces (Dymond 1999) and historic or cultural resources that are the subject of legislative protections (King 2012; Mahoney 2014).

Long-existing cemetery protections are particularly underreported in the academic literature related to archaeology, planning, and urban studies worldwide (e.g., Demirakin 2012),[3] despite recent experiences in Louisiana suggesting that the ancient legal concept of an inviolate cemetery is the strongest protection existing anywhere in the law for historic spaces of any kind.[4] Indeed, in a 1950 publication by the American Society of Planning Officials titled "Cemeteries in the City Plan," though "cemetery removal" is contemplated as a manner of managing such spaces in an urban environment, no consideration is given to the sacred nature of this land nor really of what to do with the remains interred therein (Marsh and Gibson 2015). The cemetery dedication, though often draconian for both archaeologists and developers-planners, answers questions regarding what to do when modern development encounters a cemetery. A complete understanding of these laws is essential to navigating the cemetery legal landscape for archaeological-mitigation purposes.

The ancient concept of the cemetery dedication, at least in Louisiana, has emerged as a stronger site protection tool than the more recent historic preservation legislation reviewed in previous chapters (Seidemann 2018a, 2018b). The stronger nature of the dedication laws is an interesting reality, as the latter laws were intended specifically to stem the impacts of development and the looting of cemeteries and other sites, while the former was not. The significance of the emergence of the cemetery dedication as a factor in planning and as an archaeological and historic preservation tool in Louisiana has implications across the United States, as the cemetery dedication is virtually ubiquitous in all 50 states (e.g., Cal.Health & Safety Code § 8553 [California]; T.C.A., Health & Safety Code § 711.035 [Texas]). Ultimately, this means that little-known and often underused tools for the protection of sacred spaces may be lurking in existing legal schemes in most jurisdictions, and this chapter reviews the history, existence, and usage of such tools in Louisiana.

The Legal Interplay of Ancient and Modern Cemetery Laws

The existence of such sweeping cemetery protections as the cemetery dedication, though occasionally discussed in legal literature (Tom 2016:185) and appearing a few times per year in the reported jurisprudence in the United States (e.g., Seidemann 2013), does not seem to have permeated much of the nonlegal academic literature. Although occasionally sources comment on the generally accepted notion of the sanctity of the grave (e.g., Worpole 2003:155, 158) or simply note the reality that putting land to a cemetery use places it out of commerce for other purposes (e.g., Canning and Szmigin 2010), scholars seldom look beyond the modern environmental and historic preservation movements for sources of such protections. Another especial shortcoming in the existing literature is in the field of archaeology, where much attention is paid to NAGPRA but little consideration is given to protections for non-Native American burial sites. Baugher and Veit (2014:25–29) typify this dearth when they observe that, before NAGPRA, there was virtually no protection for burial sites from unauthorized plunder and pillage or even from unintended damage. Certainly, NAGPRA was a watershed event for raising the awareness of threats to nontraditional cemeteries in the United States (Seidemann 2010a) and perhaps worldwide (Seidemann 2004, 2020), but, as discussed in the previous chapter, it provided neither a panacea of protective legislation for all burial sites nor the earliest such protection. Admittedly, because the cemetery dedication is obscure and poorly understood, Baugher and Veit's (2014) observation that cemetery site protections are minimal is probably accurate in practice even if not a technically correct read of U.S. law.

As is illustrated by the archival evidence reviewed and analyzed in other chapters, the cemetery dedication is not a universal fix for the problems of disproportionate treatment of cemetery sites either. Indeed, the cemetery dedication is merely a title cloud that carries great weight for the merchantability of property and the security of title, but it does not act as a deterrent that works on the level of combating structural violence, necroviolence, or other types of disproportionate treatments of disenfranchised peoples. However, as Ander (1986:354) states, a title cloud

> may impair the owner's ability to convey a marketable title. A buyer may refuse to accept a deed to the encumbered property unless the purchase price is adjusted or the encumbrance is removed. Further, a lender may be reluctant to commit funds in such a transaction.

In other words, title clouds such as the cemetery dedication can affect the legal ability to use the burdened property in a particular way, it can affect the resale value of the property, or it can affect the owner's ability to obtain financing guaranteed by the property. Accordingly, while such mechanisms may carry great financial weight for property owners and developers, the cemetery dedication is only useful when such individuals are concerned with these fiscal ramifications and know of the presence of a cemetery. It was precisely these fiscal ramifications that led to the archaeological excavation and protection of the St. Peter Street Cemetery in recent years. Because banks mandate clear title to issue loans for property development, the potential of a cemetery dedication title cloud on the Rampart Street property meant that adherence to current archaeological treatment of the site was necessary. In other words, financial considerations (and, perhaps to a lesser extent, civil and criminal sanctions for violations of modern laws) can drive the planning for the treatment of cemetery sites like the St. Peter Street Cemetery.[5]

Urban Environments and the Dead

The land used for the interment of the human dead is often an afterthought in planning and development circles (Rugg 2022) unless and until those dead interfere with actual real estate development (Bennett and Davies 2015; Coutts et al. 2011; Klaufus 2014, 2016). Indeed, cemeteries have occupied a binary position from a planning and public health perspective for centuries: they are known, on the one hand, as sacred and inviolate spaces, and, on the other, as nuisances and hazards that need to be marginalized and moved (Bennett and Davies 2015).[6] In this regard, the literature is replete with discussions of the historical growth of urban areas and the drive to locate cemeteries at the margins of those areas (e.g., Dedek 2017; Upton 2008:210) and the perceived public health threats of cemeteries when the urban growth reaches these "insidious" locales (e.g., Bennett and Davies 2015; Jenner 2005; Johnson 2006; Kong 2012; McCrea 2007). Not only are the needs of a community for future burial spaces often not considered at the planning stage, but cemeteries are often expensive and direct hindrances to development.

Admittedly, in many cases, when development encounters human remains or cemeteries, it is unexpected (e.g., Doran 2002; Spott 2010). Especially in rural (or formerly rural) areas, the locations of small family or church burial grounds are not well documented, and their markers are often perishable or semipermanent (e.g., Brown 2016; Yanner and Ybarrola 2003; Sloane 2018). Furthermore, many underprivileged communities were simply afforded no burial space in traditional cemeteries, and the evidence of their burial locations has been lost over time (Spott 2010). Consequently, such sites are often encountered only by accident once a development project has begun (Kay 1998; Pitts 2015), and, as Sloane (2018:129) observes, "developers have fought with communities about preserving cemeteries in the way of development, with mixed success." However, such accidental finds are not always the case. There have been well-documented examples of developers or others who are aware of the presence or probable presence of cemeteries in the path of a planned project who simply choose to ignore the problem and deal with any damage after the fact. Examples of both good and bad actors encountering cemeteries abound. One example is of a logging company allegedly driving over a historic cemetery in Illinois (Anon. 2017). Another is of developers who paid for the proper archaeological excavations to be done before undertaking a construction project nearby (Rickert 2017; see also Thomas et al. 2010). Most significantly are archaeological reports from Florida of knowing erasures of African American cemeteries from the landscape to make way for various developments (Moates and O'Sullivan 2020a, 2020b; Pelley 2022, 2023).

Perhaps the most famous of the impacts of development to Louisiana's cemeteries is the case of the Protestant Girod Street Cemetery (Dedek 2017). Girod Cemetery was located roughly in the area occupied today by the Caesar's Superdome, Champions Square, and the surrounding parking garages.[7] Discussed more fully in this and other chapters, this site was cleared in the 1950s as part of the development of downtown New Orleans. The cemetery was, by the late nineteenth century, largely full and defunct as an operating burial place. A combination of its prime location and unkempt nature led to its being reclaimed for alternative uses in the mid-twentieth century.

Although New Orleans boasts some of the most well-known cemetery reuses—spaces that were once cemeteries and were later either lawfully (e.g., Girod and the Gates of Mercy Cemetery) or unlawfully (e.g., Charity Hospital Cemetery No. 2) put to noncemetery uses—the city is not alone with such problems. Indeed, New York has recently had problems with conflicting land uses when, during the construction of a General Services Administration (GSA) building in Manhattan in 1991, workers unearthed what is now known as the African Burial Ground—the burial location of many first-generation enslaved people in North America (Wright and Hughes 1996; Frohne 2015).

Characterized as "one of the most significant unplanned historical, archaeological finds" of its time (Clinton and Jackson 2020), the GSA development resulted in protests over perceived racial biases in the treatment of the dead and considerable additional project expenses for the U.S. government.

Although such high-profile cemetery problems have not yet been experienced in Louisiana, the numerous cemetery sites improperly put to alternative uses since statehood in 1812 certainly raise the specter of such potential problems in the future. Indeed, this lack of experience now may be short-lived. The current tension between a plastics maker and descendants of those once enslaved on two plantations in St. James Parish regarding cemetery site access and preservation threatens to become Louisiana's first such contentious experience (Mitchell 2020).

The African Burial Ground project, though difficult, was not without its benefits, including considerable knowledge acquired by the descendant community and a raised awareness of the sensitivities involved in such projects. Michael Blakey (2010:61), the African Burial Ground project's lead bioarchaeologist, characterized the ultimate outcome of what began as an insensitively informed effort to expeditiously remove human remains from the path of development, following considerable protest and descendant community participation thus: "[t]he site went from desecration in 1991 to becoming a US National Monument in 2007, representing a successful example of bioarchaeology in the service of a descendant community's human rights." Despite Blakey's characterization, Weiss and Springer (2020) continued with unsupported arguments that descendant-scientific collaborations are farces. The African Burial Ground outcome represents a solidly documented rebuke to such assertions.

Occasionally, cemeteries are not completely erased from existence by development. An example of such a space is Historic Highland Cemetery in Baton Rouge. Recent archaeological excavations and historical analyses identified that Highland Cemetery, which is Baton Rouge's oldest existing Euro-American cemetery, shrank from two acres to one-half acre in size since its founding in 1813 (Seidemann and Kleinpeter 2014). In this situation, a neighborhood simply grew up around the cemetery and slowly encroached on to the graves. The general preservation of that site across its two-century history is particularly important to understanding the difficulties faced when development and cemeteries collide and is instructive of the management of these spaces in other contexts. Highland Cemetery is also significant as it illustrates that, while less common, the burial places of the privileged and elite—Highland contains the burial of Armand Allard Duplantier Sr., aide-de-camp to the Marquis de la Fayette during the American Revolution, as well as the founding patrician families of Baton Rouge—are not immune from the encroachment and destruction of development. Indeed, as reviewed in a later chapter, Highland Cemetery presents a unique archaeological laboratory to observe de jure and de facto treatment of cemetery property in Louisiana from an archaeological perspective.

The Cemetery Dedication

In terms of strict legal classifications of cemetery land in general, under the law in Louisiana, the purposeful interment of human remains in the ground (or entombment on the ground, as the case may be) creates a legal cloud on a property's title (Seidemann 2018a, 2018b). This cloud, codified at La. R.S. 8:304–307, is known as the "cemetery dedication." The cemetery dedication is a common legal concept across the United States (see table 4.1) and basically stands for the premise that once human remains have been interred in a tract of land that land is forever classified as a cemetery and cannot be put to alternative uses (Anon. 1968).

As fully reviewed in a prior chapter, in Louisiana, as in many other jurisdictions, there is a suite of additional laws aimed at protecting and preserving cemeteries. These laws exist across the legal spectrum from the federal level to the local level. Unlike the preservation and criminal laws already reviewed, when the Louisiana Cemetery Act was enacted in 1974, the legislature included in this law the dedication provisions to ensure the sanctity of cemeteries. These protections, when properly applied, appear to represent the strongest legal protections in existence in Louisiana for such spaces. These provisions have not materially changed since their original enactment. These statutes provide, in pertinent part, as follows:

> After property is dedicated to cemetery purposes pursuant to this Chapter, neither the dedication nor the title of a plot owner shall be affected by the dissolution of the cemetery authority, by nonuse on its part, by alienation of the property, or otherwise, except as provided in this Title . . . (La. R.S. 8:304[A]).
>
> * * *
>
> Dedication to cemetery purposes pursuant to this title is not invalid as violating any laws against perpetuities or the suspension of the power of alienation of title to or use of property but is expressly permitted and shall be deemed to be in respect for the dead, a provision for the interment of human remains, and a duty to and for the benefit of the general public (La. R.S. 8:305).

* * *

> Property dedicated to cemetery purposes shall be held and used exclusively for cemetery purposes unless and until the dedication is removed from all or any part of it by judgment of the district court of the parish in which the property is situated in a proceeding brought by the cemetery authority for that purpose and upon notice of hearing to the board, and by publication as hereinafter provided, and proof satisfactory to the court: (1) That no interments were made in or that all interments have been removed from that portion of the property from which dedication is sought to be removed; and (2) That the portion of the property from which dedication is sought to be removed is not being used for interment of human remains (La. R.S. 8:306[B]).[8]

As noted above, read together, these provisions stand for the proposition that once human remains are interred in a piece of property that property is forever dedicated as a cemetery. In addition, such property cannot be put to any use other than a "cemetery use" unless all human remains are removed from the property and a court of competent jurisdiction issues an order removing the dedication.

As alluded to above, these strict prohibitions are occasionally in conflict with modern archaeological preferences for preservation of cultural materials and human remains in situ when possible (Wheeler 2013) and can become draconian in practice. In other words, using modern archaeological methods, removing only the portion of a site that is to be affected by development and leaving the remainder of the archaeological deposits intact for either future excavation or for general preservation is more advisable than full and complete excavation (Sharer and Ashmore 1993). This latter approach presents a more attractive option for developers when cemetery impacts are unavoidable. Removing only what will be affected—not all human remains in the project area—is substantially less expensive to implement than a wholesale removal of all remains. This less invasive approach to mitigating cemetery impacts, while economically and archaeologically advisable, is, in most cases, not legally authorized due to the strict mandates of La. R.S. 8:306(B). Quoted above, this legal provision requires that once property is dedicated for use as a cemetery, the legal cloud that hangs over that property exists until removed by a court judgment finding that "all interments have been removed" from the property (La. R.S. 8:306). Accordingly, no alternative use of cemetery property can exist until all the remains have been removed. Whether scientifically or economically preferable, the absolute ban on alternative uses of cemetery property under the cemetery dedication is the mandatory legal manner in which cemeteries must be treated in many U.S. jurisdictions. In Louisiana, this mandate is applicable to all property in which human remains are interred based upon the following history of the law itself. The only reason that this mandate did not apply to the St. Peter Street Cemetery is because Charles IV officially decreed that the land was no longer a cemetery long before the Louisiana legislature enacted the statutory cemetery dedication. This specific decree exempted the St. Peter Street Cemetery from the later general dedication law.

The Shallow History of Louisiana Cemetery Dedication Laws

In general, the retroactive application of law is disfavored and often will not be allowed by the courts.[9] Such a reality is problematic when the bulk of the cemetery regulation laws in Louisiana, and, indeed in the United States generally, were not enacted until after Jessica Mitford's 1963 publication of *The American Way of Death* (Sloane 1991:215).[10]

Indeed, as discussed below, though the concepts undergirding Louisiana's cemetery dedication laws had existed in the jurisprudence definitively since the 1940 Louisiana Supreme Court case of *Humphreys v. Bennett Oil Corp.*, the actual cemetery dedication statutes were not legislatively enacted until 1974. For such site protections to apply to property without running afoul of the prohibition against the retroactivity of laws or otherwise representing a taking of private property by the government,[11] the protections must predate the interest acquired by the current landowners (or their ancestors-in-title, depending upon their method of property acquisition). From the review above, the cemetery-specific protection laws—NAGPRA (1990), the Unmarked Burials Act (1991), the Historic Cemetery Act (2010), or even perhaps the criminal desecration laws (1950)—clearly do not predate much property ownership in Louisiana. Thus, the key to cemetery protections for those sites located on private property in Louisiana and elsewhere lies in the ancient concept of the cemetery dedication.

Although the statutory cemetery dedication provisions were enacted in 1974, predating jurisprudence in Louisiana clearly accorded cemeteries some measure of protected status as special spaces. In particular, at least five pre-1974 Louisiana cases stand for the notion that cemeteries are inviolate pieces of property. These cases are critical, as they tacitly acknowledge the long-standing legal notion of cemetery protections.

In the early case of *Choppin v. LaBranche*, 20 So. 681 (La. 1896), the Louisiana Supreme Court wrestled with the question of whether the use of land for interment somehow disrupted long-accepted concepts of property owner-

Table 4.1. U.S. states and territories with codified or jurisprudential cemetery dedication laws

State/ territory	Dedication laws?	Citation	Original enactment date
Alabama	Yes	Ala.Code 1975 § 11-17-6	1907
Alaska	No	N/A	N/A
American Samoa	Explicit in jurisprudence	*Leiato v. Satele & Tapopo*, 2 ASR 341 (Am. Sam. 1948)	1948
Arizona	Yes	A.R.S. § 32-2194.22	1963
Arkansas	By inference	A.C.A. § 20-17-1002	1977
California	Yes	Cal.Health & Safety Code §§ 8550, et seq.	1939
Colorado	By inference	CO ST § 12-54-108	2019
Connecticut	By inference	C.G.S.A. § 19a-315	1984
Delaware	Explicit in jurisprudence	*Roe v. Doe ex dem. Town of Seaford*, 80 A. 250 (Del. 1911)	1911
District of Columbia	Yes	DC ST 1981 § 27-112	1901
Florida	By inference	F.S.A. § 497.005	1993
Georgia	By inference; explicit in jurisprudence	Ga. Code Ann., § 44-5-230	1863
Guam	Yes	6 G.C.A. § 5107	1963
Hawaii	Yes	HRS §§ 441-2, et seq.	1967
Idaho	By inference	I.C. § 27-403	1963
Illinois	Yes	525 ILCS 30/11	1981
Indiana	By inference	IC 23-14-33-7	1997
Iowa	By inference	I.C.A. § 523I.103	2005
Kansas	By inference	K.S.A. 17-1302	1913
Kentucky	By inference	KRS § 367.932	1984
Louisiana	Yes	La. R.S. 8:304-307	1974
Maine	Yes	13 M.R.S.A. § 1141	1954
Maryland	By inference	MD Code, Business Regulation, § 5-505	1992
Massachusetts	By inference	M.G.L.A. 114 § 1	2008
Michigan	By inference from jurisprudence	*Richmond Hills Memorial Park Ass'n v. Richardson*, 266 N.W. 396 (Mich. 1936)	1936
Minnesota	By inference; explicit in jurisprudence	M.S.A. § 149A.02	1997
Mississippi	By inference	Miss. Code Ann. § 73-11-71	2008
Missouri	By inference; explicit in jurisprudence	V.A.M.S. 214.200	1939
Montana	By inference	MCA 35-21-802	1999

State/ territory	Dedication laws?	Citation	Original enactment date
Nebraska	By inference from jurisprudence	*Graceland Park Cemetery Co. v. City of Omaha*, 114 N.W.2d 29 (Neb. 1962); *Sjuts v. Granville Cemetary Ass'n*, 719 N.W.2d 236 (Neb. 2006)	1962; 2006 (respectively)
Nevada	Yes	N.R.S. 451.069, et seq.	1979
New Hampshire	By inference	N.H. Rev. Stat. § 289:1	1994
New Jersey	Yes	N.J.S.A. 45:27-21	2003
New Mexico	By inference	N.M.S.A. 1978, § 58-17-3	1978
New York	By inference; explicit in jurisprudence	McKinney's N-PCL § 1506	1977
North Carolina	By inference	N.C.G.S.A. § 65-48	1943
North Dakota	By inference	NDCC, 23-21-01	1959
Northern Mariana Islands	No	N/A	N/A
Ohio	Yes	R.C. §§ 517.10, 759.08	1953
Oklahoma	Yes	15 Okl.St.Ann. § 752	1972
Oregon	Yes	O.R.S. § 97.340, et seq.	1955; 1965
Pennsylvania	By inference	9 Pa.C.S.A. § 101	1972
Puerto Rico	Yes	T. 32A Ap. IV, § 16	1979
Rhode Island	Yes	Gen.Laws 1956, § 23-18-1, et seq.	1939
South Carolina	Yes	Code 1976 § 40-8-30	1976
South Dakota	No	N/A	N/A
Tennessee	By inference	T.C.A. § 46-4-104	1949
Texas	Yes	V.T.C.A., Health & Safety Code § 711.001, et seq.	1989
United States Virgin Islands	Yes	19 V.I.C. §§ 2007; 2021	1971
Utah	No	N/A	N/A
Vermont	Yes	18 V.S.A. § 5302	1947
Virginia	Yes	VA Code Ann. §§ 54.1-2310; 57-39	1998
Washington	Yes	West's RCWA 68.24.040; 68.60.010, et seq.	1943; 2017 (respectively)
West Virginia	By inference	W. Va. Code, § 37-13A-7	2010
Wisconsin	Yes	W.S.A. 157.061; W.S.A. 157.115	1923; 1857 (respectively)
Wyoming	No	N/A	N/A

Note: The data in this table represent minimum dedication laws. Every effort was made to capture each state's or territory's laws. However, varying terminology may have caused some data to be missed. In addition, the dates indicated in this table are not intended to represent the first time a jurisdiction recognized a dedication of property to cemetery purposes, but rather is an indication of the enactment of positive dedication legislation in its current form implementing the common law dedication. Those states whose dedications are referred to as "by inference" refers to situations in which certain laws reference a cemetery dedication, but no explicit law creates that dedication (suggesting the existence of a common law dedication). The sources for cemetery dedications in various jurisdictions may be positive law, inference from definitions or from negative statements, acknowledgements in jurisprudence, or in existing legal presumptions in the respective jurisdiction.

ship. This case revolved around the rights of certain people to be interred in a New Orleans tomb and whether later disagreements over tomb ownership rights empowered the title owners of the tomb to disinter those who they no longer wanted buried in their tomb. Although the court never specifically addressed what is known as the cemetery dedication, its opinion in this case is prescient of disputes later to come when it noted that, "[t]o disturb the mortal remains of those endeared to us in life sometimes becomes the sad duty of the living. But, except in cases of necessity, or for laudable purposes, the sanctity of the grave should be maintained, and the preventive aid of the courts may be invoked for that object."[12] In other words, the court recognized that disturbance of cemeteries is disfavored, and that courts generally stand sentinel to enforce this sanctity. This precise concept is embodied in Louisiana's current statutory cemetery dedication when those seeking the removal of a dedication must apply to a court for approval of such a land use alteration.

Ultimately, the *Choppin* court did not specifically classify the type of restriction or right that a cemetery use placed on property in Louisiana. The court correctly noted that such use did not affect the underlying ownership of the property, but it also did not create a servitude (easement) in favor of the families of those interred on the property. Nonetheless, the court sidestepped an actual conclusion as to the nature of the legal classification of such property and instead seemed to hold, based upon the general disfavor with the disturbance of the dead, that the remains in the disputed tomb could not be disturbed based upon a contract during life between the tomb owner and its inhabitants. In this regard, the court was loath to create a species of property right without explicit authorization from the civil code. As is set forth below, such a jurisprudential creation is not inconsistent with Louisiana's civil law system and, had the *Choppin* court wished, it could have found ample historical support for the notion that interment creates a legal dedication that burdens the underlying (and overlying) property.

The case of *Humphreys v. Bennett Oil Corp.*, 197 So. 222 (La. 1940), represents the worst-case scenario of such interactions between the special nature of cemeteries and the violation of their sanctity. In *Humphreys,* a case reviewed in detail in a later chapter, a mineral production company thought it advisable to sink two oil wells into a rural cemetery in Acadia Parish, Louisiana. When descendants of those interred in the offended cemetery brought suit against the production company for, among other things, mental anguish, the Louisiana Supreme Court reacted harshly, with an uncharacteristically editorial decision. In this decision, the court described the problem in the following manner:

> It is admitted that this small Evangeline Cemetery, consisting of a one-acre plot of ground, was literally converted into an oil field by the drilling thereon of two producing wells. By such use, this consecrated ground, which was destined for the peaceful slumber of the dead, was transformed into an industrial site, to be exploited for material gain. . . . This use of the cemetery plot divested it of its sacred character, violated and profaned the sanctity of the graves. This was a desecration calculated to wound the feelings of the living who had relatives buried there.[13]

From the tone of the decision, the court clearly did not look favorably upon violations of the cemetery dedication. Although the court's rhetoric in this case contains a bit of purple prose, it also presages a judicial reverence for the spaces of the dead. In *Humphreys*, the court also explicitly addressed the concept of the cemetery dedication when it stated the following:

> Regardless of the laws and rules relating to the ownership and control of real property, when a plot of ground is set apart for cemetery purposes, and burials are made in the land, the ground changes its character in the minds and feelings of the community. "It assumes a sacred quality that overrides conveyances' precedents and requires freedom from profanation until, by abandonment and removal of the bodies or by complete disintegration, there remains nothing to appeal to the emotions of the survivors."[14]

With the above statement, the Louisiana Supreme Court unequivocally recognized that the presence of a cemetery on a tract of land fundamentally changes the character of that land such that the land cannot be used for anything but the interment of the human dead unless and until the remains are removed from the ground.

An interesting caveat to the cemetery dedication as espoused by the *Humphreys* court is the notion, taken from Jackson (1936:206), that the cemetery dedication can effectively disappear from a tract of land upon "complete disintegration" of the human remains therein such that "there remains nothing to appeal to the emotions of the survivors."[15] Such an exception to the cemetery dedication is certainly inconsistent with the later-enacted dedication statute, which does not authorize the removal of the dedication protections either upon the disintegration of the human remains or upon the descendant community's forgetfulness of the cemetery's existence.

Though likely unintentional, the 1974 dedication laws appear to reflect the archaeological reality of cemeteries: Though surface evidence of a cemetery may disappear and be forgotten, subsurface evidence seldom disappears. Such evidence exists in the form of bone fragments, material culture, and even in mere soil discolorations associated with grave shafts and other cultural activity (Carmack 2002; Rojas-Perez 2015; Springate 2015). Unsurprisingly, Jackson, a lawyer writing in the 1930s, was unaware of such persistent vestiges of cemeteries and human remains when he suggested that the dedication may disappear with the disappearance of surface evidence of a cemetery. Archaeological inquiries into trace evidence of a cemetery's existence can fairly be said to have been in their infancy during Jackson's time, and it certainly was not an area of scientific inquiry that influenced the law at that time. Indeed, until 1936, the terms "archaeology" and "archeology" appear in only eight reported state and four reported federal cases in the entire United States, and none of those cases relates to the practice of archaeology in cemeteries. If the advocacy that led to NAGPRA's passage and the implementation of similar laws in the past 30 years is any indication, the "emotions of the survivors" are wont to persist around a cemetery site long after its surface evidence has disappeared (e.g., Herzfeld 2020; Jenkins 2020; McConnaughey 2020).

Because Louisiana's (and other states') dedication provisions substantially predated NAGPRA's passage or even its early drafts (Seidemann 2003; McKeown 2012), the former laws cannot possibly represent a reflection of the incorporation of archaeological knowledge into the law. Rather, these laws seem to have stemmed from a jurisprudential reverence for spaces of the dead and from an aspirational, de jure, historical treatment of these spaces. Of further importance to Jackson's seemingly flippant remark regarding the disappearance of the cemetery dedication, it must be observed that the statement cannot be considered in a vacuum. Indeed, in the same paragraph, Jackson (1936:206) stated that, "[t]he sense of repulsion awakened by a desecration of the grave tends to give permanence to the devotion of land to burial purposes." With the benefit of nearly 100 years of scientific hindsight, Jackson doubtfully would maintain that cemeteries cannot disappear from the landscape. Moreover, the entirety of Jackson's support for the chapter containing this statement is not based on any court having held that the cemetery dedication can actually disappear. In other words, this statement is Jackson's supposition, not a conclusion ever (at that time) held by any court. Indeed, as is set forth below, the history of the dedication provisions supports a contrary conclusion: once a cemetery, always a cemetery. Thus, though the *Humphreys* court took an interesting caveat from Jackson in its opinion, the statement is mere dictum in the court's decision that does not appear to be supported or followed elsewhere in the history of cemetery dedication laws and it is definitely not the case today under Louisiana's statutory cemetery dedication.[16]

The proximate result for the litigants of the *Humphreys* case was less significant than for the protection of cemeteries in general. The court awarded the anguished families only $6,000.30 in damages (approximately $28,514.77 in late 2022). Nonetheless, though the descendants of those buried in the disturbed cemetery in *Humphreys* did not obtain a windfall judgment, the case is an exemplar of cemetery protections available in Louisiana before the enactment of any positive statutory law on the matter.

Despite these protections, the seemingly paltry award in *Humphreys*—a financial penalty that could be used as a deterrent to bad action—continues to be a problem today. Indeed, in the *Jetton* situation discussed in chapter 1, restoration was not a possibility. As noted in chapter 1, though the individual was arrested and evicted from the property, the damage done was so substantial as to make the restoration of the site impossible. No funds existed for work to remove the overburden or to locate the missing markers. In that case, the community had to settle for a commemorative marker on the site containing the names of those known to have been buried in the cemetery. The result for the descendants in *Humphreys* is unfortunately consistent with jurisprudence nationwide that, while acknowledging the sanctity of cemeteries, often awards little to no damages for emotional harms visited upon families when cemeteries or human remains are mishandled (Ogolla 2022; Joiner and Seidemann 2019a, 2019b; Seidemann 2013). This shortcoming does little to act as a deterrent to reckless action in cemeteries.

The cemetery dedication was again reviewed by the Louisiana Supreme Court with regard to the Girod Street Cemetery in *City of New Orleans v. Christ Church Corp.*, 81 So.2d 855 (La. 1955). At issue in the legal part of this case was whether the cemetery dedication is permanent or whether it can be removed. In this case, a curator appointed by the court to represent the interests of the unknown descendants of those interred in the cemetery argued that, when the City of New Orleans sought to expropriate, for the purposes of road expansions and other public works, the property on which the Girod Street Cemetery was located, it could not do so because the land was burdened with a cemetery dedication in perpetuity. The court in *Christ Church* rejected that argument, stating that a dedication could be removed, but that a particular process must be followed by which to remove the dedication (i.e., removal and reinterment of remains and court judgment approving of the removal). In a particularly poetic conclusion, the *Christ Church* court held that the cemetery dedication is not necessarily perpetual and that, if proper procedure is followed, such a restrictive covenant on the property use can be removed. Thus, the court concluded:

> It was with a prophetic eye that the poet of the day saw the dawning of a great transition period, and so he exclaimed to the world to ring out the old and to ring in the new. The old has been rung out, and the new rung in by keeping in step with progress and development. We cannot allow any determent of expansion by a beating of the living with the bones of the dead.[17]

In the matter of *Touro Synagogue v. Goodwill Industries of New Orleans Area, Inc.*, 96 So.2d 29 (La. 1957), the Louisiana Supreme Court was presented with a factual scenario that directly implicated the cemetery dedication some 17 years before its enactment by the legislature. The court recited the following summary of the facts in the *Touro* case:

> On April 9, 1956, Touro Synagogue agreed to sell, and Goodwill Industries agreed to buy, an abandoned cemetery at the corner of Jackson Avenue and South Saratoga Street in this city for $50,000. In this agreement Touro Synagogue bound itself to remove at its own expense and in compliance with proper religious ceremony all remains and tombstones from the abandoned cemetery to a cemetery which it is now using. Pursuant to this agreement Touro tendered title to Goodwill, but the latter refused to accept title on the ground that title was litigious and not merchantable because the property was used as a cemetery at one time and the remains of the dead had never been removed. This suit followed.[18]

In the above recitation, it is clear that by 1957 there was in Louisiana a court-recognized legal concept that property could be dedicated to cemetery purposes and that such a dedication represented a cloud on the property's title, restricting its use only to cemetery purposes.

The "abandoned cemetery" at the heart of the *Touro* case was the Gates of Mercy Cemetery, established in 1828 and, according to the reported case facts, last used in 1872. By the time of the *Touro Synagogue* case in 1957, there had been no interments made in the Gates of Mercy Cemetery in 85 years. Nonetheless, and not surprisingly, the prospective purchaser of the property, Goodwill Industries, was wary of acquiring a cemetery when the purchaser planned to use the property as a facility other than one involved in deathcare on the site of the former cemetery. As a result of this apprehension, the district court in the *Touro Synagogue* case acknowledged that Touro and Goodwill entered into a valid contract to sell the abandoned cemetery property, but that such a sale could only be properly consummated if the seller (Touro) funded the disinterment and reinterment (elsewhere) of the remains of those buried in the cemetery.

On appeal to the Louisiana Supreme Court, the court was again presented with the question of whether a cemetery could ever be put to a noncemetery use. The court answered that question in the affirmative, noting that, consistent with earlier rulings, as long as the human remains had been properly removed from the cemetery property, a cemetery could be decommissioned and the land could be put to an alternative use. Furthermore, the court found that, because the cemetery had been abandoned for active interments and because the synagogue was willing to relocate the human remains interred in the cemetery, no prohibition existed on the sale of the property for noncemetery uses. Moreover, once the remains removal was accomplished, a cemetery dedication no longer burdened the property.

Thus, while the *Humphreys* court recognized the sacred and generally inviolate nature of cemetery property in 1940, the *Touro Synagogue* court, in 1957, reaffirmed the unique nature of cemetery property but also acknowledged that cemetery dedications could be removed from property. The *Touro Synagogue* court noted that as long as certain procedures were followed, such spaces could be converted to another use. Specifically, these procedures were the "proper religious" removal of the human remains interred in the cemetery and their reinterment elsewhere.[19]

Of course, if you happen to be the king of Spain, you can apparently skip over the reverential bits and simply decree that land is no longer a cemetery—the dead be damned—as occurred with the St. Peter Street Cemetery.[20] Modern notions of decency and legal requirements no longer permit such a result.

The Deep History of Louisiana's Cemetery Dedication Laws

Although no legislative history exists accompanying the enactment of the Louisiana Cemetery Act in 1974 (of which the cemetery dedication is a part), one can reasonably presume that the cases discussed above formed the basis for the modern concept of the cemetery dedication in Louisiana. Finding support for that supposition is essential to ensuring the legally binding nature of the concept of the cemetery dedication. Indeed, such support is necessary in light of the *Choppin* court's reticence to "create law" to modify the Louisiana Civil Code property concepts that remain in force today. To this end, as noted above, portions of the *Choppin, Humphreys, Christ Church,* and *Touro Synagogue* cases are present in the modern version of the cemetery dedication law. To bridge the gap between these cases and the land titles that may predate them (without requiring a retroactive application of the dedication law), it is necessary to determine whether more ancient versions of the cemetery dedication than 1896 (*Choppin*) exist. The reason for this need is that among the sources of law in Louisiana are "legislation and custom" (La. C.C. art. 1). The legislative sources of law are easy enough to find—they are enacted and written in some compilation such as the Louisiana Civil Code or the Louisiana Revised Statutes. Clearly, the *Choppin* court did not find the cemetery dedication in any of the legislative sources of Louisiana law. The customary sources of Louisiana law present a more complex problem. According to the civil code, "[c]ustom results from practice repeated for a long time and generally accepted as having acquired the force of law" (La. C.C. art. 3). Thus, custom as a source of law must represent a pattern of practice over a period of time.

Until the enactment of the cemetery dedication, ample jurisprudence (discussed above) supported the notion that restrictions existed on property used for the interment of human dead before 1974. Indeed, among the sources of custom as law in Louisiana are prior versions of law on which Louisiana's law is based. Louisiana's legal system, now a virtual hybrid of civil and common law principles, traces its history back through various civil codes dating from 1808 through the present, and before that, through French and Spanish civil codes, all of which trace their legal origins in one form or another to the Roman Empire. Thus, legal concepts in Louisiana that are traceable to a Roman source of law carry considerable weight even if not incorporated into the positive legal codes of the state.

Although not civil law jurisdictions in the manner of Louisiana and though deriving their legal history through the English common law system, the remainder of the United States, through England's legal system, can also trace many of its roots back to imperial (especially Christian) Rome (MacMillan 2003). Indeed, as MacMillan asserts, the contemporary European civil law systems were crucial to England's acquisition of new territories during the age of exploration. Stein (1999) echoes this sentiment when he observes that, though England prides itself on its common law system, certain portions of its law are direct descendants of Rome's civil law system.[21] According to MacMillan (2003:412), "the common law possessed no doctrines for the acquisition of new territory . . . [meaning] that the precedents of land possession in civil law could be used." For areas under English dominion (the modern United States, Canada, and Australia to name a few) beginning around AD 1575 (the rough beginning of England's adoption of civilian property concepts according to MacMillan), civil law property concepts, including the restrictions on cemetery land uses, were the controlling law and continues today as a property law foundation in these jurisdictions.

Thus, in England, where "the common law might have reigned supreme," it was ancient civil law property traditions that facilitated the acquisition of colonial land (MacMillan 2003:423). Accordingly, as sixteenth-century English jurists "recognized[,] . . . the civil law, as codified by the emperor Justinian in the sixth century," was fundamental to the international legitimacy of England's colonial land claims and formed the spine of property law in these places (MacMillan 2003:409; Hogerty 1992). This confluence of legal histories is important for the use of the cemetery dedication outside Louisiana for cemetery protection purposes. Based upon this confluence, the Roman law of cemeteries (a species of property law) is the universal source of modern legal rights and constraints in all common and civil law jurisdictions, thus making an understanding of this organic law crucial to interpreting how to lawfully interact with these spaces today.

The *Institutes of Justinian*

The *Institutes of Justinian* were written in the sixth century as part of the *Corpus Juris Civilis*—a compilation of Roman civil law created at the behest of Emperor Justinian I, with various drafts being completed in AD 529 and AD 534 (Brewer 2005; Pacia and Pacia 2001). The *Corpus Juris Civilis* is seen as a fundamental source of Roman law, being the formal successor to the prior codifications in the *Twelve Tables* (ca. 450 BC) and the *Lex Aquilia* (ca. 287 BC) (Stein 1999). Moreover, as noted below, these laws also included laws enacted in prior centuries, the most recent of which was the Theodosian Code in AD 438 (Brewer 2005; Van Sickle 1928). The influence of this Roman law on Louisiana's civil code cannot be understated, leading one commentator to observe that Louisiana law represents "[t]he living institutes of Justinian" (Pacia and Pacia 2001:39, quoting Krauss 1992). Thus, the presence of positive statements related to the sanctity of cemeteries in the *Institutes of Justinian* is of no small moment in the history of the development of this legal concept as a custom practiced over time in Louisiana and elsewhere.[22]

As noted above, the *Institutes of Justinian* was by no means the first series of codified law in Rome. Rather, this document was an overhaul of existing imperial Roman law. Indeed, as Van Sickle (1928) has noted, the *Institutes of Justinian* contains headings that indicate that some portions were written by jurists during the reigns of Marcus Aurelius (AD 161–180), Septimus Severus (AD 193–211), Caracalla (AD 211–217), Alexander Severus (AD 222–235), and Diocletian (AD 284–305), with intentionally omitted references to Geta (AD 211) and Elagabalus (AD 218–222). This pre-Justinian period, characterized by Scarre (1995:85) as "the high point of Empire" in Rome was also known as "a period of good stable government lasting for over 80 years."[23]

During this stable government period—characterized by succession by adoption rather than by blood—emperors handpicked subsequent rulers based upon merit and accomplishment rather than the more tenuous qualifications often seen in bloodline successions. Also during this period, these successors began to represent a more diverse rulership, with emperors shifting from being exclusively of Italian Peninsula origin to those from other portions of the empire: Spain (Trajan and Hadrian), Libya (Septimus Severus), and Syria (Elagabalus and Alexander Severus).

The significance of this diversity cannot be underscored enough for the purposes of the laws passed under these emperors' reigns. The jurists appointed by these diverse emperors from around the realm would have brought a panoply of legal policies and concepts from throughout the Mediterranean world to bear on subsequent legal enactments. This geographic scope suggests that, as more non-Italian emperors controlled the adoption of codified law, broader policies from around the region were incorporated into the codes preceding (and feeding into) Justinian's major rewrite of Roman law. Moreover, the geographic reach of these laws due to the extent of the empire extending from the Levant and North Africa to the Baltic Sea and Britannia means that (much like the later Spanish and French laws in Louisiana), as imperial authority retreated from mainland Europe and moved to the Near East, existing legal codes, concepts, and policies were left behind in the former areas of empire that served as the foundations of later legal developments in these far-flung jurisdictions. In other words, pan-Mediterranean legal concepts and theory form the basis for modern legal traditions throughout Europe (and later the Americas) simply because existing Roman law provided a starting point for later legal developments. Indeed, today's tradition of legislating in the Western world continues to illustrate this reality, as plagiarism of existing laws in one jurisdiction by others is a bedrock of legal drafting. Interestingly, while the explicit legal concepts regarding sacred property (i.e., churches and burial grounds) first appeared in the *Institutes of Justinian,* Van Sickle's (1928) analysis of the that code's antecedents suggests that this later comprehensive legal enactment relied heavily on even pre-Christian law as its source.

Justinian ruled the empire (AD 527–565) after a period of internal chaos (AD 235–285), after the formal adoption of Christianity as the state religion by Constantine (AD 307–337), and after the shift of imperial Rome from Europe to Byzantium. During the nearly four-century span between pre-Justinian legal enactments that definitively survived into that later document (i.e., from Marcus Aurelius to Justinian), there were innumerable opportunities for new laws—even new laws regarding sacred property—to have been added to the Roman legal pantheon from which Justinian's jurists created the later code that bears his name. All of this is to say that, while it is clear that the sacred nature of cemeteries can definitively be traced to the *Institutes of Justinian,* the possibility that these notions predate even this legal source cannot be ruled out. However, it is clear that no such formal pronouncements regarding sacred property exist in the *Lex Aquila* or the *Twelve Tables.* Thus, the legal classification (and thus the dedication) of cemetery property as sacred and inviolate in Western legal traditions have a *terminus post quem* of 287 BC (i.e., the Lex Aquilla's known date of existence), but has a *terminus ante quem* of AD 534 when the *Institutes of Justinian* formally adopted these classifications. In other words, the cemetery dedication in Western law is indeed ancient—it is approximately at least 1,500 years old.

Roman Law in the United States

With the foregoing in mind, Kearley's (2007:525) assertion that "[i]n the United States today, Roman law is of little consequence for the legal profession. Relatively few law schools teach a course in it, and courts do not seek guidance from it" seems odd. Certainly, Kearley continues by acknowledging the critical importance of Roman law in modern civil law systems around the world (i.e., the majority of the legal systems on Earth), but the mere academic interest that Kearley ascribes to Roman law is not necessarily consistent with other scholars' perspectives or the writings of high common law courts. With specific regard to the *Institutes of Justinian,* Humfress (2005:162) observes that

> the Age of Justinian is nothing short of pivotal. [Those] . . . interested in the so-called reception of Roman law in later times and places must look back to Justinian and his law books.

This latter characterization seems to be the prevailing perspective of most legal scholars and many courts today.[24] This statement is not to suggest that Kearley (2007) is necessarily incorrect. Explicit reference to original Roman law is infrequent in modern American jurisprudence. However, much like ever-evolving linguistic lexicons, syntaxes, and grammatical rules that derive influence from sources both modern and ancient, today's legal systems, when viewed in an anthropological and historical evolutionary context, cannot discount the continued presence—even if in transubstantiated form—and continued influence of Roman law today.

However, even if taken at face value, Kearley's assertion that Roman law has little importance in 49 out of 50 of the United States,[25] the analysis remains of critical importance to the protection of cemetery sites outside Louisiana. Because the majority of the world's legal systems are civilian, the ancient Roman protections of cemeteries is either controlling (i.e., codified) reality or a persuasive (i.e., customary) authority in most nations.[26]

In the *Institutes of Justinian*, book 2, title 1, articles 8–10 (Moyle 1913), the following is stated as the sixth-century Roman law of sacred spaces:

> 8. Those things are sacred which have been duly consecrated to God by His ministers, such as churches and votive offerings which have been properly dedicated to His service; and these we have by our constitution forbidden to be alienated or pledged, except to redeem captives from bondage. If any one attempts to consecrate a thing for himself and by his own authority, its character is unaltered, and it does not become sacred. The ground on which a sacred building is erected remains sacred even after the destruction of the building, as was declared also by Papinian.
>
> 9. Any one can devote a place to superstitious uses of his own free will, that is to say, by burying a dead body in his own land. It is not lawful, however, to bury in land which one owns jointly with some one else, and which has not hitherto been used for this purpose, without the other's consent, though one may lawfully bury in a common sepulchre even without such consent. Again, the owner may not devote a place to superstitious uses in which another has a usufruct, without the consent of the latter. It is lawful to bury in another man's ground, if he gives permission, and the ground thereby becomes religious even though he should not give his consent to the interment till after it has taken place.
>
> 10. Sanctioned things too, such as city walls and gates, are, in a sense, subject to divine law, and therefore are not owned by any individual. Such walls are said to be 'sanctioned,' because any offence against them is visited with capital punishment; for which reason those parts of the laws in which we establish a penalty for their transgressors are called sanctions.

In the above excerpt, the redactors of the *Institutes of Justinian* clearly held out a narrow category of property considered sacred and consecrated. Pursuant to article 8, consecration can only occur through the actions of "God's ministers" and can only apply to things "dedicated to His service." However, article 9 appears to hold that the ground in which someone is buried "becomes religious" and, along with other such sacred and religious things listed in article 10, becomes subject to divine law. Because the sixth-century Romans classified burial sites as religious property, with certain restrictions attendant thereto, one can reasonably assume that this early approach to burial grounds as deserving of special treatment represents an ancient version of Louisiana's and other modern jurisdictions' cemetery dedication, and, indeed, may be a direct ancestor of the modern concept. This is not to suggest that historic Europeans actually always practiced what they preached. As Iserson (1993:529–533) has noted, history is replete with stories and evidence of the deconsecration and moving of cemeteries since the time of the *Institutes of Justinian.*

The Law from Rome to Spain

The ancient Roman origins for Louisiana's cemetery dedication laws are continued in the Spanish law enforced in the state during its early years. Bridging the temporal gap between the *Institutes of Justinian* in the sixth century to the drafting and implementation of Spain's *Las Siete Partidas,* first compiled in the thirteenth century is a series of subsequent civilian codes seldom reviewed by scholars today. Madden (2013) observes that, in Europe following Justinian's death, various parts of the *Institutes of Justinian* were carried forward by several Germanic groups who adapted these laws to their unique cultures while retaining much of the structure and content of the original Roman source material. *The Burgundian Code* (ca. AD fifth to sixth centuries), the *Law of the Lombards* (ca. AD seventh to eighth centuries), and the *Law of the Salian Franks* (ca. fifth century) all heavily borrowed from prior Roman law and remained in force in much of continental Europe until the later Middle Ages when European powers began again to draw from old Roman legal sources (primarily the *Institutes of Justinian*) in the creation of various modern civil law systems (Madden 2013).

Volume 1 of *Las Siete Partidas* contains the Spanish law regarding cemeteries that was largely the civil law system in effect when the United States acquired Louisiana in 1803 (Yiannopoulos 1992). Certainly by the time Spain administered Louisiana (AD 1762–1800), the inviolate nature of cemetery property that appears to have originated in Christian Rome or earlier is cemented in the positive codal law. In this regard, *Las Siete Partidas* contains a prohibition against the use of cemetery property for anything but cemetery uses, thus: "The churches . . . enjoy certain privileges and extraordinary exemptions. . . . [I]t is proper to speak in this Title of the exemptions and privileges which they, as well as their cemeteries, enjoy" (Scott and Burns 2001:166). Explaining that "[a] privilege means a special law," the redactors of *Las Siete Partidas* go on to list prohibited activities in churches and cemeteries, including taxation (of the church or cemetery property), resolution of secular disputes, the conduct of criminal proceedings, and trade (Scott and Burns 2001:166). This concept is consistent with the modern legal principles that dedicated cemetery property cannot be put to noncemetery uses and that cemetery property is exempt from taxation. Early Spanish law also prohibited the alienation of church (and by extension cemetery) property (Scott and Burns 2001:182–188). That Roman and Spanish law through the age of exploration considered cemeteries and churches together for legal treatment is unsurprising, as it was not until later in the nineteenth century that the concept of secular cemeteries emerged in the United States and elsewhere (Sloane 1991; Melville 2022). The treatment of spaces of the dead was thus cemented in early modern legal traditions before the secular cemetery movement and the legal limitations of the past attached to both religious property and cemeteries thereafter.[27] Through these protections of cemetery property and prohibitions on the alienation of that property in Roman and Spanish law, one can easily trace the history of the inviolate nature of cemeteries in civil law traditions through the present, and that the antecessors to Louisiana law clearly held such lands as specially protected. Importantly, a review of the early Louisiana Civil Codes (the Digest of 1808 and the 1825 and 1870 Civil Codes) reveals that, from the time that Spanish law was in force in Louisiana until the enactment of the Louisiana Cemetery Act in 1974, no positive codal law existed in Louisiana related to cemeteries to alter any of these ancient concepts.[28]

Although, as noted above, the retroactive application of law to people's vested property rights is disfavored, if not outright unconstitutional.[29] That cemeteries have been singled out as deserving of special protection as a class of property since at least the sixth century strongly suggests that no current landowner in Louisiana or elsewhere in the United States acquired any of his or her property under circumstances in which a cemetery dedication was nonexistent or to which the application of that law would occur.[30] Accordingly, requiring that landowners comply with the cemetery dedication in Louisiana regardless of the antiquity of their title or the age of the cemetery on their property is neither unreasonable nor unconstitutional. Of course, Louisiana landowners have not often adhered to such restrictions, leading to the demolition of cemeteries and the reuse of those spaces across the state.

Arlington Cemetery's Departure from the Norm

The ancient nature of the cemetery dedication has also been documented in Virginia in one particularly bizarre instance dating to the 1860s. The dedication provisions have, on at least one significant occasion, been used as a sword rather than a shield to ensure that certain property would not be used for anything other than a cemetery again. In 1864, out of both necessity and spite, Union Quartermaster General, Montgomery Meigs, directed the conversion of General Robert E. Lee's property into the national cemetery that we now know of as Arlington. Meigs, enraged by the death of his son in a Confederate ambush, began burying Union dead on Lee's plantation grounds (Poole 2010; DeVito 2015). According to Poole, this act was directly calculated to ensure that the Lee family would never be able to use their estate again. In this case, the Union dead were not just interred on the plantation property, but were buried in the prized gardens, and, as Mary Custis Lee described in a contemporary letter, "They are even planted up to the very door without regard to common decency" (DeVito 2015:123). However, this offensive use of the cemetery dedication was generally supported at the time as indicated in a contemporary news report (DeVito 2015:112):

> There is in the vicinity of Arlington House, indeed on the part of the property, a romantic spot in which hundreds of Union heroes murdered by the orders of Mrs. Lee's husband, or by her husband's troops, are buried. These sacred remains shall not be profaned by the unhallowed touch, much less outraged by the usurping demands, of this race of savages and traitors.

The Arlington situation is unique. Nonetheless, it demonstrates the strength, both the legal and psychological, of the placement of human remains in the ground. Indeed, the Lees never again occupied this property, and it now serves as the crown jewel in the U.S. National Cemetery system.

Structural Violence in the Law from Rome to the Present

These ancient legal sources—both the *Institutes of Justinian* and later Spanish, French, and American laws—were not without fault even if their pronouncements on cemeteries today provide for strong protection of these sites. Scholars and casual observers have long acknowledged the overt and inherent structural violence of these sources of law. This violence was not always directed at the typical objects of that violence today: people of color, the poor, and other minorities. Brewer (2005) and Ben-Sasson (1976) have documented structural violence in the *Institutes of Justinian* directed at Jews. As Brewer (2003:127) observes, under the *Institutes of Justinian,* Jews went from being "a '*religio licita,*' a permitted religion" under the Theodosian Code of a century earlier to being classified as an "outsider" (along with non-Catholic Christians, pagans, and Samaritans) and subject to direct and overt discrimination and unequal treatment under the law.

These structurally violent practices were continued more explicitly by the French *Code Noir,* a series of laws later adopted by Americans in Louisiana. In addition to the obvious object of this series of laws—those with dark skin—Jewish persecution also continued. Indeed, though it is doubtful that this law was put into universal practice, the first article of the Louisiana's *Code Noir* of 1724 decrees the expulsion of Jews from the colony.[31] Under the *Institutes of Justinian* and the *Code Noir*, it is doubtful that the burial places of the Jews or enslaved Africans were accorded protection (de facto) inherent in the law (de jure) of that time. For example, it is known that non-Catholic Christians, Jews, and the enslaved were buried outside the walls of St. Louis No. 1 Cemetery in New Orleans. This property has been subject to many noncemetery uses since at least the early twentieth century, a fact laid bare during the demolition of the Iberville Housing Projects following Hurricane Katrina, when archaeologists documented human remains interred in-ground across the site, both in open areas and underneath the foundations of the former housing structures (Godzinski et al. 2013).[32] Importantly for the Jews, an argument can be made that their cemeteries were explicitly excluded from the above-discussed protections for sacred (i.e., Catholic) lands in the *Institutes of Justinian*. Any other non-Catholic burial ground could similarly be excluded from these protections. Because Spanish law exclusively recognized "those dying in communion with the Catholic Church" as deserving of funeral and burial services (Martínez-Fernández 1992:35), it is unsurprising that the graves of non-Catholics were allowed to be obliterated around St. Louis Cemetery No. 1. Such overt and de jure violence that is essentially enabled by the prejudices of their respective times is disappointing but not surprising. These exclusionary protections are now either nonexistent or unenforceable in both de jure and de facto scenarios in the United States as a result of the equal protection clause of the Fifth and Fourteenth Amendments to the Constitution.[33]

In recent years, planning scholars, lawyers, archaeologists, and legislators have apparently looked back only as far as the 1960s when looking for both mechanisms to regulate the protection of cemeteries and other historic properties and for mechanisms to limit the use of certain historically important property. This myopic approach may seem logical, as the modern environmental movement began in the late 1960s with the primary laws related to the protection of the environment and historic properties enacted in 1970 (NEPA) and 1966 (NHPA), respectively, and the deathcare industry came under close scrutiny following the publication of Mitford's (1963) book (Sloane 1991:215). However, when dealing with cemeteries, the inquiry should be temporally deeper. However, when combined with freedom of religion (First Amendment), the abolition of slavery and its "badges and incidents" (Thirteenth Amendment),[34] and equal protection (Fifth and Fourteenth Amendments), the broadly cast sacred land protections that predate modern environmental laws must today be interpreted to excise the inherent structural violence of prior enactments. In other words, discriminatory though they may have been, these old sources of law established broad, nondiscriminatory protections for all cemeteries (the discriminatory provisions were elsewhere in these ancient laws) that have now been filtered through modern notions of equal protection to (at least in de jure scenarios) eliminate structural violence in the protection of cemeteries in the United States (and maybe elsewhere). To be clear: neither the *Institutes of Justinian* nor the *Siete Partidas* were concerned exclusively (or even primarily) with cemetery or human remains protections. Rather, relevant portions of these legal schemes can support a special treatment for spaces of the dead that was ingrained in the United States' (and other countries') legal schemes long before modern property rights became guaranteed by the U.S. Constitution.

As noted above, this need to look deeper for cemetery site protections can be a double-edged sword. While such spaces are inviolate and can only be invaded for other uses following strict guidelines, the mandate to remove all remains from a site may run counter to best archaeological practice concepts and techniques. Thankfully, because of Charles IV's action in 1789, this potential conflict of law and best practices did not arise in the St. Peter Street Cemetery excavations. However, the next case may not be as cleanly resolved.

Based upon this review, while the object of modern environmental and historic preservation laws may have been to protect sites, cemeteries have apparently never fit well or easily into the modern milieu of such laws (King 2012). The existence of the cemetery dedication makes apparent that perhaps it is unnecessary to attempt to fit a square peg into a round hole to ensure the protection of cemetery sites under the guise of protecting the environment or preserving history. The reverse may be the case, though. Cemeteries such as Concord, Massachusetts's Sleepy Hollow Cemetery was dedicated by Ralph Waldo Emerson and other Transcendentalists for the express purpose of preserving the surrounding environment (Melville 2022), and modern green burial cemeteries may be used for the same purpose. Indeed, the well-known protections afforded by most twentieth-century environmental and historic preservation laws are only relative protections at best (Seidemann and Moss 2009). In this regard, while a developer may have to "consider" the impacts of a project on a historic structure or an archaeological site for historic resources and value before demolishing that structure or site (Seidemann and Moss 2009:454), if the site is a cemetery, the developer has no option but to avoid a cemetery or to fully mitigate the impacts to that site in order to be in compliance with the cemetery dedication laws. Should a landowner or developer not be beholden unto financial or title considerations for a particular project, it is possible that the dedication provisions have little power to protect cemeteries. However, the provisions carry no actual civil or criminal penalties aside from affecting the merchantability of title. Although the history of these laws substantially bolsters the constitutionality and authority of modern laws such as NAGPRA and the Unmarked Burials Act, the actual reuse of the cemetery property may only be limited by the requirements of these more recent laws if landowners or developers do not seek merchantable title. Notwithstanding the possibility that ignoring these laws and reusing a cemetery might constitute criminal desecration, ignorance of the dedication laws alone only creates a financial burden on the landowner in the form of a title cloud.

Surely, the existence of the cemetery dedication provisions cannot be linked to any effort to temper the effects of structural violence on the disproportionate treatment of certain groups and their dead. The history of these provisions is too intimately intertwined with basic Christian religious notions to be said to represent a concerted effort to right past wrongs or to provide disenfranchised groups with agency for the protection of their dead and their spaces of death. However, the ability to employ such protections for the same ends as exist in modern laws created to provide such agency cannot be overlooked. The dedication provisions represent actionable legal theories for enfranchised and disenfranchised people alike to create their own agency in the protection of deathscapes, and the pairing of such ancient laws with modern archaeological practices and legislative protections creates a strong means for controlling human remains and spaces of death by descendant communities.

What this research means for other jurisdictions is perhaps that legal practitioners and preservationists may have been looking in the wrong place when trying to protect cemetery sites. Certainly, Louisiana has been at the forefront for many years in the enactment of specific legislation designed to protect and preserve burial sites. However, while that legislation has accomplished the goal of professionalizing the disinterment process required for the removal of the cemetery dedication, the protection of the site itself did not necessarily require legislation. Virtually every state in the United States has a concept of the cemetery dedication in its law (see table 4.1). While the specific language of any particular law will certainly vary from state to state, a high likelihood exists that stronger and more absolute protections exist for cemeteries in these antiquated and often forgotten enactments.

5

Archival and Archaeological Evidence of Historical Cemetery and Human Remains Treatment in Louisiana

In recent years, archaeological excavations at various sites in New Orleans and Baton Rouge have provided insight into the historical de facto treatment of both cemetery sites and human remains in Louisiana. Archival evidence, though scant on the topic of cemetery and human remains treatment, also exists in the form of the court records of some of the cases reviewed in previous chapters. These materials provide some insight into the historic treatment of cemetery spaces. This chapter contains reviews of that work and the implications presented therein regarding the treatment of these sites and materials over time, including a consideration of whether structural violence, based upon the evidence reviewed here, played a part in the treatment of these sites.

The Available Archival Record

The Louisiana Supreme Court archives contain a sampling of documents sent to the state's highest court. In some cases, these materials constitute the complete record of a case from its instigation at the district court, through its appeal, and then to it ultimate review by the Supreme Court. In other cases, the materials in the Supreme Court's records are more scant, representing just the briefs filed at the Supreme Court and the court's decision. The materials available for the cases reviewed here span that range. The two primary cases presented to the court that touch on questions of the power of the cemetery dedication and the handling of human remains removed when such sites are sought to be moved—the cases regarding Gates of Mercy (*Touro Synagogue*) and the Girod Street Cemetery (*Christ Church Corp.*)—are threadbare. In the case of the *Humphreys v. Bennett Oil* matter, the litigation that, in 1940, first positively addressed the effect and power of the cemetery dedication laws in Louisiana, the archival situation is considerably different. A trove of materials exists in this collection, including photographs and the trial transcript with testimony from descendants about the treatment of their loved ones' graves after they learned that an oil company had established a mineral production worksite in a cemetery in Acadia Parish.

The Humphreys Archival Record

The Louisiana Supreme Court case of *Humphreys v. Bennett Oil Corporation* is the only reported case in Louisiana's jurisprudence in which the cemetery was intentionally damaged during development activities rather than attempts to mitigate harms by seeking court authority before undertaking development. In this case, which made it to the Louisiana Supreme Court in 1940 and whose reported decision was reviewed in chapter 4, late 1930s mineral exploration and production in Acadia Parish resulted in a corporate decision to locate a drilling and production facility directly atop an existing cemetery. Evangeline Cemetery had been first used in the late 1880s or early 1890s by settlers in the Rayne area in southwest Louisiana.[1] This case's voluminous archival record provides important and scarce insight into the psychological effects on descendants when such destruction occurs. Moreover, the lasting jurisprudential implications of this case continue to ripple through Louisiana law, forming, in part, the basis for later legislation to protect cemetery sites (see figure 5.1).

Filed in Acadia Parish on July 15, 1938, the original petition in this matter establishes that the plaintiffs are family and descendants of those interred in the Quaker Evangeline Cemetery and alleged that the cemetery was damaged in the financial amount of $20,000.00 ($436,580.14 in late 2023 dollars) when Frank W. Bennett and later Bennett Oil Corporation "carried on drilling operations in said cemetery from May 20th, 1937, continuously."[2] The plaintiffs further alleged

> [t]hat the defendants, continuously, during repetitive periods of the illegal drilling operations, have, with ruthless and utter disregard of the sacredness of the spot, performed every act in furtherance of a frantic effort on their part to advance their financial ends, to the great mental anguish and heart-rending suffering of your petitioners and others, because of the desecration of the graves of their loved ones.[3]

At trial, in support of their allegations of cemetery damage and mental anguish, the plaintiffs called several witnesses whose family members were buried in Evangeline Cemetery. Mr. Joseph Chetagnier testified that he and his wife had buried a daughter in the cemetery in 1932 and that the mineral production activity on the site "destroyed" the grave and the beautification

Figure 5.1. The approximate location of Evangeline Cemetery (encircled) based upon the site description provided in the court record. This image is a 2013 aerial derived from the Louisiana Department of Natural Resources' SONRIS website.

work done to it.[4] Crucially for the plaintiffs' case, Mr. Chetagnier had spent his career working in the oil industry and testified to the jury regarding that industry's best practices and that, even if minerals underlay Evangeline Cemetery, the site did not need to be disturbed (see figure 5.2 and figure 5.3 for examples of this disturbance). In this regard, Chetagnier testified in the affirmative to such loaded questions by counsel for the plaintiffs as:

> Q: As an experienced oil man could an operator properly keep up a one acre graveyard in which burials had been taking place since 1895, could an operator go into that graveyard one acre, put down two wells, have five boilers and necessary slush pits and necessary roadways in and out, engines, tool room and material stack without desecrating the one acre?[5]

Chetagnier testified to the complete unnecessary destruction and that directional drilling could have avoided the cemetery entirely. In other words, the plaintiffs used Chetagnier not just to pull on the heartstrings of the jury, but to demonstrate that the oil company, by exercising some discretion, could have avoided damage to the cemetery.

Chetagnier's wife, Mrs. Celestine Matt Chetagnier, testified to symptoms of anxiety when informed of the industrial operations ongoing in Evangeline Cemetery, stating that, "I never went while they were drilling. I couldn't stand it. I was nervous."[6]

When asked how it made her feel when later she was unable to find her daughter's grave, Mrs. Chetagnier testified that "if I would have seen the one

Figure 5.2. Imagery of Evangeline Cemetery introduced into evidence in the *Humphreys* matter. The derricks for the two wells are clear in the background of this image. The photographer of this image is unknown, but the image is dated to June 1939 in the court record. This image comprises part of the *Humphreys* case file held at the Louisiana State Archives.

that done it I felt like shooting him and it wouldn't hurt me a bit."[7] On cross-examination, Mrs. Chetagnier doubled down on her feelings of anger and grief in the following exchange with the oil company's attorney:

> Q: It made you very angry[?]
> A: It makes me mad yet.
>
> * * *
>
> A: It hurt me and when you hurt you do most anything. It made me mad but I wasn't only mad. I stayed about three months that I couldn't eat and sleep. To me it was just like the day that she died.
> Q: But you were mostly mad[?]
> A: I was sorry too.
> Q: You wanted to shoot somebody?
> A: I felt like it.[8]

Figure 5.3. Imagery of Evangeline Cemetery introduced into evidence in the *Humphreys* matter. This image shows a grave marker in the foreground with a tank battery and the well derricks in the background. The photographer of this image is unknown, but the image is dated to June 1939 in the court record. This image comprises part of the *Humphreys* case file held at the Louisiana State Archives.

The plaintiffs also called Mrs. E. J. Green as a witness. Mrs. Green testified that she had buried a child in Evangeline Cemetery and that, without her authority, Bennett Oil Company disinterred the child and relocated the remains to another cemetery. In a statement that substantially resonated later with the Louisiana Supreme Court, Mrs. Green testified that "[t]hey took her out and they took the little tomb stone and made steps out of it"[9] (figure 5.4).

Another witness, Mr. Milo Hunt, a resident of California, came to Louisiana to testify about the state of his father's grave, which, upon seeing the mineral operations at the site, he characterized as, "[a] scene to make the heart sick, the most abominable thing I ever saw in this United States of America."[10] Importantly, as elicited in cross-examination, Hunt admitted that his father's grave had not been directly affected by the industrial operation on the site, but that the general impacts to the cemetery, in his mind, constituted a desecration.[11] When asked why he joined as a plaintiff in this lawsuit, Mr. Hunt stated that "[t]he revulsion of feeling that every man who regards a cemetery as a sacred burial place must feel when he knows such conditions exist as were reported to exist"[12] at Evangeline Cemetery. This is an important observation anecdotally reported and clarified how indirect desecration is perceived as offensive by descendants of those not directly affected by a cemetery desecration. Indeed, a later witness, Dr. A. C. Wilkins, testified that, in his medical

Figure 5.4. The much-discussed child's grave marker used as a step to the site office in the *Humphreys* matter. The photographer of this image is unknown, but the image is dated to June 1939 in the court record. This image is part of the *Humphreys* case file held at the Louisiana State Archives.

opinion, he believed that the stress of knowing what had become of the cemetery substantially contributed to his wife's premature death.[13]

The oil company representatives seemed to be largely remorseless for any hurt or harm caused by their actions, ultimately resulting in their loss of this case. More significantly for modern legal protections of cemeteries in Louisiana, this case had an impact on the Louisiana legislature and the jurisprudence. Within the year, the Louisiana legislature enacted a law now codified at La. R.S. 8:901. This law, clearly a direct result of the *Humphreys* litigation, states:

> A. It shall be unlawful to use, lease or sell any tract of land which is platted, laid out or dedicated for cemetery purposes and in which human bodies are interred, on any part of such tract, for the purpose of prospecting, drilling or mining; provided that the prohibition of leasing contained in this section shall not apply to any oil, gas, or mineral lease that contains a stipulation forbidding drilling or mining opera-

> tions upon that portion of the leased premises which is included within the cemetery.
>
> B. Whoever violates this section shall be fined not less than one hundred dollars nor more than five hundred dollars, or be imprisoned for not less than thirty days nor more than six months, or both, and each day during which drilling, mining or prospecting is conducted or prosecuted shall be considered a separate offense.

Thus, the *Humphreys* case carved out a special misdemeanor statute that criminalizes mineral exploration and production in Louisiana cemeteries. This law has been used many times over the years as a deterrent to such activities.

The Gates of Mercy Archival Record

In the case of *Touro Synagogue v. Goodwill Industries of New Orleans, Inc.*, 96 So.2d 29 (La. 1957), the archival record makes clear that a curator appointed to represent the interests of the deceased and their unknown descendants worked diligently to upend the transmission of the Gates of Mercy Cemetery property to Goodwill Industries, the latter of which intended to erect a retail facility on the property in Central City, New Orleans. Much of this anemic Supreme Court record revolves around the legal question of whether land dedicated to cemetery uses can be put to other uses by de-dedicating the land. These materials clarify that the representatives of all involved parties (the synagogue, the curator, Goodwill, and the City of New Orleans), acknowledged that the human remains from this in-ground cemetery established in 1828 must be removed before the land's use as anything but a cemetery. Little detail is provided regarding how this human remains removal would be accomplished aside from a notation that the removal would be overseen by the New Orleans Rabbinical Council and that the remains would be reinterred in Hebrew Rest No. 1 Cemetery in New Orleans. Although the case fails to clarify who would undertake this removal work, the record strongly implies that the removal would be done with little or no meaningful oversight by individuals with intimate knowledge of human skeletal material.[14] The probable result of such action would be to leave behind substantial amounts of human remains when the bodies are encountered in various stages of decay (Williams 1994; Seidemann and Seidemann 2020), thus meaning that, though legally no longer a cemetery, it is likely that the space practically continues to contain human dead.[15] Despite this reality, recent excavations have not identified any human remains at the former cemetery site (Hahn et al. 2017; Halling, pers. comm. 2022).

Although the curator for the Gates of Mercy dead expressed grave concern about the de-dedication of the property, he does not appear to have considered the possibility that many remains may be left behind during any removal and subsequent reuse of the property. Rather, the curator's focus in this matter was to seek the Supreme Court's order that a cemetery dedication cannot ever be removed once remains are committed to the ground. Because this case preceded the enactment of the Louisiana Cemetery Act and the formal articulation of the cemetery dedication therein, this effort was not unreasonable. Ultimately, however, the court agreed with the other parties that the land could be made merchantable once the human remains were removed. The court went further to hold that the removal of the remains would be accomplished at the synagogue's cost,[16] but it specified no standards for the removal of those remains.

No transcript for this case has survived, and none of the record evidence presented at the district court is available in these materials. Thus, though the curator refers to communications that he received from several descendants expressing their opposition to the property's reuse, the *Touro Synagogue* record is not particularly enlightening regarding the impacts of the cemetery's removal on the descendant community at the individual level. Certainly, the community, through its religious leaders and the court-appointed curator, had agency in this dispute and in the property transaction. However, whether that agency represented the true intentions of the individual community remains unanswered following a review of the available documentary evidence.

The Girod Street Cemetery Archival Record

Similarly anemic is the Louisiana Supreme Court record for the dedication removal associated with the Girod Street Protestant Cemetery in New Orleans ("Girod") in the matter of *City of New Orleans v. Christ Church Corp.*, 81 So.2d 855 (La. 1955). Unlike the Gates of Mercy situation, the trial transcript is available for the Girod matter. However, the transcript is bereft of testimony from but a few descendants, and then only regarding matters of reimbursement for unused grave spaces from the City of New Orleans.

In this case, the city sought to expropriate the Girod property to convert its use to roadways in advance of the construction of, among other things, the U.S. Post Office building on Loyola Avenue. While the case file contains scant information on the impacts felt by descendants of those interred in the cemetery and even less on the process for removing the remains from the site, the testimony of the city public health officer and a city engineer is insightful with respect to the general treatment of cemetery sites in New Orleans at the time of the lawsuit—the late 1940s and early 1950s.

With specific regard to the disposition of disinterred remains from Girod, the Protestant church's attorney stated on the record that, along with compensation for the land that the city sought to expropriate in this dispute, the church also expected that the city would "remov[e] and reinter elsewhere with perpetual care of all human remains from the cemetery."[17] Clearly from the record, the church was concerned about disrupted human remains as a result of the road construction and it had certain expectations for the management of those remains. Throughout the record, though, no indication exists regarding what constituted an appropriate removal of these remains. Similarly, though contemporary news reports noted that the remains would be removed from this cemetery that then exhibited a "ghoulish appearance," no details were provided regarding how this move would be accomplished (Anon. 1954b:1). The record indicates that at least some of the "white remains were reinterred in Hope Mausoleum and those of the Negro dead were removed to Providence Memorial Park" during a two-month period in 1957 (Huber and Bernard 1961:83). By inference from other record statements in the Girod matter, many descendants of those interred in the cemetery were apparently notified of the city's plans to convert the space to an alternative use. One church official interviewed in early 1954 indicated that the Protestant church that owned the cemetery had plans to "have someone identify the tombs from church records and inscriptions, box the remains found inside, catalog and reinter them in appropriate places" (Anon. 1954a:7). However, that same article indicates that that work had been planned for many years and was not started at the time of the expropriation suit. Further, an attorney for some of the descendants stated that, "we had received notice in this particular case to remove the remains, which we did, and the remains are now temporarily in a temporary place of abode."[18] Reflecting a shift in obligations for such activity between the time of this case and the present, the descendants were expected to make arrangements for those remains removed from Girod. Today, the law places the onus on the cemetery authority, landowner, or developer to cover the costs of such removals.[19] Indeed, part of the purpose of the descendants' presence in the case was to seek "such funds to purchase a new plot and tomb, or, in the alternative, [for the city or church to] furnish us with the tomb or expenses of reinterment."[20] While some of the descendants made appearances in this case through their own counsel, a court-appointed curator represented most of the Girod dead and their descendants. This curator had no funds for the removal of remains. Although some known descendants had unilaterally undertaken such removals, as evidenced by the above quotation, the lack of a clear funding source for such removals raises a concerning question regarding what became of the remains of those for whom descendants did not speak.

What is particularly interesting in the Girod record is the absence of any meaningful dispute regarding the fate of the cemetery or the human remains contained therein. The predetermined notion of this portion of the litigation is abundantly clear. The parties appeared in court not to dispute the removal of the cemetery, its dedication, or the remains contained within it, but rather they were in court to contest the compensation due for this property reuse.

To be sure, the city made a record of the need for the expropriation of the property. The city's attorneys called public health experts and planners to establish both the harmful nature of the existing cemetery and the need for that specific property to be used for road construction purposes. However, none of this testimony is particularly directed at justifying the need to move a cemetery. Rather, the testimony satisfied the threshold requirement that an expropriation, to be lawful, must be undertaken for a public purpose. The ostensible public purpose here was protection of the health and the safety of travelers on New Orleans's road system. Any of the implications that this testimony justified the actual need to close and move a cemetery were mere coincidences and asides. This predetermined outcome is apparent from the lack of meaningful opposition to this testimony by the descendants and the curator. That Girod was going to be closed and moved was a fait accompli before the city instigated this suit.

Nonetheless, to justify the public purpose of the expropriation, the testimony regarding the condition of the cemetery—especially that elicited from Dr. Walter P. Gardiner, director of Health, City of New Orleans—is telling of the perspective of many regarding cemeteries at this time. When asked what conditions in the cemetery effect "the health of the City of New Orleans," Dr. Gardiner testified that the cemetery

> is in a marked condition of dilapidation; tombs are opened; some of the caskets have been pulled out. There is evidence of vandalism. There's also evidence all throughout the cemetery where tramps are living in the tombs.[21]

Dr. Gardiner went on to observe that rats infested the cemetery and that the site existed as a breeding ground for mosquitos (figure 5.5). Seemingly most disturbing to Dr. Gardiner, though, was the presence of those he described as "tramps." He further testified that

Figure 5.5. Historic imagery of Girod Cemetery from the Hogan Jazz Archive, Special Collections, Howard-Tilton Memorial Library, Tulane University. Top (OPH000404_2) and bottom (OPH000402) were photographed by William Russell in 1956.

> with the type of individuals who are using that place as a means of abode, it is quite apparent that they are from a very low type social strata from unknown communities, so that the potential hazard for malaria infestation, and as well as rats, subsequent typhus infestation is very marked.[22]

From these characterizations, when Dr. Gardiner was asked whether he "consider[ed] all those conditions to render the further use of this area as a cemetery in the condition that it is in a hazard to the health of the City of New Orleans?,"[23] the doctor stated,

> Well, the answer to that is certainly yes, and the old saying of words fail to adequately describe the scene is definitely applicable in this instance. I think one view of the cemetery will convince anybody that it is of no further use.[24]

As his subsequent testimony suggests, "one view of the cemetery" may have been the extent of Gardiner's own forays into the site. Importantly, no questions were asked to rebut either Dr. Gardiner's sense of the condition or future prospects for the cemetery should it remain as a cemetery. In other words, to the fait accompli nature of the judicial decision in this matter, no discussion occurred regarding the possibility of preserving or rehabilitating Girod to abate the identified public health hazards or to continue its use as a functioning cemetery. Indeed, Gardiner volunteered (without prompting) that "the Health Department felt that to restore the cemetery would be such an expensive program that it would be absolutely impracticable, and in no ways feasible."[25]

Dr. Gardiner's characterizations of Girod evoke a vivid picture of the place as one of debaseness and possible debauchery, and certainly one of festering disease. However, the descendants' counsel, Sam Roccaforte, initiated a bit of pushback to Dr. Gardiner's assessment at one point when he pressed Gardiner regarding how closely he had examined the cemetery. Roccaforte's questioning was not intended to preserve the cemetery, but rather to demonstrate that certain families kept their tombs in better shape than what Gardiner had suggested with his prior testimony. In this regard, Roccaforte stated that "You see, I am representing [a party] who is claiming that they have kept the tomb and plot in excellent condition and shape up until the time they received orders from the Church to remove the remains."[26] Such better condition, presumably, would lead to higher compensation rates for the expropriation. In answer to this question, Dr. Gardiner equivocated on his prior statement that the entirety of Girod was in a dilapidated state, and he further noted that "I didn't go through the place and take a chance of having my clothing torn with vines and crawling over the collapsed tomb."[27] Such a statement does not particularly instill confidence in Dr. Gardiner's sweeping assessment of Girod's condition.

However, by this point, this testimony undoubtedly and substantially affected the court's thinking regarding the continuation of the site as a cemetery. Indeed, even after Gardiner's equivocation, the court characterized his testimony thus:

> Well, Doctor, I understand from you you consider the Girod Street Cemetery not only a deserted but an abandoned village, even though it was formerly occupied by the dead, and it has been constantly desecrated by vandals and what not, to the point where it has become a menace to the health and welfare of the City?[28]

Moreover, because the court immediately after that characterization began questioning Gardiner about health risks related to planned development in the area, the testimony clearly had already convinced the court of the unsalvagability of Girod.

The city's next witness in the Girod matter was the director of the Planning Commission, Louis Bisso. Mr. Bisso's frank testimony regarding his perspective on the Girod Street Cemetery provided that

> without any reflection or disrespect on any of the bodies in the graves, since I'm not competent to speak on any of that, we can say that the use of that particular property is incongruous with all the other uses that are within this area.[29]

Clearly, Mr. Bisso testified from a strictly planning perspective—Bisso did not speak to the merits or detriments of the cemetery property, but rather confined his testimony to the problems of routing urban traffic around such a site. This perspective, though, was the other component to the city's demonstration of the public purpose behind its expropriation of the Girod property and Bisso demonstrated that purpose well. Bisso made clear to the court that the Girod property was the only available and appropriate property over which to run the roads necessary to develop the Tulane-Gravier/Central Business District area. Again, the fait accompli nature of this expropriation is evident in Bisso's testimony:

> Q: All right. Now, will you state, or can you state that the route of the proposed street and of the expropriation can not be diverted to any other area without great public loss or inconvenience?
>
> A: I would definitely say that any other substitute plan would be in contravention with good planning principles, and the further you go away, the more you attempt to compromise, the more inconvenience, the more possibility of loss of lives, loss of property, and all the other complications that develop when you get away from the smooth expedition, which is the only one we plan to try to fight for.[30]

According to Bisso, the city had one plan for the development of the roads in this area—straight through Girod Street Cemetery—and the alternative to that plan would result in the "loss of lives" and the "loss of property."[31]

The testimony of the city's witnesses alone did not condemn the Girod Street Cemetery to the annals of history. Although no such witnesses testified at the trial of this matter, it is apparent from concurrent newspaper articles that not all New Orleanians were dispassionate regarding the fate of Girod. One letter to the editor in 1952 (MLH 1952) lamented that

> What is happening to the historic Girod Street cemetery sets a bad precedent. The most appalling feature is the way New Orleans now

> treats the memory of its pioneer dead. . . . In the name of common decency, let the pioneer dead rest in peace.

Oddly, as noted above, several descendants also supported the city's demolition of the site and testified that the site represented a public health hazard. In this regard, the pro se party, Lydia Hollingsworth, testified about the state of the cemetery because she, "was interested . . . for the simple reason that my sister was very ill with an incurable disease, and was expected at any time to die."[32] Speaking of her experience upon visiting Girod to inquire into the condition of her family's tomb there, Hollingsworth stated that the cemetery "was in such a deplorable condition that we just couldn't believe it possible."[33] Miss Hollingsworth went on to testify that

> the sexton said to me, in your tomb it's all broken. He says there is a metal casket; would I like to see it, and I said, "Horrors, no!" That was my favorite aunt who was buried in there, and he said it was preserved, the body you could see it, but I couldn't bear to see my sister buried in there.[34]

Hollingsworth, when asked by the court whether she believed the cemetery to be "abandoned, neglected," answered "[o]h, frightfully so."[35] She rounded out her testimony by asserting that

> it is only right that the people that are buried there, the heirs, to those should be willing that the City use that of the expropriation so that we can improve our city, but I contend the terrible expense that my sister went to for the doing over of the tomb twice and being broken into, and, of course, the metal casket, and then the expense of having to bury my sister elsewhere because we couldn't bury her there, I think she should be reimbursed. I don't care.[36]

Hollingsworth's testimony stands in contrast to the general tenor that Huber and Bernard (1961:81) suggest existed among the descendants when they noted that "[m]any people, particularly those whose ancestors had been interred in this place, felt that the church should have continued to keep a sexton on the grounds to maintain the old cemetery." If any descendants opposed the cemetery's demolition, no such testimony was presented in the legal proceedings. Moreover, though the court held over Hollingsworth's questions of compensation to a subsequent trial (a common expropriation practice), it acknowledged Hollingsworth's testimony regarding the state of the cemetery as part of its analysis of the public purpose of the expropriation. In this situation, based upon Huber and Bernard's (1961) assertion, many descendants seemingly were not given voice in this dedication removal process.

The court ultimately approved the expropriation of the Girod Street Cemetery. The record clearly indicates, particularly from statements made by the appointed curator for the dead and their descendants, J. Richard Reuter Jr., that possibly hundreds of people inquired into their rights in the to-be-demolished cemetery. However, no documentary evidence exists regarding the resolution of these interests or the descendants' concerns about the treatment of the remains in the cemetery. Reuter mentioned the letters from interested parties only to raise the point to the court that many people would have to be compensated for the expropriation. The court and the parties appeared wholly unconcerned with how the human remains from the site would be handled and how those remains would be disinterred and reinterred. Ultimately, this substantial task merited only a passing mention in any of the surviving documentation and none that provides any insight into the details of the management of these materials. However, if Miss Hollingsworth's testimony is any indication of the feelings of the descendant community on the demolition of the Girod Street Cemetery, then it seems that the descendants believed that their civic duty recognized the relocation of their ancestors for the betterment of the city.

The Available Archaeological Record

For the Gates of Mercy and Girod Street cemeteries, archaeological analyses of the property years later provide insight suggesting that, though the de jure legal mandates were at least superficially followed at these sites, the de facto cemetery site treatments fell short the law's requirements. In addition to these sites with both archival and archaeological records, archaeological research has been conducted at the Locust Grove and Charity Hospital Cemetery No. 2 cemeteries in New Orleans and at Highland Cemetery in Baton Rouge that provide further de facto insight into the treatment of cemetery sites in Louisiana in the nineteenth and twentieth centuries. No correlative archaeological data exist for Evangeline Cemetery in Acadia Parish, so that site stands on its archival record, which, because the case centered on actual desecration, sufficiently demonstrates the distinction between de jure and de facto cemetery site treatment in Louisiana in the mid-twentieth century.

The Gates of Mercy Archaeological Record

On behalf of the Federal Emergency Management Agency, archaeologists from Coastal Environments, Inc., undertook post–Hurricane Katrina archaeological investigations on the property formerly occupied by the Gates of Mercy Cemetery in New Orleans (Hahn et al. 2017). In large part, this postmortem analysis of the Gates of Mercy site provided a unique opportunity to assess the efficacy of the legal requirement in the 1950s that all the human remains were to be removed from the cemetery before the removal of its dedication and the reuse of the property for noncemetery purposes. After Hurricane Katrina ravaged New Orleans in 2005, one site slated for rehabilitation was the Allie Mae Williams Multi-Service Center in the Central City neighborhood of the city. The structure was partially located on the former Gates of Mercy Cemetery site that was the subject of the *Touro Synagogue* litigation. For this reason, archaeological monitoring, survey, and limited excavation occurred when the original facility's slab was removed in 2014–2015 to determine what impacts, if any, future work would visit upon the portion of the former Gates of Mercy Cemetery site underlying the original slab.

Because the *Touro Synagogue* case in the 1950s had removed the cemetery dedication of the Gates of Mercy property, partially under representations that all human remains would be removed from the site, this land has since been put to alternative uses. Thus, any archaeological findings of human remains, though significant under more recent laws such as the Unmarked Burials Act, have no legal impact on the use of the site and must merely be mitigated to the satisfaction of the Louisiana state archaeologist (i.e., consistent with archaeological best practices).

The archaeological monitoring and limited surveying and excavation of the Gates of Mercy site resulted from a 2013 finding of "one *ex situ,* potential human bone [that] was found" by Federal Emergency Management Agency archaeologists (Hahn et al. 2017:iii, 3). This bone was later identified as "[o]ne human bone fragment" (a possible femoral head) (Hahn et al. 2017:106, 111). The subsequent monitoring, survey, and excavations revealed little to no positive evidence of human remains at this site. The archaeologists working this project cautioned against too broadly interpreting their negative findings, noting that their analysis of the site constituted only 4 percent of the former cemetery property and that, "[w]hile no identifiable human remains were encountered by the current study, there could well be human remains, both in situ and *ex situ,* within the remainder of the project area and/or within the site as a whole" (Hahn et al. 2017:iv).

Despite the statement that archaeologists found no human remains at the site, their faunal analysis of materials recovered from the fieldwork, observed that, "[f]ive specimens were recovered that compared favorably to human bone and because the material originates from a cemetery setting, it is highly likely that these fragments are human" (Hahn et al. 2017:148).[37] Astutely, Hahn et al. (2017:262–263) observe that "[a]lthough it is possible, it seems unlikely that past disinterment activities were 100 percent successful in recovering all human remains within the cemetery limits." They further note that "[h]ow rigorous the disinterments were of any burials made in those areas remains an open question" (Hahn et al. 2017:263). Such a reality, coupled with the substantial disclaimer quote above, strongly supports a supposition that the supervision of remains removal by the Rabbinical Counsel of New Orleans was not to archaeological standards and that any future work on the site must proceed with caution. Nonetheless, a reanalysis of the faunal bone fragments excavated in the 2014–2015 field season by bioarchaeologist Christine Halling and this author confirmed that none of the fragments was human (Halling, pers. comm. 2022). Instead, these excavations yielded mortuary material culture in the form of gravestone fragments that have since been returned to the descendant community and are located in the Hebrew Rest cemeteries.

The Girod Street Cemetery Archaeological Record

Archaeological investigations at the Girod Street Cemetery have been far more opportunistic, sporadic, and uncontrolled than those reported for the Gates of Mercy site. Indeed, in personal communications with Douglas Owsley, formerly a physical anthropologist associated with Louisiana State University, he recounted one road construction project in the 1980s in the vicinity of Girod in which he was given mere hours to observe and salvage any human remains exposed by subsurface activities (Owsley, pers. comm. 2020). The only documentation of any reconnaissance archaeology at the site of this former cemetery comes from a four-page site form (16OR115) completed by Mary Manhein in 1987. In her limited site access to the former Girod property at this time, Manhein identified human bone fragments that she concluded represented a minimum number of 100 individuals, clearly indicating that the remains removal was less than complete at this site in the mid-twentieth century. Manhein's finding is even more troubling when considering that Girod was a largely above-ground cemetery, suggesting that the remains should have been easier to identify and remove than those in the entirely in-ground interments of the Gates of Mercy Cemetery. As Manhein correctly notes, the site holds significant potential for future research and should be carefully monitored during any ground disturbances in the area. What is clear from Manhein's findings is that neither the church nor the City of New Orleans completed a systematic removal of human remains from Girod. Such a conclusion is substantially supported by the minimal testimony in the trial court record in which at least two individuals indicated that they had received notices to remove the remains of their loved ones at their own expense. Presumably, most, if not all, of the remains of those whose family members did not respond to that call were simply left on the site and were demolished along with the above-ground tombs and constructed over when the city was undertaking its road improvements.

The Locust Grove Cemeteries Archaeological Record

The Locust Grove cemeteries in Central City, New Orleans, mentioned previously have no court record of a dedication removal. These cemeteries were the subject of archaeological investigations in post-Katrina New Orleans for the purposes of determining whether the land on which they were situated—property later converted to use as a school (Thomy Lafon Elementary)—could again be repurposed using federal funding following the storm (Hahn and McCarthy 2012). The Locust Grove cemeteries served as New Orleans's pauper cemeteries in the middle portion of the nineteenth century and were overfull by the turn of the twentieth century (Hahn and McCarthy 2012), by which time these sites had been given over in favor of Holt Cemetery as the city's pauper burial ground (Branyon 1998; Hahn and McCarthy 2012; Seidemann and Halling 2019). At the time, the Locust Grove cemeteries were slated for repurposing as school properties, despite the knowledge that burials existed therein. Indeed, then-Mayor Martin Behrman indicated as much when he directed by ordinance in 1905 that the land be converted to a school and that the human remains be removed from the property before that conversion (Hahn and McCarthy 2012; Seidemann and Halling 2019). After a city attorney opined that it was permissible to reuse cemetery space, an ordinance issued in 1905 by the City of New Orleans removed the dedication from Locust Grove Cemetery Nos. 1 and 2 and authorized the construction of the Thomy Lafon School on top of them (Hahn and McCarthy 2012). A concurrent ordinance directed the school contractor to "remove with due respect any remains found in Locust Grove Cemetery No. 1 to Locust Grove Cemetery No. 2" (New Orleans City Ordinance No. 2945, March 15, 1905).

At the time of Ordinance 2945's passage, no positive law in Louisiana mandated that a court must approve the removal of a cemetery dedication. In 1905, the legal authority to direct property use (here, Mayor Behrman) provided for the removal of remains before the land's reuse for noncemetery purposes.[38] Appropriate city officials never actually removed the remains from the Locust Grove cemeteries, as borne out by subsequent archaeological work (Branyon 1998; Hahn and McCarthy 2012). The question remains whether city officials made some effort to undertake at least a symbolic removal of some human remains from the Locust Grove cemeteries so as to show compliance with the ordinance or whether they entirely ignored the directive to move the remains. Post-Katrina archaeological work proves that the ground of the former Thomy Lafon School is literally choked with human remains (similar to Holt Cemetery in Mid-City, New Orleans, today), and that any improvements to this property would impact multiple burials. However, from a legal perspective, it is probable that it was the thought that counts regarding the dedication removal at these cemeteries. Today, though the ground of the cemeteries is full of human remains, it is no longer legally a cemetery and any future use of the land merely requires a removal of the remains in the potential impact zone in a manner consistent with modern archaeological practice and subject to a permit from the state archaeologist under the Unmarked Burials Act.

As with both the Girod Street Cemetery and the Gates of Mercy Cemetery, adherence to the de jure requirements for putting former cemetery property to an alternative use (i.e., the removal of the cemetery dedication) cannot be interpreted as proof positive that the requirements of that removal were fully or even partially accomplished. In each of these instances, substantial evidence adduced by modern archaeological inquiries has demonstrated that such de-dedications may have been largely paperwork transactions before the advent of laws such as the Unmarked Burials Act and its mandates to apply archaeological precision to the excavation and removal of burials from a cemetery site.

The Charity Hospital Cemetery No. 2 Archaeological Record

New Orleans also presents evidence of cemeteries that were simply ignored in the face of development. Most notable of these cemeteries is Charity Hospital Cemetery No. 2, a site today situated beneath the south end of Canal Boulevard in Mid-City New Orleans. The presence of this site underneath the roadway has been long known (Smith and Stone 2014). The cemetery located at this site is, as described by its name, the site of burial for those who died at Charity Hospital in New Orleans. Along with its extant counterpart (Charity Hospital Cemetery No. 1) on Canal Street, Charity Hospital used its Cemetery No. 2 for interments from ca. 1849 to 1910 (Godzinski et al. 2008). Charity Hospital sold the property in 1910 for road development, and research indicates that, "except for a reference of Act 119 of the 1904 Louisiana Legislature authorizing the sale of Hospital property, there is no mention at all of the tract being in use for more than a half a century as a cemetery, and at that time containing remains of thousands of burials" (Godzinski et al. 2008:27). Although Beavers et al. (1993) indicated that, though a necessity existed to advertise that burials could be moved from the cemetery, no documentary evidence verifies such a publication (Godzinski et al. 2008). Thus, while Beavers et al.'s (1993) basic assessment of the legal requirements to remove a cemetery dedication appears to be, at least in part, correct for its time, no evidence exists that Charity Hospital, the private developers lobbying for the extension of a major thoroughfare over the cemetery toward Lake Pontchartrain, or the City of New Orleans made any efforts to comply with those laws. Thus, though the law was known at this time—Mayor Behrman signed the Locust Grove ordinance just five years prior (and was still in office in 1910)—it was seemingly ignored for Charity Hospital Cemetery No. 2. Therefore, no compliance with that law in 1910 is evident. After the paving of what would later be renamed Canal Boulevard, the collective consciousness of New Orleans seems to have largely forgotten about the cemetery located thereunder only to be periodically reminded during roadwork that invariably disrupts remains. Based upon the work undertaken by Godzinski et al. (2008) and Smith and Stone (2014), archaeology substantially altered the treatment of this site in future development from a mere roadway to a cemetery that must be managed in accordance with the Unmarked Burials Act. In this case, the de jure protections for cemeteries were entirely ignored during the development of Canal Boulevard. Such a disregard for these laws should have, and for a time did, represent substantial barriers to development in this area prospectively. Over several decades of road and streetcar-line improvements, both archaeological removal of remains and legal de-dedications of project footprints were required by the State of Louisiana and undertaken by developers (Seidemann 2014c). This compliance came to an abrupt end when, seemingly under the cover of COVID-19 stay-at-home orders, a considerable portion of Charity Cemetery No. 2 was redeveloped as commercial space. As figure 2.5 and figure 2.6 illustrate, this location that now houses a coffee shop and burger joint was once the heart of Charity Cemetery No. 2. No permitting or archaeological reconnaissance of this area occurred. Once identified as a fully complete construction, all evidence to make a case of the disturbance of the cemetery and a violation of the dedication laws now underlie substantial construction and are out of reach of regulators. It can only be hoped that post-Katrina building code elevation requirements mean that these elevated structures were built atop the burials and not through them. Any future ground-disturbing work at this site must be accompanied by archaeological monitoring to ensure that such a shameful treatment of a burial place does not continue to be perpetuated.

The Highland Cemetery Archaeological Record

A final archaeological example of the failure of de jure cemetery protections comes from outside the New Orleans area. Historic Highland Cemetery ("Highland") is today located on an approximately half-acre tract along Oxford Avenue in the College Town neighborhood in Baton Rouge, Louisiana (Coastal Environments, Inc. 1975) (figure 5.6). Although the earliest known interment in the cemetery is that of Captain John James Neilson, which occurred in 1813 (Thom 2005 [1974]), documentary evidence of the cemetery's existence first appears in the public records in 1819 when the then-owner of the property, George Garig, donated "one superficial arpent"[39] to the Roman Catholic Church of East Baton Rouge Parish for use as a cemetery. Although the actual donation did not occur (which represented a formal recognition of the existence of the cemetery under the law) until 1819 (Seidemann 2018a), the act of donation acknowledges the preexisting burial ground when its authors note that the area, "is fenced in and has been used as a grave yard by the said Roman Catholic Congregation for the purpose of burying their dead for the space of three or four years past."

Highland Cemetery was expanded by a subsequent property owner, Robert Penny, who added his own "family's burying ground, which he described as being thirty feet square" (Thom 2005 [1974]:11), presumably to allow for the burial of his Protestant family outside the Catholic confines of the existing cemetery space. The Penny addition, based upon the 30-foot description, would only amount to an addition of 0.0007 acres, bringing the total acreage for Highland Cemetery by the time of Penny's death in 1825 to 1.263 acres. By 1876, a survey of the area for the heirs of Penny's successor-in-title to the land surrounding Highland Cemetery shows the cemetery as two acres in size. Thom (2005 [1974]) provides no explanation for this increase in size nor is there any known indication in the available historical records to explain the increase. However, maps that postdate this time also show a much larger cemetery than the original donation, with some individual graves identified beyond the original boundaries, thus lending credence to the potential expansion. Thom (2005 [1974]:11–12) notes several other land transactions between 1876 and 1923 that expanded the size of Highland Cemetery. However,

Figure 5.6. Google Earth imagery modified to show the location of Historic Highland Cemetery in Baton Rouge. The appearance of relatively neat rows of anomalies in this image is actually weed-eaten areas around survey nails used during site excavations as well as a few grave markers.

it is apparent that this information may be based upon oral history as there is no currently known documentary support for the expansion.

Highland Cemetery again appears on official survey records in 1923 when the College Town neighborhood was platted. At this time, according to Thom (2005 [1974]:12) the surveyor, A. C. Mundinger, produced a map dated June 23, 1923, that shows Highland Cemetery as 1.48 acres in area and shaped like a rectangle. However, when Mundinger filed his final plats of the College Town neighborhood on November 23, 1923, the actual dimensions of the cemetery were omitted, leading to continuing problems in the identification of the cemetery's boundary to this day. Recordation problems such as this have resulted in known portions of the cemetery being meted out to surrounding landowners over the years, and it is unclear what occurred to the burials in those areas between the 1930s and 1960s (Thom 2005 [1974]:13). Further, the Catholic Church's general apathy with the long-term preservation of Highland Cemetery led to further losses of property, including a servitude from the nearby Parker Boulevard and blurred property lines where fences were not maintained.

The last known interment in Highland Cemetery is that of Octavine Favrot in 1939, thus ending more than a century of mortuary activity at the site. Highland Cemetery today exhibits surface evidence of 65 burials (by way of marked graves), but documentary and archaeological evidence suggests that this number is potentially substantially lower than the actual number of those interred in the site (Haley 2003; Kleinpeter and Seidemann 2013; Seidemann and Kleinpeter 2013, 2014; Thom 2005 [1974]). Indeed, as one might expect for a small cemetery that was in service for more than a century, probe data, ground-truthed by ground-penetrating radar and controlled archaeological excavations suggest that 200 or more unmarked burials exist in and beyond Highland Cemetery's current roughly 0.5-acre boundaries (figure 5.7).

In 2018, two excavation units were completed at Highland Cemetery for the purpose of archaeologically verifying, if possible, evidence of definitive encroachment of the surrounding neighborhoods onto burials at the cemetery. In addition to the above-noted Oxford Avenue western boundary, Highland is currently bounded on the south side by the College Town neighborhood, the east by an East Baton Rouge Parish Parks & Recreation Commission park and the LaHavre neighborhood, and the north by the LaHavre neighborhood (Seidemann 2018c). In addition to the above-noted historic maps that suggest encroachment on the cemetery by the College Town neighborhood beginning sometime in the early 1940s, 2008–2011 probe data from the cemetery indicate that anomalies representing grave shafts extend under the southern wall that now purports to divide the cemetery from the College Town neighborhood (Kleinpeter and Seidemann 2013; Seidemann and Kleinpeter 2013, 2014).

The north side of the cemetery is a bit more problematic for archaeologically evaluating encroachment. Although the LaHavre neighborhood was constructed later than the College Town neighborhood (ca. AD 1970s), neither the probe data nor historic maps show any signs of anomalies or graves outside the modern cemetery fence. Although the cemetery hopefully represented a natural rise in the landscape and the burials were confined to the higher ground (which is now largely contained within the cemetery fence), reality may not have been so simple. The original topography of the LaHavre

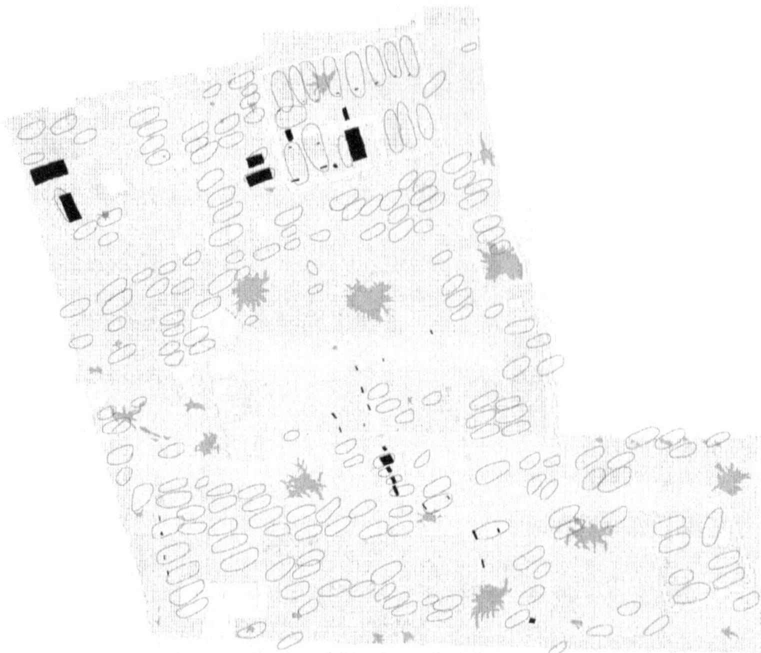

Figure 5.7. Mosaic probe map of Highland Cemetery. Each of the black shapes represent existing markers in the cemetery. The gray areas are rough outlines of tree root balls identified in the probe. The roughly oval shapes represent areas of little to no resistance to the probe throughout the cemetery and have been interpreted as probable grave shafts. Archaeological excavation has supported these interpretations. Image courtesy of Kenneth P. Kleinpeter.

neighborhood seems to have been lower and swampier than it is today. The area was substantially filled by dredged materials from the creation of the LSU Lakes in the early to mid-twentieth century (Thom 2005 [1974]). If this history is correct, with the nearest LaHavre residence less than 2 m from the northern cemetery fence, it is possible that additional burials in the lower areas north of the fence (and thus into the LaHavre neighborhood) are now obscured by massive amounts of fill and are beyond the reach of remote-sensing technologies.

Using the existing probe map anomalies as a guide, the excavation area for this small project was selected in the southern portion of the cemetery along the cinder block wall that separates the cemetery from College Town.[40] The specific anomaly on the probe map was an area of negative probe returns in the general shape of a partial grave shaft. What this amounts to is an area in which the person using the probe encountered little to no resistance when depressing the probe to its maximum depth of 1 m.

This anomaly was wholly contained within the first of two 1×2-m units excavated in 2018. This anomaly along the south wall appeared to show only a portion of a grave shaft within the cemetery, with the other portion continuing under the wall and disappearing. The first two arbitrary 10-cm levels of this unit were plagued with substantial root intrusion from bushes and vines planted to hide the cinder block wall and from construction materials from the wall itself. Indeed, the material culture recovered from these levels consisted mainly of cement from the wall, cinder block fragments, some ferrous materials, and some gardening tools. By level three, the material culture dropped off precipitously and a discoloration in a roughly rectangular shape began to emerge in the rough center of the unit, disappearing beneath the wall. Level four was devoid of all material culture. By this level, which bottomed out at roughly 55 cm below datum, a clear outline of what can only be described as a human grave shaft was visible within the unit and clearly extended under the wall into the College Town property to the south (figure 5.8). Because the shape of this feature was consistent with other grave shafts encountered at the site, and because no compelling reason justified disturbing the remains likely contained therein, the feature was fully documented and the unit was backfilled. Although it is impossible to state with certainty that human burials exist beyond the southern wall of Highland Cemetery based upon the single excavation unit completed in that area to date, the probable grave shaft feature is strongly suggestive of this likelihood and helps to archaeologically confirm the above-noted suspicions based upon the existing maps of the area.

This excavation provided information useful to the interpretation of the relationship of Historic Highland Cemetery to the broader landscape of the vicinity. Most importantly, the results of the excavation appear to substantially support the encroachment of the College Town neighborhood into the historic boundaries of the cemetery.

The combination of probe and excavation data from Highland Cemetery paint a picture of the treatment of this site during the time between its abandonment as an active burial location (i.e., 1939) and modern efforts to preserve the site (ca. 1975). The story told by these data strongly suggests that suburban development adversely affected burials in Highland Cemetery. Such impacts represent violations of the de jure legal protections in place for cemetery sites at the time of these disruptions. Although no positive law representing the cemetery dedication existed in Louisiana until the year before the Highland preservation efforts (i.e., 1975), as has been discussed at length in prior chapters, jurisprudential protections mandated a certain methodology for reusing cemetery property. The probe and archaeological data from

Figure 5.8. South-facing image of the floor of Level 4, the 1×2-m excavation unit at 514 N, 502 E at Highland Cemetery in 2018. The dark stain in the rough center of the excavation unit is a probable grave shaft whose north end terminates within the unit and whose south end extends under the fence into the College Town Neighborhood.

Highland demonstrate either an ignorance or a willful disregard of such mandates when the developers of College Town encroached on the cemetery in the 1940s. The practical reality of this encroachment amounts to clouds on the titles of every landowner along at least the southern boundary of the cemetery.

In both the Girod Street Cemetery and the Gates of Mercy cases discussed above, the *Humphreys* matter was cited for the proposition long held in Western legal traditions that once human remains are interred in a plot of land or entombed thereon, that land is a cemetery in the eyes of the law and shall remain dedicated to that purpose until the dedication is properly removed (Seidemann 2018a, 2018b). Those later cases revolved, in part, around the removal of that dedication. As has been belabored at length in the legal literature (Seidemann 2018a, 2018b), the only proper manner by which to remove a cemetery dedication is by accomplishing two things: (1) removing all human remains from the property; and (2) demonstrating to a court that those remains have been removed and that the land is no longer a cemetery. Both the Gates of Mercy and Girod Street Cemetery cases ultimately resulted in such court orders removing the cemetery dedication. Thus, in those cases, the de jure protections of cemeteries that existed for centuries but that were cemented in Louisiana law by the *Humphreys* case were vindicated, and the respective courts were convinced that all human remains had been removed from those pieces of property such that they could be put to alternative uses. However, modern archaeological investigations of these tracts of land suggest that, though well-intentioned and seemingly in compliance with the applicable law, these mid-twentieth-century efforts to remove all remains from these two cemeteries were less than successful.

The archival and archaeological evidence reviewed here demonstrates several things. First, the existence of de jure protections for certain property does not ensure de facto protection. Moreover, even when superficial evidence of compliance exists with the de jure protections (e.g., the dedication-removal efforts at Gates of Mercy, Girod, and Locust Grove), no guarantee exists that such efforts translate to actual de facto protections. However, recent archaeological work clearly indicates that cemeteries should be better protected in Louisiana today than in the recent past. In this regard, the mitigation of cemetery impacts by archaeological means at Charity Hospital Cemetery No. 2 for road and streetcar-line improvements and the decision not to proceed with development at Locust Grove Cemetery Nos. 1 and 2 because of the archaeological requirements of such work are hopeful indicators that de jure protections are now equating to de facto protections for cemeteries in Louisiana. The one major recent deviation from this modern regulatory framework—the conversion of Charity Cemetery No. 2 to commercial uses—should only represent an unfortunate blip on the radar screen of modern cemetery protection efforts in Louisiana. Finally, the archival evidence related to Evangeline Cemetery supports the notion that cemetery damage on the scale seen in New Orleans causes the type of psychological (and perhaps even physical) damage to descendant communities that rises to the level of Galtung's (1969) concept of structural violence. As the following chapter demonstrates, this violence, while substantially mitigated by modern de jure and de facto laws and applications of those laws, can likely never be eliminated entirely. Some burial sites are simply too ephemeral to be protected.

6

Isolated and Clandestine Burials

In 1830, Agnes Magnúsdóttir and Friðrik Sigurðsson were the last people executed in Iceland under that country's capital punishment laws. The duo, convicted of murder and whose sentences were not commuted by a ruling from Copenhagen, were led, at dawn, to a hillock on a remote northwestern peninsula near the town of Þrístapar. On this hillock, Sigurðsson fell under the blow of an executioner who used a large axe to decapitate him. Magnúsdóttir was next. The attendants at the execution buried the convicts' bodies in a hastily dug grave in the near-Arctic desolate landscape.

Agnes's and Friðrik's severed heads were placed on pikes and were publicly displayed for some time as a deterrent, with conflicting reports as to their ultimate fate: some suggesting eventual interment at the execution site; some suggesting thefts; some suggesting interment or disposal elsewhere (Vatomsky 2018; Þorgrímsdóttir 2005). Today, the execution site in the countryside is an easily missed pull-off of the Ring Road (Route 1) with minimal signage. The actual location of the beheadings is a raised berm surrounded by sheep farms, and the space where the headless bodies were originally interred in their unmarked graves is now commemorated by a single engraved granite marker.

Magnúsdóttir's and Sigurðsson's bodies remained interred from the time of their execution in 1830 until 1932 when, based upon unclear motives, Sesselja Guðmundsdóttir successfully campaigned for their disinterment for transport to a churchyard on the same northern peninsula (Þorgrímsdóttir 2005). Once accomplished, Agnes's and Friðrik's skeletal remains were placed into a single box and reinterred in the churchyard at Tjörn, some 56 km from the execution site.

One of the striking aspects of the reinterment is its diminutive size. As indicated in contemporary accounts, Agnes's and Friðrik's reinterments were not full-body inhumations; the final grave is simply too small. Such a reality raises questions of skeletal completeness at the Tjörn burial site. As has been well documented from archaeological recoveries of secondary burials, it is often that something less than comprehensive recovery of all skeletal elements is accomplished (Ubelaker 1994; Williams 1994; Damiata et al. 2017). Among the (roughly) 206 separate bones of an adult human skeleton, fully 30 such bones from the ankle and wrist (i.e., 14.6 percent of a person's bones) are virtually indistinguishable by nonexperts from gravel or small pebbles. Further, many other small bones and teeth are often missed during nonarchaeological excavations and taphonomic processes often lead to disarticulation and poor preservation of many skeletal elements (Zöega 2016). Because contemporary accounts of the execution and primary burial indicate that the bodies were not interred in any container, it would have been easy to miss such small pieces and probable fragments in the disinterment a century later. Thus, based upon the available archaeological evidence from other contexts, the chances that multiple bones or bone fragments were left at the execution site is highly likely.

The probability that some of Magnúsdóttir's and Sigurðsson's skeletal remains remained at the execution site is more than a mere academic curiosity. As the sites are treated at this time, the Tjörn cemetery (Tjörnkirkja) is a formal cemetery, presumably subject to standard Western legal site protections for burial places, while the execution site is a historic site rather than a burial site.[1]

With the rise of dark tourism (Miles 2015), urged on by television shows such as Netflix's "Dark Tourist," which seems to suggest that the trade in human remains is an acceptable practice, and because the execution site is a substantially unregulated and unmonitored historic site, the risk to Þrístapar of increased traffic resulting in site disturbance and possible damage to what is certainly the original and continued burial places of Agnes and Friðrik is real. This probable increase in tourist traffic necessarily includes the possibility that some of their skeletal remains will be carted off as curiosities.[2]

These dual burial places of Magnúsdóttir and Sigurðsson present an interesting window within which to examine how and whether the law protects isolated or clandestine interments of human remains when buried or entombed on land that does not fit the definition of either a traditional Western burial or even of a cemetery site that might be recognized as entitled to protection under various modern cemetery or archaeological site protections. The example of Magnúsdóttir's and Sigurðsson's initial burial site at the location of their execution would merit protection under existing American and most Western legal regimes as the bodies were intentionally interred at that site, though later, and likely incompletely, moved to another location. Moreover, Icelandic law also provides at least some protection for such sites. The question of which protection becomes more complex the more clandestine or accidental a burial is determined to be remains.

Archaeologically and legally, isolated and clandestine burials are more complex than any other human burial site. From both perspectives, it is virtually impossible to protect something when its location is vague or unknown. The Icelandic burial sites of Magnúsdóttir and Sigurðsson, though originally opportunistic, are at least known. Legal protections can be applied to these spaces, and their known locations—both original and secondary burial sites—can be protected. More difficult reckonings occur at sites of clandestine burials.

Although deserving of and entitled to protection as the intentional burials of human dead, vague assertions regarding the location of these sites are not enough to blanketly limit the use of whole swaths of land. In this regard, American notions of private property rights make impractical (and costly) the laying aside of large tracts of land on a supposition that one or more burials have occurred somewhere on the property. This is a case in which archaeology and its associated fields are crucial to the application of legal protections to cemeteries and burial sites.

Although not clandestine, two recent examples of how archaeological and other methods can be used effectively and ineffectively to protect such sites have occurred in Louisiana. Louisiana's River Parishes region—the roughly 110 river km between Baton Rouge and New Orleans that is also known today variously as "Cancer Alley" (Bullard 2000) or "the Industrial Corridor"—was the historic home to large numbers of antebellum plantations on which countless enslaved peoples toiled and died. This fact is known. What is often not known is where these people were buried. Although there is no doubt that these burials exist, as testified to by Louisiana's state archaeologist, Dr. Chip McGimsey, and University of New Orleans archaeologist, Dr. Ryan Gray, where these burials are is often unknown.[3] In a 2022 court hearing, both of these archaeologists testified that these enslaved people found their final rest often in discrete cemeteries on plantation property on which they lived, but that most knowledge of the whereabouts of those cemeteries has long ago been lost. Moreover, due to more than a century of agricultural and some industrial activity on these former plantation sites, most surface evidence of their existence has vanished.

That 2022 court hearing occurred in a dispute between the descendants of former enslaved peoples in St. John the Baptist Parish, near the town of Wallace, and the parish government over the rezoning of former plantation lands from agricultural uses to industrial. A company was planning to construct a grain elevator along the Mississippi River near Wallace—a town now largely inhabited by the descendants of former enslaved peoples—on former plantation property (now sugarcane fields). Among the descendant community's challenges to this proposed project was an objection to its impacts on enslaved burial grounds. At the time of the hearing, basic archaeological reconnaissance of the project area was complete (Erickson 2020; Somers 2021). This reconnaissance followed state law requirements and was necessary as part of the permit process for activities located in the state's coastal zone. The archaeological work identified no definite or even probable burial sites in the project area, even though no real dispute exists as to the presence of such interments somewhere on the plantation property.

At the hearing—a miniature evidentiary trial on whether injunctive relief should be imposed on the project's progress—the descendant community called a witness to testify who had undertaken georeferenced cartographic analyses of the project area. This analysis clearly showed unexplainable anomalies on the plantation property (though not within the project footprint) that were not identified by the probabilistic-based archaeological testing of the land. Unfortunately for the community, this witness was excluded from testifying for legal-procedural reasons. Nonetheless, these anomalies, known at the time to the regulatory agencies involved in permitting the site, did not fall within the project footprint and were too vague to actually raise suspicions that they represented unmarked burials. Because of this disconnect between anomalies identified in historic records and remote-sensing versus reasonably certain burial sites, private property rights intervened to both keep the regulatory agencies from mandating exploratory archaeology beyond the scope of that required by law (which was already complete and approved) and to otherwise restrict the use of the broader property on suppositions that burial sites existed somewhere on the land. As of this writing, the Wallace grain elevator project has been ended by the company. Although this project will not proceed, it is possible that burial sites may be found before the beginning or completion of any other construction that would alter the legally authorized uses of portions of the former plantation property.

Even if such sites were identified on the grain elevator land, this fact does not amount to a complete restriction of all uses of the entire property. In 2020, a site just upriver from Wallace, in St. James Parish, was slated for the construction of a plastics plant on another plantation site. As with the Wallace project, pursuant to federal and state permitting mandates, archaeological testing was done on the project area (Coastal Environments, Inc. 2020a, 2020b). Historical records for this site—actually spanning two plantations—clearly indicated the presence of enslaved peoples' burial sites in or near the project area. Despite being on high alert for human remains, the archaeology at the site identified no cemeteries.

Convinced that the probabilistic-based archaeological testing, though compliant with the law, was simply missing the known cemeteries, descendants of those once enslaved on these plantations contracted with a separate cultural resources management firm. The historians and archaeologists with this second firm used cartographic regression of modern aerial photography and historic maps to locate highly probable areas for the locations of the lost cemeteries (Coastal Environments, Inc. 2020a, 2020b). In this situation, the weight of this new evidence was sufficient to require additional archaeological testing. This subsequent round of testing—above and beyond that initially required by law—definitively revealed the location of one cemetery and strongly supported the archival evidence for the location of the second. Based upon this work, the plastics plant was forced into a decision: replan its plant design or work with the state regulators and the descendant community to archaeologically excavate and respectfully relocate the burials in the cemeteries. Initially, the company placed the now-known site off-limits and fenced it to protect it from construction and plant uses. The second site (i.e., the probable cemetery), as of the time of this writing was still in a state of flux as to how to actually manage it. Prior industrial activity on the property had likely substantially, if not completely (though seemingly unknowingly), destroyed the site with the placement of a pipeline directly through it. Thus, the site's integrity was substantially compromised and the ability to archaeologically recover remains for later move and reinterment elsewhere is doubtful. Nonetheless, it is hoped that this second area will be similarly placed off-limits for future use, but, as of the time of this writing, litigation over other components of the plastics plant have stalled any final planning and construction. Thus, the fate of these River Parishes enslaved peoples' cemeteries is unknown at this time.

What is important in both of the above Louisiana scenarios is that, though cemeteries—even isolated or clandestine sites—if of a known location, can only protect the discrete areas in which burials exist. This is a reality across the United States. The discovery of a cemetery site does not equate to control of the reuse of entire swaths of property. In many environmental justice suits today, the presence of these sites is but a single tool in efforts to fight potentially offensive or discriminatory uses of land. When such sites are found, entire industrial projects cannot necessarily be scuttled. However, the discrete areas of known burials must be reckoned with, as those specific areas cannot be reused for industrial purposes without complying with modern archaeological laws and applying modern archaeological techniques to any disturbance of those burials. Moreover, such reuses also must contend with not only modern archaeological laws but also ancient laws that apply to cemetery property such as the cemetery dedication.

The two Louisiana projects—Wallace and St. James—illustrate the limitations of both archaeology and the law and their roles in protecting burial sites. For the legal protections to apply, the archaeological, historical, and archival evidence must demonstrate or strongly suggest the actual presence of burials in a proposed reuse area. Supposition and untested anomalies are not legally sufficient to place such areas off-limits to reuse. In such cases, constitutional protections of private property rights will undoubtedly prevail over vague data and suppositions to restrict regulatory archaeologists and descendant communities from restricting the use of such lands. Moreover, even when cemeteries are identified in a proposed project area, these sites do not represent comprehensive restrictions to environmental disputes or land reuses. Such sites are crucially important, and the law mandates their special treatment when known or discovered. However, such sites are but one item in the toolkit of property control. Archaeology, no doubt, occupies a special and important place in environmental protection (e.g., Seidemann 2007; Douglass and Cooper 2020), but it is not the panacea for environmental justice that was hoped for by the descendant community in the Wallace grain elevator case.

Occasionally, but very rarely and unlike the Wallace grain elevator case, the social justice of locating clandestine graves tips the balance of interests for a while to allow for exploratory remote sensing to be accomplished, as was the case at the Dozier School for Boys in Marianna, Florida, in the 2010s (Kimmerle 2022).[4] In this case, a groundswell of public support to locate the clandestine burials of boys believed to have died at a juvenile penal school in the early to mid-twentieth century coupled with extensive archival and oral history research by the project's archaeologists combined to provide for a unique social justice project. Boys who had died at the school between its founding at the turn of the twentieth century and its closure almost a century later, many at the hands of guards and other public employees at the site, had been rumored to be buried in multiple unmarked locations around the massive working farm and industrial site that once constituted the institution (Kimmerle 2022). This former school was slated for sale and development in the early part of the twenty-first century, and descendants and relatives of those thought to be buried in these unknown, rumored cemeteries on the property were concerned that any new development would result in the destruction of graves and end any hopes that the families harbored for learning the fates of their loved ones. Because of the salacious nature of the stories told by former school detainees, including inhuman physical treatment often meted out to African American boys and conditions that resembled antebellum slavery, families and archaeologists were able to persuade politicians and bureaucrats to forestall sale of the property to allow for the exploratory archaeology (Kimmerle 2022) that could not occur at the Wallace grain elevator site. It was also fortuitous—at least for the purposes of this project—that the land was public property, and thus such exploratory activities did not constitute a regulatory taking of private property. This is also a key difference between the Dozier Project and the Wallace grain elevator situation in which the latter was located on wholly private property.

Although ultimately able to conduct considerable remote-sensing and archaeological excavation in search of unmarked and clandestine graves at the Dozier School, Kimmerle (2022) still reports substantial institutional obstacles to this social justice project. As Kimmerle (2022) has recently observed through her work at the Dozier School, it occasionally occurs that the cemetery protection laws, rather than being used to protect the integrity of the burials, are used to thwart truth and justice-seeking. These obstacles included bureaucratic roadblocks to permitting cemetery excavations, archaeological questioning of motives for the work, as well as criminal complaints of desecration by white community members who were concerned about what the possible truths this archaeological work would reveal about their community's history. In such situations, the archaeological community and regulators charged with enforcing burial protections should tread carefully before denying permits that are supported by descendant community members as was the case at Dozier. Ultimately, the agency that has been denied many of these disenfranchised communities over time can be found through the excavation and analysis, and indeed, the cooperative applied archaeology that occurs when it is the descendant communities' well-defined questions that are answered by archaeology about these long-past injustices. Whether the archaeological and bureaucratic communities considered these matters in the Dozier situation is not known. However, the case is illustrative of the continued need for the archaeological and regulatory community to place descendant community interests—especially when those interests are in favor of archaeological excavation and bioarchaeological analysis—on an equal footing with scientific and regulatory decision-making.

The initial roadblocks to the Dozier social justice research were noticeably absent from the recent efforts in the United Kingdom to locate the remains of King Richard III, suggesting that even an institutionalized archaeological dichotomy exists when confronted with the burial spaces of the disenfranchised and the enfranchised. When archaeological efforts began in earnest in 2012 in Leicester, England, to locate the long-lost remains of King Richard III, the obstacles were not questions of research integrity and motives, but rather the more logistical management of expectations associated with searching for centuries-old unmarked graves and disrupting modern uses of property (Pitts 2015). To be sure, between the time when Richard was killed on Bosworth Field, ending the Wars of the Roses in 1485, and his interment in an unmarked grave, his remains suffered from the treatment often seen in cases of structural violence against marginalized peoples (Pitts 2015). This is unsurprising treatment for the remains of a vanquished royal whose remains were controlled by his enemies in war. Richard was reputedly treated as a pauper when he was buried on the fringes of a monastery cemetery in Leicester immediately following his defeat, being provided no pomp and circumstance (or even a coffin or the basic trappings of a respectful burial) typically associated with royalty (Pitts 2015).

The similarities between the cemeteries in which the Dozier boys were reputed to have been buried and where Richard III may have been buried were striking. There was no certainty that many of the unaccounted-for Dozier boys were buried on the school's property just as there was no certainty that Richard's remains were interred in a pauper's grave, dumped in the nearby River Soar, left to rot on the battlefield at Bosworth, or otherwise lost to history (Pitts 2015). Effectively, in death, these disparate human remains were treated with equal disrespect and disregard—their postmortem-narrative journeys, though separated by centuries, were similar. Indeed, the nature of one of Richard's possible final resting places (the one that turned out to be correct) seems to violate the most basic notions of cemetery reuse discussed in this book. The monastery cemetery where Richard was ultimately found was later buried beneath a car park in Leicester with no apparent effort to remove the human remains resting therein and with seemingly no regard for the common law cemetery dedication or sacredness of sepulchre. Although this conversion seems to have occurred slowly as the cemetery first became a garden (an often-consistent use of cemetery property) and then later was converted to other uses. Thus, though a violation of basic land use laws, it is possible to imagine how the current use came about through the collective memory loss of the cemetery's presence.

However ignominiously Richard III was buried at the time of this death and then treated in postmortem popular culture (history was not kind to Richard), the difficulties of searching for his lost burial place—ongoing contemporaneously with the Dozier School project in the United States—did not include attempts by established archaeologists and members of the public to stop the work (cf., Kimmerle 2022). Certainly, for both projects, funding was a problem as was skepticism regarding the chances for success (Kimmerle 2022; Pitts 2015). Such is often the expected response to the search for a needle in a haystack that is common when attempting to locate lost clandestine graves. But the seemingly race-based vitriol that Erin Kimmerle and her crew faced when working on the Dozier School project was absent from the Richard III project. Of course, race was not a component of the Richard III project, but it was a search for a much-reviled royal and yet the project garnered the international spotlight without the attendant opposition to the work from within the archaeological community and various members of the public. Perhaps more than 500 years of water under the bridge with respect to Richard III's reputation and the more open wound of racism and the temporal proximity of the events at Dozier (less than 100 years and with some participants and many close relatives still living) can explain the dichotomous treatment of these projects by the public, but there is no explanation for the pushback from the professional community reported by Kimmerle (2022). The Dozier Project was one that was undertaken with the blessings of and at the behest of the descendants and families of the decedents using modern archaeological and forensic methodologies. Under those circumstances, archaeological opinions regarding the treatment of the site and the remains must defer to the collective wishes of the descendants. For those descendants, thankfully, the Dozier School project proceeded and was able to answer some of their questions and to bring them some amount of closure.

Further complexities exist when there is only oral history to suggest the location of a cemetery or burial when a proposed use of property is thought to threaten an unmarked burial site. In his recent book *Red Summer: The Summer of 1919 and the Awakening of Black America,* Cameron McWhirter (2011) provides several examples of how violent events that can lead to the creation of clandestine cemeteries are difficult to protect. McWhirter recounts various events around the United States following the World War I in which African Americans, expressing their frustration with their second-class status after fighting in Europe, brought the rage of American white people to bear in clashes that resulted in massive numbers of gruesome minority deaths in the plain sight of and often with the support of the American legal establishment (see also Ifill 2018). McWhirter (2011:13) reports that NAACP records "show at least 25 major riots and mob actions erupted and at least 52 black people were lynched. Many victims were burned to death." During these deadly months, in Mississippi, Eugene Green, an African American alleged to have injured a law enforcement officer "was dragged from jail, hanged, shot, and dumped in a river" (McWhirter 2011:29). Of the incident, Governor Theodore Bilbo commented that Green "'"was 'advanced' all right"'" for his crime "'"from the end of a rope, and in order to save burial expenses his body was thrown in the Yazoo River"'" (McWhirter 2011:30). Other terrifying accounts of the troubles of 1919 include a mass killing of African Americans in a riot in Elaine, Arkansas, in which local fraternal lodges paid for 103 grave spaces, and it is estimated that an additional 73 victims remained unaccounted for. A *New York Times* account of this event observed that "'[t]he bodies of other Negroes probably will be found in the woods by searching parties'" (McWhirter 2011:225).

The human remains unceremoniously disposed of during such terrible events present the most problematic fate from both an archaeological and a legal perspective. Eugene Green has no grave. His burial will not be protected as his remains were dispersed down the Yazoo to the Mississippi and ultimately to the Gulf of Mexico. Although countless human bodies have been dumped or ceremonially disposed of at sea, the Gulf of Mexico does not meet the legal definition of a cemetery. Thus, there is no site at which to mourn the memory of Eugene Green nor one to protect as a burial site.

As is currently being demonstrated in Tulsa, Oklahoma, places of mourning and remembering of the 1921 massacre of African Americans in that city can, in part, be found and commemorated. Recent archaeological efforts in that city have identified numerous unmarked burials in existing cemeteries (Razek and Wolfe 2022). This work is laudable because it provides closure to some, voice and agency to others, and confirms the historic record and oral traditions surrounding this dark event in American history. These burials, though previously unmarked, were part of an existing cemetery and they were and are protected by the laws discussed in prior chapters. What have not been found are the countless clandestine burials of this massacre that occurred outside existing cemeteries.

However, as with the victims of the Elaine, Arkansas, massacre, those of the Tulsa Massacre, whose bodies were not placed into known cemeteries but rather were unceremoniously dumped in the rural areas or left where they were killed, are virtually impossible to find. Under the law, a cemetery exists where a human dead body was intentionally interred or entombed. Thus, as development comes to places such as Elaine, Arkansas, and Tulsa, Oklahoma, care should be taken to watch for the mass and individual graves likely in undeveloped areas and marked on no map. These sites, too, are entitled to the same protections, reverence, and respect as established cemeteries. However, with only ancient recollections and vague oral histories of the locations of these interments, the identification and protection of such sites becomes more remote with each passing year. In addition, because such cemetery protections as the dedication laws rest on intentional interment or entombment, if remains are left where they were killed with no intentional burial, such land is likely unprotected as a legal cemetery. Certainly in this case, general restrictions on the disturbance of human remains would apply, but the property itself likely would not be protected or protectable as a dedicated cemetery rather, as happened in New Orleans following Hurricane Katrina, the spaces where the victims came to rest were crime scenes rather than cemeteries (Seidemann 2010e). The same reverence accorded cemeteries should be extended to these ancient crime scenes for whom there is no one left to prosecute even if the law does not provide them with protection.

Because the dedication laws rely on intentional burial, the location of crime scenes and natural disasters doubtfully will be protectable as isolated or clandestine cemeteries. A good example of this difficulty would be if the Space Shuttle *Columbia*'s crash site were to be legally classified as a cemetery. This site, substantially scoured for human remains after the 2003 disaster (though no doubt missing many fragmentary remains), covered a spatial area of 5,180 km^2 (2,000 mi^2) (Leinbach and Ward 2018).[5] Such massive swaths of land—areas that encompassed cities, towns, residences, and businesses—where the astronauts' remains happened to fall to Earth and not where they were actually interred would cause dedication restrictions and other burial protection laws to apply to tens of thousands of places never actually containing human burials. Such a reality is practically and politically untenable and not legally supported. The lack of legal support derives from the absence of intent in the locations where the remains came to rest. These spaces were not intentional burials and thus are not subject to the dedication laws.

One extreme deviation from this notion in many ways is the Ground Zero site of the September 11, 2001, terrorist attacks in Lower Manhattan. This site where so many people died is considered sacred by many descendants, families, and friends. Indeed, many of them regard this site and the surrounding areas where human remains were found on rooftops at some distance from the World Trade Center towers as a cemetery (Aronson 2016). This situation appears to be the closest to a site that represents no intentional burial being considered sacred enough by many to be a cemetery. Legally, the land is not a cemetery. Even those remains contained in the memorial facility on site are not intended to be in permanent repose on the site, and, despite the sacred nature of the site to some, the land has been repurposed for commercial uses (Aronson 2016). Certainly, this repurposing does not remove a cemetery dedication that might have existed, but despite the fact that many people regard the site as a cemetery, the absence of intentional burials thereon defeats any legal classification of the land as such.

In the Katrina situation, federal and state emergency response agencies were concerned that they would have to adhere to the somewhat draconian implications of the classification of a place of natural disaster death as a cemetery. In such cases, it would be impossible to rehabilitate a property destroyed by the storm unless and until the remains were archaeologically removed from the site and the legal requirements to remove the cemetery dedication has been accomplished. Again, the dedication provisions rely on intentional interment or entombment for their application. Modern archaeological protections for deathscapes defer to law enforcement in cases of crimes or natural disasters. Thus, the places of death of disaster victims do not constitute burials or cemeteries as contemplated by the law. Any commemorative restrictions to such sites would have to be applied to these lands irrespective of cemetery laws.

More confusing from a legal perspective is the opportunistic identification of sites such as individual burials and lynching locations. Because murder has no statute of limitations, the places where single or small numbers of executions occurred may represent crime scenes when discovered. As a matter of practicality, as the perpetrators of such crimes as lynching die off, these sites become more than just crime scenes; they become places for memorialization (Aronson 2016; Williams 2007) and occasionally, as with the execution site of Magnúsdóttir and Sigurðsson, even if the majority of the remains were moved elsewhere for burial, are still cemeteries under the legal definition of that term. McWhirter (2011:68, 70) recounts one such event in Ellisville, Mississippi, in 1919 with the execution of John Hartfield, an African American accused of attacking a white woman.

> "Lynchers cut off Hartfield's fingers. They let him dangle from a branch, then they shot him. They burned the corpse . . . not less than 2,000 bullets were fired into his body. One of them finally clipped the rope. John's body fell to the ground, a fire was built around it, and John was cremated." An hour later, nothing remained of Hartfield but a pile of ashes.

In this case, as in the situation of Magnúsdóttir and Sigurðsson, it is virtually impossible that pieces of Hartfield do not remain at or near his execution site (to say nothing of the morbid trophies actually taken from his body as mementos).[6] The location of this execution exists only in the memories of those present. Even with vague knowledge of its location, it is doubtful (but not impossible) that this site could be identified archaeologically. Without that archaeological evidence, John Hartfield's final place of rest will never be protected. In such cases, as was shown in the Wallace grain elevator case, archaeology is necessary to trigger the legal protections for both places of violent demise that retain human remains as well as for the final resting places of those whose lives were spent in forced toil and whose burial location is now forgotten.

7

Discussion and Conclusions

During the course of this writing, CBS's *60 Minutes* news program broke a story about the mistreatment of an African American cemetery in Clearwater, Florida (Pelley 2022). Although shocking to the reporters and the general public, this story is all too common in the world of archaeology.

In Clearwater, archaeologists with the Florida Public Archaeology Network and the University of South Florida, working on tips from a descendant community and partially funded by the local NAACP, conducted ground-penetrating radar on a now-developed area in the city to determine whether oral tradition that the site had once been an African American cemetery was true (Moates and O'Sullivan 2020a, 2020b). Over several days of fieldwork in 2020, Jeffrey Moates and Rebecca O'Sullivan conducted systematic surveys of an unused parking lot and the entrance area to a commercial structure on South Missouri Avenue in Clearwater (Moates and O'Sullivan 2020a, 2020b), identifying remote-sensing anomalies that are consistent with the presence of dozens of likely burials. They had found the St. Matthew Baptist Church Cemetery. With this information and especially with the national media attention, questions presented from this initial research are: (1) how did this happen; (2) what is to be done with this site now that probable burials have been found; and (3) were any laws broken or are any laws being broken by the presence of these offending structures atop this cemetery site? Certainly, the second question is the most complex, requiring considerable consultation with the descendant community, which is now, understandably, angry and hurt by this desecration of their ancestors' final resting place (Pelley 2022). These questions also must grapple with issues related to private property rights.

Florida's unmarked burials law predates NAGPRA by three years (Quetone 1987). Enacted in 1987, this law provides protection against unmarked burial disturbance, among other things. By the time that this law was enacted, burials at the St. Matthew Baptist Church Cemetery had ceased by almost 50 years (Moates and O'Sullivan 2020a, 2020b). Based upon historic records research by Moates and O'Sullivan (2020a, 2020b), it seems that most, if not all, of the cemetery was constructed over by a Montgomery Ward store and parking area by 1962. It is disappointing but unsurprising that this African American cemetery in the southern United States was erased from the landscape in the heat of the civil rights movement in the 1960s. However, this is consistent with the treatment endured by other African American places and people during this time (Wilkerson 2010). Thus, as with the many Louisiana cemeteries discussed in this and previous chapters, modern burial protection laws did not provide any protection against this erasure because they did not yet exist.

However, what the landowners and developers did in the 1950s and 1960s by erasing the surface evidence of this cemetery has now effectively cursed the current landowners. With virtual proof positive of the existence of a cemetery on this property in the form of ground-penetrating radar results and oral histories,[1] the current landowners are burdened, at a minimum, by bad press and the common law cemetery dedication. As Moates and O'Sullivan (2020a, 2020b) indicate, the current owners likely came to this property with clean hands due to the lack of records regarding the cemetery in the then-existing public documents. Thus, they presumably did not knowingly violate any laws by the construction of the current structure and parking lots (unless construction crews actually witnessed but did not report the presence of human burials). But with the knowledge of these burials' presence now, no reuse of the land can occur unless and until the cemetery is properly protected or archaeologically moved pursuant to a lawfully issued permit and consultation with the descendant community.

More than anything, the St. Matthews Baptist Church Cemetery erasure in Clearwater is emblematic of the disparate treatment of the disenfranchised dead in the United States historically and, sometimes, even in the present. Laws exist and have existed for centuries to avoid such treatment. These laws failed in Florida (St. Matthew's) and in Louisiana (Locust Grove, Girod, Charity No. 2, and Stonewall) and have likely also failed across the country as modern construction is revealing more disenfranchised cemeteries that were plowed under by development.

The purpose of this research has been to examine the treatment of cemetery sites and human remains and how the treatment of those materials and spaces are indicative of the treatment of disenfranchised peoples. This review also examined the extent to which, if at all, recent legislation (particularly, NAGPRA) and evolving archaeological standards influenced and informed such protections. The above reviews of archival and archaeological evidence from the past 80 years have demonstrated that the treatment of cemetery sites and human remains substantially changed over that period. The changes trended from a general disregard for burial places and human remains (e.g., *Humphreys*) to substantial regulation of such sites and the scientific and respectful treatment of human remains (e.g., Charity Hospital Cemetery No. 2). This trend tracks archaeology's own history with human remains as Arnold and Jeske (2014:326) note: "the present generation of scholars is atoning for acknowledged discipline-wide abuses of colonialism." Indeed, when viewed through the analytical lens of structural violence, one can easily conclude that many of New Orleans's former disenfranchised residents, especially the poor, have experienced unequal treatment in death just as they did in life (Halling and Seidemann 2017; Seidemann and Halling 2019). The same can be said of communities across Louisiana (e.g., Stonewall Cemetery) and the rest of the country (e.g., St. Matthew's in Florida). However, with the advent of modern laws and archaeological standards, additional agency is and has been provided to such groups in ways that enhance their ability to control their postmortem histories.

Considering the foregoing review, definitively connecting all these changes to the passage by Congress of NAGPRA in 1990 is impossible. Little doubt exists that NAGPRA, as highly visible federal legislation, represented something of a catalyst for states to implement similar legal protections for human remains and burial sites within their respective jurisdictions. Moreover, NAGPRA and its progeny have altered the management of cemetery sites as historic and cultural resources by professionalizing their management within archaeological contexts (cf. the treatment of Charity No. 2 in 2014 [Smith and Stone 2014] to the treatment of Stonewall Cemetery in the 1950s through 1970s [Servello et al. 2003]). However, as the extensive congressional record leading to the passage of NAGPRA demonstrates, this law's passage addresses matters related to providing agency to Native Americans, Native Hawaiians, and Alaska Natives with regard to the repatriation and protection of their ancestors' human remains (Lannan 1998). NAGPRA's passage led states like Louisiana to adopt and expand protections with the passage of its Unmarked Burials Act in 1991, though it is probable that such site protections were often tangential afterthoughts to the main thrust of these laws (i.e., human remains protections).

The Cemetery Dedication Is a Helpful Site-Protection Tool, but It Is Fallible

As the review of the cemetery dedication laws demonstrate, most states have had cemetery protection laws in place for decades, if not centuries, before the passage of NAGPRA. Thus, some legislators possibly did not see a need for increased cemetery site protections before NAGPRA. While definitively linking NAGPRA to a largely modern increase in cemetery and human remains protection in the United States broadly is not possible, NAGPRA likely provided a framework within which states and descendant communities could begin to address such matters as grave protection and human remains treatment from legal and cultural perspectives.

However, as also noted, a cemetery dedication's protection, while an important tool for the prospective protection of known cemeteries, is reliant on knowing that a cemetery exists. As Lemke (2020) demonstrates with cemeteries in Texas, identifying the presence of a cemetery, especially one that is the final resting place of disenfranchised people, may be the most difficult task in the process of protecting those sites. Thus, if a cemetery's location is unknown or known but not recorded, the protection of those sites is entirely dependent upon those encountering cemeteries to self-report their findings—a situation that may be contrary to their own fiduciary and land use interests.

Among the enhanced protections for cemetery site preservation in the United States may be mandatory archival reviews such as that undertaken in Texas (Lemke 2020). In this review, the Texas Historical Commission's Missing Cemeteries Project compared historic and modern maps in the state to identify where once-documented cemeteries disappeared from United States Geological Survey quadrangle maps. Along with additional archival research, numerous previously forgotten cemeteries in Texas were documented for posterity and protection, the majority of which were cemeteries for disenfranchised peoples. Such cartographic regression analyses have also been undertaken in Louisiana to verify the locations of enslaved peoples' cemeteries (Coastal Environments, Inc. 2020a, 2020b). With the passage of the African American Burial Grounds Preservation Act in 2022, the National Park Service is poised to fund, up to $12 million within a four-year period, a similar undertaking to what Texas has accomplished (Seidemann 2023). Such an outcome would be well worth the use of taxpayer dollars, and, by accompanying the research with mandatory transmission of such findings to respective State Historic Preservation Officers and local clerks of court, protections like the cemetery dedication can be brought to bear almost immediately—a veritable (but not complete) game-changer for protecting the mortuary spaces of many of America's disenfranchised peoples.

No doubt exists that this sort of research is fruitful for the identification of many such cemeteries. What is unknown is whether these identification efforts meaningfully protect such sites from destruction by most forms of development. As Lemke (2020:606–607) notes, the Texas study's data were added "to a geographic information system (GIS) database used by professional archaeologists and cultural resource management (CRM) companies in the state." Louisiana and many other states also maintain such a database of site-locational information. However, because of the aforementioned concerns about publishing site locations representing invitations to looters, such locational data often are not readily available. Thus, the only benefit from documenting these cemetery locations is that when CRM professionals are engaged for a particular project—the vast minority of large development projects in the United States—they will be able to benefit from the restricted recordation of such sites in their informing of development. Although such identification is laudable, as noted in chapter 4, its utility is substantially hampered without the recordation of such sites in the public conveyance records (Rainville 2009), thereby placing all on notice of the presence of a cemetery on a particular tract of land.

Since 2008 in Louisiana, this recordation of the cemetery dedication (and the correlative establishment of a cemetery) has been mandated by law (La. R.S. 8:304; La. Acts 2008, No. 423, §1). While important for keeping geographic track of constantly formed small and family cemeteries, such mandatory recordation is prospective only and does not help to identify or document the thousands of existing cemeteries in the state. Only amendments to various laws mandating the public recordation of existing cemeteries that predate the 2008 amendments either immediately (for known sites) or as they become known (for unknown sites) will make any meaningful difference for the protection of the many cemeteries of disenfranchised people in Louisiana. The same can and should be mandated elsewhere.

The other shortcoming of the cemetery dedication as a site protection tool is the lack of penalties for its violation. No explicit penalties exist in Louisiana law for violating the cemetery dedication laws (La. R.S. 8:304–307). This problem is endemic nationwide. While Louisiana's Unmarked Burials Act and the Historic Cemetery Act contain substantial penal provisions and the Human Remains Trafficking and Control Act elevates crimes against human remains to the level of felonies, all that failing to comply with the dedication laws results in is a cloud on the property's title. Although this burden is not insignificant for landowners and lenders (Curtin 2013) affecting the merchantability of title, the punishment is not a direct deterrent with anything more than financial implications for those who would violate the law. Simply adding criminal sanctions for violations of the cemetery dedication laws would enhance the deterrent significance of these laws greatly.

Archaeological Contributions to Cemetery Site Protection

Over the past 50 or so years, archaeological practices and ethical standards substantially developed to a point that the removal of human remains from a cemetery context became a controlled scientific practice that does not resemble the haphazard removals that occurred at the Girod Street and Stonewall cemeteries in Louisiana. The practical changes in archaeological excavation techniques in the United States are bolstered by theoretical approaches to interpretation of excavation results, especially those that incorporate multiple perspectives and voices on the past. The combination of these changes substantially altered the nature of archaeological interpretation and practice. Moreover, since the passage of NAGPRA and its state analogues, in many cases, archaeological methods are employed meaningfully in the removal of human remains from cemetery contexts in advance of development. Thus, in a post-NAGPRA world, much of the human remains removal and relocation in the United States includes such modern archaeological hallmarks as detailed recordkeeping (through field notes, unit-floor and profile sketches, and photographs) and collection or excavation proceeds by planned and structured (generally) hand excavation of square or rectangular units within a metric grid that spans all or part of the site at a pace of arbitrary levels, interrupted by natural stratigraphy changes that might signal important cultural or geological shifts in site function. The implementation of these modern archaeological techniques in cemetery contexts has shifted the development interactions with these sites from haphazard body and tombstone removal to a controlled, scientific process that incorporates analytical techniques calculated to recover not just the remains, but, through the application of modern archaeological theory, the stories of those who were interred in these sites, too.

Indeed, according to Wilkie (2005), modern historical archaeology seeks to interpret multiple pasts as seen through the lenses of different participants observed in the archaeological record. Such aspirational goals are not always attainable from the available archaeological records. In this regard, Burnston (1997:101) notes of excavations and analyses of enslaved peoples from a Maryland site that "[w]hile historical archaeology has been called the record of the people who had no share in the written past, it must be pointed out that in this case our best efforts archaeologically have told us next to nothing about these peoples themselves, about what mattered to them, nor about their beliefs, values, and aspirations."

Gray (2011:55) also notes that "identity as an analytical category to be applied to the past" is becoming an increasingly popular method of inquiry. This multivocal approach to archaeological interpretation has enabled historical archaeology to pioneer the use of race-, sex-, class-, gender-, and ethnicity-specific perspectives on the past, and these perspectives are now brought to bear on cemetery interpretation in ways not heretofore employed. The use of such interpretive methods as applied to cemeteries resulted directly from the placement of most cemetery impacts permitting under the jurisdiction of archaeologists—such changes correlate substantially with the enactment of NAGPRA and its state analogues.

Although some measure of special treatment of cemetery spaces has been present in extant legal traditions for a long time, from a review of the sources in this research, modern archaeology has clearly influenced the development of both legal protections as well as notions of what constitutes a cemetery. As seems to be the case in Florida's St. Matthew's Baptist Church Cemetery and Louisiana's Girod Street Cemetery scenarios, if a cemetery and its human remains were out of sight, they were also out of mind. In other words, superficially erasing these sites from the landscape by removing visible evidence of their existence often sufficiently satisfied or otherwise sidestepped the law and perhaps even the descendant communities at the time. Today, modern archaeological methods mandate a higher level of precision in the removal of human remains from a particular site. Simply removing visible evidence of such remains does not suffice for the removal of a cemetery. Moreover, modern archaeological methods have demonstrated that many cemeteries are larger than they appear to the untrained eye. So many cemeteries contain unmarked graves (Jones 2011) that merely mitigating potential impacts to the known graves is now fairly well accepted to be an insufficient manner of ensuring that a cemetery is fully out of the path of development (Kay 1998). Some amount of archaeological reconnaissance is now required in most situations to ensure that unmarked graves on the periphery of known cemetery sites are not going to be influenced by development before an area can be cleared as a cemetery.

Archaeology and the law that has evolved over the past century has demonstrated that the perspective of those such as Rugg (2000) that characterize cemeteries as ordered constructs is somewhat myopic. In her efforts to classify types of cemetery sites and burial features, Rugg focuses on the regimented nature of such sites as Père Lachaise (Paris) and Mount Auburn (Cambridge, Massachusetts) while ignoring other examples—often complex mortuary landscapes with traditions of multiple uses and superimposition of burials—of human burial sites. According to Rugg (2000:260), citing Kolbuszewski (1995), traditional concepts of cemeteries do not include mass body disposal locations such as the site of massacres. However, the reasoning for such exclusion is inconsistent with modern American law as informed by archaeology. These sites—ones in which victims of the Tulsa Massacre and many lynching victims find their permanent rest—though likely not the locale of interment that would have been chosen by those buried therein, certainly can become imbued with the sacred aspects of traditional cemeteries, both as a space that embodies the suffering leading to the deaths of its inhabitants and as a final resting place of those people. Under the law, such a site would be a cemetery, and archaeologically, it could be considered both a burial place and a sacred site. This characterization is not made lightly. Although Rugg is a UK researcher, the scope of her article overtly includes within its classification schemes the United States, Europe, and Australia. While certain of those jurisdictions may have a custom of distinguishing between cemeteries, churchyards, and other burial spaces, Rugg's (2000:272) suggestion that "cemeteries constitute a particular type of burial space" is inconsistent with law and custom in much of the United States and is certainly incorrect in Louisiana. Indeed, this suggestion is inconsistent with one of Rugg's earlier publications that defines a cemetery as, "any place in which the dead are buried" (Dunk and Rugg 1994:9). While an effort to classify burial sites for cross-comparative purposes is a laudable goal, caution should be employed to ensure the proper use of terminology as lax standards in this regard could create a legal basis to undermine existing protections.

Such efforts to delineate certain sites as cemeteries and others as "churchyards" or "places of disposal" represents a semantic discussion that does not change the legal or archaeological reality of such land: these places of burial, whether ordered or disordered, are cemeteries. Most modern legal traditions provide equally for the de jure legal protection afforded to such sites as Mount Auburn as to sites such as Charity Hospital Cemetery No. 2. Such inclusive-exclusive semantic discussions threaten what little agency has been provided to disenfranchised descendant communities by threatening to remove from existing protections certain types of deathscapes that do not conform to traditional models. Because these protections often rely on semantic classifications (i.e., what is and what is not a cemetery under the law is crucially important to that site's protection), such academic parsing of terminology can have real-life detrimental impacts on site preservation and protection (especially when the term "cemetery" is commonly used, at least in the United States, as an inclusive rather than an exclusive legal term).

The futility of such classifications is highlighted through Rugg's (2000:262) observation that cemeteries (as opposed to other burial sites), "will be divided by roads and paths: each grave will have an established 'address.'" Archaeology has borne out the fallacy of this ordered notion of places of burial, and the law, through such enactments as the Unmarked Burials Act, has followed archaeology's lead to extend legal protections to such unordered spaces. While some portions of what even Rugg (2000) might consider a cemetery follow these rules, even those contain disorganized sections of unmarked burials with no distinguishing markers or physical "addresses." An example of such cemeteries includes the potters' field in Fort Smith, Arkansas's Oak Cemetery. This unmarked field in an otherwise orderly cemetery contains undocumented pauper graves and the graves of convicts hanged on the town's nearby courthouse lawn (Seidemann 2014b). Archaeological investigations into traditional cemeteries have demonstrated the tendency of graves to stray beyond the known boundaries and to defy burial conventions (Seidemann and Kleinpeter 2014). Moreover, such sites as enslaved peoples' cemeteries are no less cemeteries because they do not contain marked graves or internal mapping or order.

Attempts to distinguish between such sites risk undermining the applicability of the legal protections reviewed here. In other words, to create a classification system in which places of interment or entombment are not identified as cemeteries is to strip those spaces of the protections that they have heretofore been afforded. While a semantic interest in such classifications may exist, the practical legal realities are too risky for site preservation purposes and are inconsistent with modern archaeological notions of what constitutes a cemetery.

Structural Violence and the Law's Role in Cemetery Site Protection

The evolution of theoretical concepts such as structural violence and the application of those concepts in archaeological and bioarchaeological contexts have resulted in a recognition of the social and psychological implications of the mistreatment of cemetery sites and human remains on descendant communities. By no means is this trend of increased scientificization and cultural awareness at an apex. As with any evolutionary process, the treatment of cemeteries and human remains will continue to change in response to external and internal pressures, most likely informed by the increasingly vocal interests of descendant communities.

The legal review contained in this research demonstrates that all the legislative efforts to enhance the methods for dealing with human remains and cemetery sites have been largely guided by the academic and legal elite. Absent from many of these laws is meaningful or substantial agency for the descendant communities to participate in the process of managing such sites and materials. NAGPRA is a single example of substantial agency provided to the descendant community in burial site and human remains protection legislation. With NAGPRA, the descendant community is a consulting party to such efforts at several stages of the process. In Louisiana, the only agency provided to the descendant community in the state's NAGPRA analogues (the Unmarked Burials Act and the Historic Cemetery Act) exists in the provisions that control the ultimate disposition of human remains following their excavation and removal from a cemetery. This shortcoming is not the fault of bureaucrats who enforce and administer these laws. Rather, it was caused by the intentional or unintentional shortsightedness of legislators. Greater agency for descendant communities at all levels of the cemetery interaction process is essential for the avoidance of structurally violent acts such as unilateral cemetery destruction and removal witnessed in Clearwater, Florida, and elsewhere. In most American jurisdictions, such agency, within the limits allowed by law, rests with the legislature to provide.

All the laws discussed herein operate within the general American limitations on the governmental controls of private property (Wright 2015). To be clear, neither NAGPRA nor its Louisiana analogues represent an absolute ban on the destruction of cemeteries—at least not those on private property. Because of the constitutional protections of private property rights embodied in the Fifth and Fourteenth Amendments to the U.S. Constitution, whether to repurpose a cemetery located on private land is solely within the discretion of the private property owner.[2] Certainly, such repurposing must be accomplished by adherence to the regulatory requirements of the applicable cemetery preservation laws, and no law sanctions a landowner's destruction of a cemetery. However, United States and Louisiana law permits the legal removal of the sacredness of a cemetery site by way of the removal of human remains and the cemetery dedication (Seidemann 2018a, 2018b). All of this activity can be accomplished without any input from, and indeed over the direct opposition of, descendant communities.

While recent legislative moves at the federal (African American Burial Grounds Network Act)[3] and state levels (Louisiana Slavery Ancestral Burial Grounds Preservation Commission)[4] seek mechanisms to provide increased agency to descendant communities of those whose cemeteries are most likely to be affected by development, such efforts are limited by the protections of private property embedded in the applicable constitutions. Moreover, with the recent passage of the African American Burial Grounds Preservation Act by Congress, it is also clear that legislators still do not understand the importance of providing agency to descendant communities when enacting ostensible burial protection legislation. This new law, while beginning as a meaningful African American analogue to NAGPRA, has been rendered largely impotent by amendments and wholly fails to provide any descendant community agency in any decisions or grants made by the National Park Service under the law (Seidemann 2023).

Unless amended at the constitutional level, descendant community agency powerful enough to supersede a private landowner's decision to remove a cemetery will never exist under federal or state law in the United States. Nonetheless, descendant community agency can be enhanced under existing laws by simply providing such people with input earlier in the cemetery removal process. Such changes can allow for descendant control over the types of narratives created from the moving of their ancestors' remains by mandating that certain types of scientific testing be done on human remains as part of the removal process or by limiting such testing.[5] Thus, while a comprehensive ban on the moving of cemeteries and human remains is unlikely in the United States under existing law, it is possible for descendant communities to have more control over the narratives that result from such impacts.

There can be little doubt that recent events such as the African Burial Ground project, coupled with increasing agency among underprivileged communities and the rise in consideration of multivocal archaeologies, have led to the passage of such laws as the Louisiana Human Remains Protection and Control Act. Such laws were specifically enacted to vest law enforcement and descendant communities with the ability to protect and reclaim human remains unlawfully looted from cemetery contexts. Laws such as these, though inspired by NAGPRA, bear little resemblance to their earlier forebears.

Can Louisiana's Protections Work Elsewhere?

As discussed in chapter 1, one of the primary purposes of this work is to determine whether the protections afforded cemeteries in Louisiana would be useful elsewhere for the protection of such sites. A few examples of the application of Louisiana law to other places follows as hypothetical possibilities of the utility of these protections elsewhere.

Among the many locales that have experienced cemetery damage partially as a result of inadequate legal protections is Dallas, Texas. In the 1940s, highway construction in North Dallas damaged a one-acre (0.4 hectare) portion of the North Dallas Freedman's Cemetery, an African American burial ground in use between 1869 and 1907 (Davidson 2007). During this time, there was no positive statutory cemetery dedication in Texas.[6] As in Louisiana at his time, however, there was a jurisprudentially recognized dedication of cemeteries that should have stopped the conversion of the Freedman's Cemetery to a roadway.[7] The law was apparently ignored and, similar to the St. Matthew's Baptist Church Cemetery in Florida and Charity Hospital Cemetery No. 2 in

Louisiana, the Freedman's Cemetery was simply converted to a road. In other words, Louisiana's dedication law, which, until 1974, was also only recognized jurisprudentially, is unlikely to result in any alternative outcome in Texas for the Freedman's Cemetery. Simply, this law only works when it is recognized and applied.

The outcome of the excavations of the remaining parts of this cemetery in the 1990s may have been different, though, at least from a descendant community perspective, had Texas implemented NAGPRA-style laws as early as did Louisiana. By the time of the road widenings in the 1990s that resulted in the excavation of 1,150 unmarked burials from the Freedman's Cemetery (Davidson 2007), Louisiana's Unmarked Burials Act was already in place and provided some measure of agency to descendant communities. Conversely, Texas's similar law was not enacted until nearly 20 years later (Seidemann 2012), thus leaving the African American community descended from those interred in the Freedman's Cemetery voiceless with regard to any disinterment, study, and reinterment plans for their ancestors' remains. Admittedly, even in Louisiana, these descendants today would only have agency with regard to reinterment decisions. However, in practice, since the passage of the Unmarked Burials Act, Louisiana state archaeologists have made efforts to consult with descendant communities throughout the entire process of development's interactions with cemeteries. No such equivalent existed in Texas at that time. Thus, from the perspective of descendant agency, whether those descendants are marginalized peoples or not, Louisiana's law has longer provided for their participation in the management of cemetery site impacts.

Perhaps a more striking example of a scenario in which Louisiana's cemetery protection laws could have changed the course of a structurally violent episode than the situation in Dallas is the African Burial Ground in New York. Because at the time of the African Burial Ground's discovery New York had no dedication or unmarked burials statutes in place, even those with the best intentions for that site's management had no legal guidance or direction. By the 1991 discovery of the African Burial Ground during the construction of the GSA building, Louisiana's legislature had enacted its Unmarked Burials Act—a law that provides a concise structure for the management of such sites. There is no doubt that, even as Louisiana's law stands today, it would not have provided the appropriate level of agency to the African American community in New York. However, the mismanagement of the site would likely have been substantially minimized by the framework of a law that contemplates some consultation with descendant communities. What is most stunning about the African Burial Ground situation in its early days is that the landowners—the U.S. government—had just months before passed sweeping empowerment legislation for the Native American community in the form of NAGPRA and yet it pushed ahead with its development plans for the African Burial Ground site in a manner that seemingly disregarded the disenfranchised African American descendant community. At that time, Louisiana's law—as would the law of such states as Missouri and Florida—would have mandated at least some meaningful consultation in analogous scenarios. Moreover, the Louisiana cemetery dedication laws, which still do not exist as positive statutory law in New York, would have mandated a full archaeological excavation of the African Burial Ground or a complete abandonment of the area containing burials for the GSA building to be constructed in compliance with the law. Arguably, though because, as discussed in a prior chapter, the dedication laws have long existed at general common law, their statutory and jurisprudential absence in New York to this day is irrelevant. As a common law state that inherited its legal tradition from Christian Rome by way of England, New York has courts where the notion of dedication laws exist, and such laws should be applied by them.

With the foregoing stated, Louisiana law also has far to go in providing meaningful agency to descendant groups. But again, Louisiana seems to be in the forefront of these efforts. Following Shell Oil Company's decision to set aside, preserve, and memorialize the site of a former enslaved people's burial ground on its Assumption Parish property in 2018 (McGill 2018), the state representative from that district, Kenneth Brass, recognized that this event was unique and that he wanted to ensure similar legislative protections for other enslaved people's cemeteries in Louisiana prospectively (Brass, pers. comm. 2018). The result of this event—the Slavery Ancestral Burial Grounds Preservation Commission—charges the Louisiana Department of Justice with identifying loopholes in cemetery site protection in Louisiana, especially for the burial sites of formerly enslaved people. LDOJ has not completed its review as of this writing. However, while a combination of the existing laws reviewed herein ensures the substantial protection of all cemetery sites in Louisiana (Seidemann 2014a, 2018a), what is still missing is descendant agency. This agency, to combat the landscape structural violence that is so often meted out disproportionately to disenfranchised peoples' spaces of death (Seidemann and Halling 2019), must be provided on the front end of the cemetery protection process. Descendant groups must have a voice in decisions regarding whether to disrupt a cemetery, how to disrupt a cemetery if that is the ultimate decision, what evaluations will be performed on human remains, and what questions will be asked from those tests. All these measures are essential to ensuring the protection and preservation of such sites and the according of proper respect and human dignity to the descendants of those dead. Indeed, contrary to the assertions made by Weiss and Springer (2020), such decisions cannot and should not be made only by those in the scientific community. Other stakeholders, most importantly descendant communities, are entitled to agency when making such decisions even if such decisions are to place the sanctity of the grave and human remains above the interests of scientific inquiry. Or, as was eloquently noted by Alfred Kroeber when asked if the remains of his friend, Ishi, could be anatomized, Kroeber stated "[i]f there is any talk about the interests of science, say for me that science can go to hell" (Shea 2000:49). Descendant groups should have the agency to provide the same response.

All the foregoing changes—legal and archaeological—must today be used to inform planning and development theory and practice. The expansive legal view of cemeteries informed by modern archaeological practice is of particular importance in planning circles (Kay 1998). Problems related to cemeteries and development are particularly acute at the intersections of modern development and former land uses.[8] As Kay (1998:1) observes:

> land developments, particularly those on the urban fringe of metropolitan areas, increasingly pressure once-rural cemeteries, small family plots, and unmarked or forgotten burial sites. . . . Existing urban cemeteries are also in conflict with more intensive land uses that may generate higher tax revenues for cash-strapped municipalities.[9]

As Kay (1998:5) further notes, the consequences of these interactions of development and cemeteries can have substantial planning, cost, and sometimes even criminal ramifications (see also Harvey 2006; Pitts 2015). Moreover, the threats to these cultural resources by development are not insignificant, and, in many cases (Kay 1998), the adverse impacts of development on cemeteries are meted out disproportionately on underprivileged groups whose burial sites may represent the nontraditional locales excluded from Rugg's (2000) definition of a cemetery. Importantly, it is precisely the efforts that led to the passage of NAGPRA and its successors in the 1990s and beyond—public awareness and activism—that represents the largest threat to developers who would run afoul of cemetery protections (e.g., Mitchell 2020). As Kay (1998:7) notes, "Native American protests have stopped or altered the development of such projects as a golf course in the Chicago area, a discount store in California, and a manufacturing facility in Minnesota." Thus, these sites and a sensitivity to their treatment is an essential part of the planning and development process today.

In many areas, more dead are present than the living (deSousa 2015). With the suite of laws currently in existence to protect the dead, planners must ensure that historic and prehistoric considerations are undertaken to account for the possibility of affecting cemeteries before beginning projects. Moreover, if remains are encountered during development, the penalties for not mitigating such sites are increasingly strong. At the heart of these admonitions is the reality that, in many cases, planners should be collaborating early with members of local communities to ensure that their concerns and desires are considered if cemeteries are encountered during development. Providing this agency to the descendant communities will often pave the way for cooperative mitigation of such sites if they are discovered. Indeed, as Paredes (1997:487) once observed of the agency granted to Native Americans by the passage of NAGPRA,

> Through the powerful medium of appeal to the widespread value of "respect for the dead," American Indians who lobbied so strongly for NAGPRA have forced the larger society to meet native peoples on an equal footing and accord them respect as fully human rather than treating them as objects, as merely the "Other."

In this way, as J. Anthony Paredes argues, "NAGPRA is not about the dead but about the living" (Paredes 1997:487). This statement is true of much that occurs in relation to mortuary sites and landscapes. The dead do not complain, but their descendants can and should be quite vocal regarding how the treatment of the dead and their landscapes affect the living (e.g., Aronson 2016). Presumably, increased agency provided through recent and proposed burial protection legislation in some states (e.g., the Slavery Ancestral Burial Grounds Preservation Commission in Louisiana) should have similar impacts on other disenfranchised groups.

Indeed, both archaeology and the law appear to be trending in the direction of increasing agency for descendant communities and protection for cemetery sites. Recent examples of these trends are the Society for American Archaeology's position statements regarding the progress of Indigenous and archaeological collaborations in the wake of NAGPRA's passage (Watkins 2020) and the organization's support for such legislation as earlier versions of the African American Burial Ground Network (Preservation Maryland 2019). In Louisiana, such examples are present in the recent passage of the Human Remains Trafficking and Control Act in 2016—a law that provides for strict protection of human remains and provides law enforcement with the authority to stem the illicit trade in such items and to collaborate with descendant communities for the respectful return of misappropriated remains.

Further support for disenfranchised groups' plight and lack of agency in cemetery and human remains studies is evident from the archaeological establishment's recent rebuke to the agency-stripping approaches to the study of the past advocated by Weiss and Springer (2020) (e.g., Boutin 2020). Such increased agency and collaboration are essential to the future protection of human remains and cemetery sites. This notion is not new (Franklin et al. 2022), but it is a critical component to both the preservation of culturally, psychologically, and archaeologically important deathscapes. These rebukes are good starting points for increasing the agency of black and Indigenous people as well as people of color (BIPOC), but they are not enough. BIPOC agency can be informed by such statements, but must be provided by state and federal legislation to have binding and meaningful effect, and local law enforcement must be trained regarding the harms of such lack of agency in order to provide the protections that this research has identified as historically meted out to the deathscapes of the underprivileged.

GLOSSARY OF LEGAL TERMS

These definitions are the author's own distillations of often complex legal concepts that have evolved over centuries. To ensure accuracy, the definitions were checked against Garner (2019), but the substance of the definitions are original.

amicus curiae A friend of the court. This term is often used to refer to entities or people who are not parties to a particular case but who have an interest in the case's outcome and who, because of this interest, submit informational briefs to the reviewing court.

ancestor-in-title Someone (individual or entity) in a chain of title before the current title holder.

attorney general This is, in the United States, generally an elected position in each state. The attorney general in most American jurisdictions serves as the chief legal officer of a state. Most attorneys general have broad civil and limited criminal jurisdictions. The U.S. Attorney General is an appointed position.

civil law A system of law present in the majority of the world. In a strict sense, the term refers to those jurisdictions that rely primarily on codified (written) legal codes. Although the historic development of this system is divergent from that of the common law system, most of the concepts in both systems are largely analogous and are simply referred to with different terms. In the United States, Louisiana is the only civil law jurisdiction.

cloud on title A problem in the title of a piece of property. Clouds on title may be adverse claims to ownership or other things that could make the property difficult to sell or to use to as collateral.

codify Written law as passed by a legislature.

common law The predominant legal system in the United Kingdom and its former colonies. This system of law is largely based upon jurisprudential precedent (judge-made law) to interpret parties rights.

corporeal movable A tangible thing that can be moved (i.e., a bone or an artifact).

corporeal immovable A tangible thing that cannot be moved (i.e., land or a structure).

curator For the purposes of this book, a party appointed by a court to represent the interests of unknown, unknowable, or uncontactable parties with an interest in particular litigation. This person is typically a lawyer.

decision A formal conclusion of a court or agency based upon the facts and the law that is typically accompanied by written explanations for the conclusion. At the appellate level, a decision must be that of a majority of the panel of judges sitting on a case.

dedication A particular designation for the use of land. Dedications are typically made by a then-current owner of the land and can be used to establish public roads or other such burdens. Cemeteries are also dedications, but, as discussed in the text, such dedications do not require a positive act (or even concurrence) of a landowner. These property burdens typically affect land indefinitely and require a specific judicial process for removal. These burdens also typically affect the value and allowable uses of the burdened property.

de facto In the context of this book, this term refers to the law as it is (or was) applied, not necessarily as it was written.

de jure In the context of this book, this term refers to the law as it was written and not as it is (or was) necessarily applied.

desecration For the purposes of this book, the intentional damage or destruction of a grave space or the human remains in that space.

detention The physical custody of a thing. This term typically refers, at least in a property law sense, to the possession of a movable thing and not necessarily to its ownership.

dictum The nonbinding discussion in a court decision. In court decisions, there is often a fair amount of context and set-up for the actual legal conclusion. Dictum is the term used to refer to this discussion. Although it is often incorrectly interpreted to be a part of a court's holding, it is (theoretically) intended to have no precedential value. In practice, all of what courts say is important and even the nonbinding discussion can have substantial impact on the interpretation of similar legal concepts in future cases.

discovery The process of obtaining relevant information for a legal case in advance of actual trial. This is the process during which the parties exchange information, documents, and testimony that they believe supports their position. If requested by an adverse party, this information is typically believed to be defeating to the opponent's case.

dissent In cases in which more than one (typically no less than three) judges sit on a panel to decide a case and one or more of them disagrees with the majority opinion, those disagreeing judges can author joint or individual opposing opinions to the majority. These opposing opinions are called dissents. Although they carry no precedential value nor do they have any impact on the outcome of that decision, they can be used as a basis to support further appeal by the losing party or to support similarly situated parties in different litigation. Dissents are exclusively the province of appellate courts.

district attorney In the United States, a district attorney is typically the highest elected legal officer for a particular county or parish. District attorneys exercise primary criminal jurisdiction for alleged violations of the law within their districts. This jurisdiction is limited only by recusals or requests for expert assistance from the state's attorney general or for those matters exclusively under the jurisdiction of the United States (as opposed to state law violations). District attorneys also have joint civil jurisdiction with state attorneys general in the former's district.

expropriation A process for the government (or other authorized party) to acquire private property or rights in the United States. In most cases, such acquisitions are required to be for public purposes (cf., *Kelo v. City of New London, Conn.*, 545 U.S. 469 [2005]) and are often opposed by the private landowner. Pursuant to the U.S. Constitution and state constitutions, such authority may be exercised through the payment of "just compensation" for the property. Expropriation is also often referred to as exercising the power of eminent domain.

holding The formal conclusion of a judicial decision. This portion of a court decision is often fairly short and concise, stating the ultimate conclusion for the outcome with little extraneous discussion. Holdings are distinguished from dictum, with the former containing the precedent-setting outcome and the latter containing various discussions and explanations of facts and law that are nonbinding.

incident In the context of this book, this term refers to an accompaniment to property ownership (i.e., the right to exclude is an incident of ownership).

judgment The implementing directive from a court for the holding. The judgment is typically a brief directive for the holding to be implemented. The term may also be used interchangeably with the term holding. The judgment carries the force of law once signed by a judge.

jurisdiction In the context of this book, this term refers to both the geographic limits of a legal officer's (i.e., attorney general or district attorney) authority and the legal limits of that authority. In terms of the legal limits, the maximum extent of that authority is set by constitution and statute.

jurisprudence Case law. In common law jurisdictions, jurisprudence has controlling effect. The term refers generally to any prior court decision, typically to a published decision.

jurisprudence constante The concept in civil law jurisdictions that stands for the proposition that the written (i.e., codal) law is the fundamental source of law and that, should a judge believe that a particular decision must depart from earlier jurisprudence, such a departure is authorized in the interest of adhering to the plain language of the law. This concept is seldom used in modern practice (cf., *Crooks v. Department of Natural Resources,* 2019–0160 [La. 1/29/20], 340 So.3d 574, in which the district judge explicitly invoked *jurisprudence constante* to depart from more than 200 years of court precedent).

law Generally, this term refers to the formal pronouncements of an entity imbued with lawmaking authority. In civil law jurisdictions, the law derives from state legislation, agency regulation, local ordinances, and, to a lesser extent, from court decisions. In common law jurisdictions, the general sources of law are the same with more authority placed on court decisions. Various jurisdictions also recognize historic custom as a secondary source of law (see, e.g., La. C.C. art. 1).

legislation Law created exclusively by elected representatives, whether at the state level by legislatures or general assemblies or at the local level by city councils or the like (also by the Foro in American Samoa, the Council in the District of Columbia, and the Commonwealth Legislature in the Northern Mariana Islands).

merchantable title Property title that is burdened with no clouds or defects and is immediately sellable.

occupancy Generally refers to the possession of property, whether movable or immoveable. One who occupies property is in possession of the property.

ordinance Law created by local tribunals such as city, county, or parish councils and the like. Such law is effective only within the geographic jurisdiction of the particular lawmaking body.

ownership Rights that create in the holder the reduction of a particular thing to direct, immediate control. Ownership is usually characterized by the right to use, benefit from, and alienate all or some of the property.

penal In the context of this book, this term refers to a law that carries criminal penalties and sanctions for its violation.

plenary authority Refers to a governmental body's complete ability to control something. For example, the U.S. Constitution confers plenary authority on Congress in terms of the ability to regulate interstate commerce and to regulate patents and bankruptcies. States cannot impinge on this exclusive authority.

prosecute The litigating of a matter, whether criminal or civil, by a government actor.

published decision Generally, court decisions only hold precedential value if the issuing court authorizes their publication. In this sense, publication means that the decision is authorized by the rendering tribunal for inclusion in case law books. The majority of these decisions occur at the appellate level (except in federal courts), and each state sets its own rules on the viability of unpublished decisions.

redact In the context of this book, this term is synonymous with the drafting of legislation.

regulation Contrasted with legislation, regulation is law created by government agencies pursuant to authority granted by a legislature. Although law, regulations are considered to be of lesser constitutional stability because they are drafted by bureaucrats as opposed to legislatures.

remand In appeals, an appellate court may send a case back to a lower court for consideration of all or a part of the matter in a manner consistent with the higher court's directives.

sepulchre From the Latin, sepulchre literally means "grave." The right of sepulchre is a common law concept that certain relatives have the right to control the disposition of the remains of their loved ones. This concept does not equate to ownership of the remains, but merely to a right or control. A similar concept exists in civil law jurisdictions.

sepulture In some cases, different spelling of sepulchre. In other cases, the placement of something in a grave.

servitude A burden on land such as a right-of-way or a right-of passage that benefits one estate to the detriment of the servient estate. Often known in common law as an easement. This is a right to use land that is short of full ownership of that land.

sine qua non For the purposes of this book, this term refers to essential things (i.e., something that is necessary and crucial).

standing The legal right to sue.

stare decisis The common law concept that courts are bound to follow prior precedent, Unlike *jurisprudence constante* in civil law jurisdictions, this concept does not allow for the discretionary departure from past court decisions when the legal questions are identical.

statute Generally, and for the purposes of this book, laws enacted by a legislative body at the state or federal level.

strict scrutiny A standard of review typically applied by courts to equal protection cases that requires courts to find a compelling interest that justifies a law or action when discrimination is alleged as against a suspect class of individuals.

suspect class In equal protection cases, this term refers generally to individuals and groups who are typically the subject of discrimination (i.e., race, national origin, sex, religion, etc.).

taking Term applied to the acquisition of property by a government or by a party acting under color of law. Takings are not necessarily illegal so long as they are accompanied by a right to due process and to just compensation.

tribunal In this book, this term is used to refer to an entity before which legal cases are presented for decision. These might include courts, administrative agencies, or similar such bodies.

vested constitutional right This is a right guaranteed by a federal or (relevant) state constitution that is owned by a particular party. In the absence of that ownership (i.e., vesting), the law recognizes no right to protect. Conversely, once such rights are owned, a party has standing to protect those rights.

NOTES

Chapter 1. Introduction

1 Importantly, in 2010, Louisiana's law related to desecration or disturbance of graves was substantially weaker than it is today. This case would have been much simpler to bring, both civilly and criminally, under the current law discussed throughout this book.

2 This high standard of proof (in a criminal context) was recently reviewed in federal cases for human remains, and cultural items trafficking and the implications for viable prosecutions are dire (McKeown 2023).

3 As is often the case with legislation, many U.S. jurisdictions simply copy others' existing laws when enacting similar legislation. In this regard, Texas's definition of "cemetery" is identical to Louisiana's definition. Tx. Health & S. § 711.001(4). Admittedly, even Louisiana's and Alabama's definitions cited here, though distinct, are substantially similar. Contrarily, some states (e.g., Mississippi) provide no statutory definition for cemeteries.

4 These sites are addressed in chapter 6.

5 This eventuality is purely a result of modern cemetery functionality that allows for the legal dedication of land to cemetery uses before any remains are buried in the land.

6 There are certainly examples of nonhuman burials prehistorically and historically. One example is the human and animal interments at the ancient site of Ur in Mesopotamia (Greenfield et al. 2022) (admittedly, many of these animals are believed to have been sacrificial). See also Collier (2016) recounting animal and human burial in various contexts. In such situations, it is the presence of human remains that imbues the land with special legal status. This is important as various jurisdictions (e.g., Louisiana and New York) begin to authorize pet burials in otherwise human cemeteries. The interment of the pets does not declassify the land as a cemetery (though a pets-only cemetery would not classify as a cemetery under this definition). Rather, the presence of human remains affords the entire site a protected status.

7 Professional physical anthropology has also had a troubled history (see chapter 3). The prevailing term for the postmodern field of physical anthropology is "biological anthropology" and both terms are used in this book in their appropriate contexts to distinguish modern scientific inquiry from the troubled past of the field.

8 While the *ownership* of human remains may be legally settled in the United States, various interests, and to some extent, the Native American Graves Protection and Repatriation Act (NAGPRA), have continued the debate over whether such items should be owned at all. Basic U.S. law is fairly consistent with regard to who has the authority

to *control* human remains for the purposes of disposition within a generation or so following death (e.g., La. R.S. 8:655). However, this *control* is not *ownership.* It is a right of *control* and it extends to only a few people. *Ownership* of human remains is nonexistent (*possession, occupancy,* or *detention* lesser property rights than *ownership* may apply to human remains). Contrary to all other laws, NAGPRA purports to create a category of human remains—Indian, Native Alaskan, and Native Hawaiian—that can be "*owned*" (25 U.S.C. § 3002). Even the "*ownership*" of NAGPRA, from a strictly legal standpoint, appears to function more like *control* and *possession* of human remains than actual *ownership.*

9 The words "Indigenous American," "Native American," and "Indigenous" are used throughout this book. These are different terms signifying different people. "Indigenous American" is the term used to refer to all peoples indigenous to the Americas (and Hawaii). "Native American" is the term used (unless used as a defined legal term) to refer to American Indians (i.e., excluding other Indigenous Americans such as Alaska Natives, Native Hawaiians, Canadian First Nations, and the Indigenous inhabitants of Central and South America and the Caribbean). "Indigenous" is the term used to refer to the original peoples inhabiting any particular place (e.g., Australian Aborigines) or native people inhabiting an area before or at the time of European colonization (e.g., the Inca, the Taínos, et al.). Finally, the term "Indian" is used only in direct quotations from other sources.

10 The term "New World" is used in this book. Some authors have indicated that this term is a colonial holdover that should now be avoided in the academic literature (e.g., Adame 2023). Other scholars recognize the colonialist origin of this term as it is applied to Earth's Western Hemisphere lands. They do not propose a wholesale rejection of the term but merely a recognition of the colonialism from which it derived (e.g., Parsons 2021). In this book, I reject the former and employ the latter perspective regarding the term "New World." While, as Adame (2023) notes, this term was first applied to the Americas by Amerigo Vespucci in AD 1503, and is thus directly derived from European colonizers, so, too, are the more specific names for places in the Americas that Adame suggests as substitutes (e.g., "Caribbean," which is known to have derived from the name given to a region by Europeans and even then based on a corrupted interpretation of the name used by the Taínos for groups in the southern Caribbean—"Carib"—referring to these peoples as cannibals) (Keegan 1992). While sensitive to decolonializing anthropology, I do not view the term "New World" as overtly or necessarily colonial. Scientific reality tells us that the Western Hemisphere lands were among the last, if not the last, parts of Earth to be colonized by humans (e.g., Dillehay 2000; Pigati et al. 2023). Indeed, many areas of the Pacific were settled by humans by or before 40,000 BP (Irwin 1994). On both a geographic and anthropological time scale, the northern, central, and southern continents of the Western Hemisphere are "new" to humanity, not just to Europeans. For this reason, I retain this commonly understood and not overtly colonialist term for ease of reference in this book.

11 Knick v. Township of Scott, Pennsylvania, 139 S.Ct. 2162, 2187–2188 (2019) (Justices Ruth Bader Ginsburg, Steven Breyer, and Sonia Sotomayor also joined in this dissent).

Chapter 2. Cemeteries as Windows into Structural Violence on a Landscape Scale

1 Horn (2018) also recounts similar events in New York City in her recent book on the nineteenth-century asylum, almshouse, workhouse, and prison on Blackwell's Island.

2 This federal legislation, NAGPRA, was inapplicable to this site because that law protects only certain Native American burial grounds and is particularly useless for non-Native cemeteries (Blakey 2010; Seidemann 2010a).

3 3 N.Y.2d 37, 43 (1957) (recognizing restrictions on land put to cemetery uses).

4 In this regard, historic newspapers demonstrate that the New Orleans government was actively involved in efforts to repurpose Charity Hospital Cemetery No. 1 as a gas station (Anon. 1930). Moreover, under cover of COVID-19 lockdowns, the City of New Orleans permitted the constructions of eating establishments atop a portion of the Charity Hospital Cemetery No. 2 in a location long-defended from such invasions by State of Louisiana actors.

5 In the interest of completeness, it is important to note that portions of St. Louis Cemetery No. 1 are not fully extant. A large portion of the cemetery lies beneath structures and green space in the blocks west and north of the visible cemetery boundaries (Godzinski et al. 2013). How these portions of the cemetery came to be used for noncemetery purposes is unclear, but it is believed that these are the graves of non-Catholics and underprivileged (i.e., Jews, Protestants, enslaved peoples, et al.).

6 While the relevant part of this translation (i.e., that regarding the closing of the old cemetery to make way for residences and the opening of a new cemetery outside the city) is clear and correct, the typed transcription of the original Spanish should be viewed with caution. As Carlin (2014:xvii) has observed of written Spanish of this period: "the Spanish writers of this time . . . wrote with great syntactic and orthographic latitude[:] . . . spelling was inconsistent and variable[, and] punctuation did not exist in any useful form. . . . In addition, the scribes made extensive use of original, creative, and curious abbreviations." Thus, even with high-resolution scans, caution is required with regard to the remainder of the transcription.

7 Although not the subject of this research, there has been debate in the past regarding whether the decree that removed the dedication from the St. Peter Street Cemetery was validly obtained (see Morazán 1972 and Gray 2017 for a review). Nonetheless, the legal effect of the decree as it relates to the cemetery dedication removal, especially this long after its issuance with later parties relying in good faith on its existence, is that there is no longer a cemetery dedication burdening this property.

8 96 So.2d 29, 33 (La. 1957).

9 81 So.2d 855 (La. 1955).

10 It is interesting to note that, though much of the bereavement literature acknowledges the negative impact of grief to individuals' personal growth (Hogan and Schmidt 2002:619–620), recent work has also shown that there may be later personal growth rebounds as a result of the grief (Riley et al. 2007). Indeed, as recently noted, personal growth deriving from grief is considered a "successful adaptation" to a loss and not a sine qua non of such an experience. (Anderson and Gaugler 2006:304, citing Hogan et al. 2001, and defining "personal growth" as "increases in tolerance, compassion, forgiveness, and hope").

11 E.g., Verified Petition for Temporary Restraining Order and Injunctive Relief, Rise St. James and Sharon Levigne v. FG LA, LLC, Docket No. 39963, Div. D, Twenty-Third Judicial District Court, Parish of St. James, State of Louisiana (filed June 15, 2020). See also Complaint, Inclusive Louisiana, et al. v. St. James Parish, et al., Docket No. 2:23-cv-00987, Eastern District of Louisiana (filed March 21, 2023).

12 For the purposes of this book, I acknowledge that the legal permitting scheme created by Louisiana's legislature in 1974 and today enforced by the LCB is probably, in and of itself, structurally violent to many African American communities. In this regard, because many African American cemeteries in Louisiana began as enslaved peoples' burial grounds, little or no written record of their ownership exists and even less is known about the use and location of the interments in these sites. Because Louisiana law requires title to a cemetery (or the permission of the titleholder) as well as a map of all burials in the cemetery to operate, a de jure reading of the existing law sets many African American communities up for failure when attempting to comply with the law. The reasoning for these legal requirements is sound: (1) to ensure that the actual landowner has authorized the interment of human remains on the land so that the dead are not at risk of eviction; and (2) to ensure that each person's burial place is known and can be avoided in future interment activity. However, this reasoning often does not fit with the historical realities of African American cemeteries' histories. It is beyond the scope of this research to fully analyze this potential problem and to suggest amendments. However, the LCB's staff often works with such communities to ensure that this de jure situation is minimized in a de facto application of the law.

Chapter 3. The Native American Graves Protection and Repatriation Act and Its Louisiana Progeny

1 An unresolved dispute still exists regarding who actually attained the North Pole first: Peary, Dr. Frederick Albert Cook, Admiral Richard Byrd, or Roald Amundsen. Although each of the former three made claims to be the first to the North Pole, only Amundsen and his dirigible crew in 1926 can definitely be said to have been the first (Bown 2012).

2 This was not a first for Peary, as he "supplied" 59 live Labrador Inuit for the 1893 World's Fair ethnographic displays (Hinsley 2016:40). As with the AMNH situation, tragedy also befell many of these earlier exhibited people by way of deaths and harsh treatment.

3 In this regard, Katarzyna Person (2021:107) characterized Jews serving in the Odnungsdienst—a semi-voluntary Jewish police force in World War II–era ghettos—as "react[ing] in a way that would preserve their self interest," whereby a seeming collaboration with the Nazis often was done as a means to protect one's own family. See also Randall Kennedy's (2008) accounts of African Americans acting similarly with their white oppressors in the Jim Crow American South. Isabel Wilkerson (2020) addresses these similarities by demonstrating how the Nazis took cues from the practices of southern American white people in the implementation of their own oppression and terror tactics.

4 25 U.S.C. §§ 3001 et seq.; P.L. 101–601. McKeown (2008) states that this lobbying began in earnest in 1986, but later (McKeown 2012) notes, along with Thomas (2000), that the effort was a longer-running process.

5 NAGPRA was not the first statement by legislatures in the United States on the treatment of Native American human remains (Zimmerman 2014). It was preceded at the federal level by the National Museum of the American Indian Act, P.L. 101–195; 20 U.S.C. § 80(q), which regulated repatriation of the Smithsonian Institution's collections. Additionally, a few states issued burial protection laws before 1990. Missouri's RS MO. 194.400–410, passed in 1987, is an example of such a state law (Price 1988).

6 Senator John McCain (R-AZ), Congressional Record, October 26, 1990, p. S17173. See also Lynge (2008), which observes that repatriation law in any country is human rights legislation.

7 S. Rep. No. 96–179 at 1, 6 (1979); H.R. Rep. No. 96–311 at 7, 13 (1979).

8 S. Rep. No. 96–179 at 6 (1979).

9 H.R. Rep. No. 96–311 at 13 (1979).

10 The Archaeological Resources Protection Act of 1979; and the Frederick Law Olmstead National Historic Site: Hearings on S. 490 and S. 495, Before the Subcomm. on Parks, Recreation, and Renewable Resources, 96th Cong. at 40 (1979).

11 *U.S. v. Diaz,* 499 F.2d at 115. This case involved the criminal trial of a man who had taken some Apache face masks that were made by a medicine man in 1969 or 1970 from a cave on the San Carlos Indian Reservation in Arizona. Writing for the Ninth Circuit, Judge Merrill found the absence of a definition of the term "object of antiquity" in the Antiquities Act to render the law unconstitutionally vague and in violation of the defendant's due process rights. The court noted that "[o]ne must be able to know, with reasonable certainty, when he has happened on an area forbidden to his pick and shovel and what objects he must leave as he has found them." *U.S. v. Diaz,* 499 F.2d at 114. This language substantially undermined the utility of the Antiquities Act as a looting deterrent as well as its use for future criminal prosecutions.

12 H.R. Rep. No. 96–311 at 7 (1979). See also Ades (1995).

13 The term "Native American" is used as a general moniker in this book roughly referring to those who ethnically and culturally identify themselves with the Indigenous peoples of the New World. The use of this term is with cognizance of the reality that "Native America" is made up of diverse and individual cultures, identities, and belief systems (see Afrasiabi 1997; Dunbar-Ortiz 2014). This is a reality often missed by the legal community, evident when authors speak of "Native American religion" rather than "Native American religions."

14 Arndt (2023:469) argues that, though the most memorable portion of Deloria's work, the anthropology critique was not intended to be the thrust of his book, which was federal recognition and its termination. Rather, these "hyperbolic statements about anthropologists" are sometimes taken to "provoke action" against the profession. Instead, Deloria's critique was intended to be a clarion call to anthropologists to assist Native Americans in their recognition battles. Whether intended or not and whether hyperbolic or not, these critiques have paved the way for tensions between anthropologists and Native Americans for some time.

15 The HeLa cell research referred to here is the continuing research on cancerous cells extracted from Henrietta ("He") Lacks ("La") in the 1950s without her or her family's consent that today forms the basis of genetics-based cancer research around the world (Skloot 2011). The poor, African American Lacks became the unknowing and unconsenting donor of cellular material when she was being treated for cervical cancer

at Johns Hopkins University Hospital and has recently become the standard example of failures of medically informed consent and the use of disenfranchised peoples as unwitting medical test subjects.

16 The Tuskegee syphilis research was longitudinal research on African Americans at the Tuskegee Institute in the early to mid-twentieth century sponsored by the U.S. government and others whose researchers were later shown to have been withholding critical aspects of the research and available treatments from the test subjects. The study took advantage of the patients' lack of agency to use them as "'clinical material, not sick people'" (Thomas and Quinn 1991:1501). This research was later characterized as "almost like genocide" by the Centers for Disease Control and Prevention (Thomas and Quinn 1991:1502).

17 Indeed, one reviewer has characterized the case studies in this source as "outdated and comically selective" (Kakaliouras 2021:645).

18 This U.S. Supreme Court case was a constitutional challenge to a fundamentalist-passed law in Louisiana known as the Louisiana Balanced Treatment for Creation-Science and Evolution-Science in Public School Instruction Act. The law, which sought equal footing of Christianity-based creationism in science classes in which evolutionary theory was taught, was intended to "provide persuasive advantage to a particular religious doctrine that rejects the factual basis of evolution in its entirety." *Edwards*, 482 U.S. at 592. The court held that such a blatant favoring of "a particular religious belief, the Act endorses religion in violation of the First Amendment." *Edwards*, 482 U.S. at 593.

19 An example of the actual recovery and repatriation efforts of human remains as representing additional cultural and historical information regarding the remains—especially when those remains are of unknown individuals—can be found in Seidemann (2017). What this source demonstrates is that, though sometimes repatriation results in an end to data collection on a particular set of remains, the story of that individual continues to inform anthropology and history through its broader postmortem-journey narrative.

20 Such perspectives are not limited to Indigenous Americans as Muyard (2016) has demonstrated among the Indigenous inhabitants of Taiwan.

21 Throughout this book, the term "other" is used to refer to nonwhite people. Such a distinction between those in power (in this case, privileged white people) and those not in power (here, the underprivileged and, more often than not, people of color) has become an important area of inquiry in historical archaeology in the past few decades (Little 1997; Wilkie 2005; Gray 2011).

22 This term is used here in quotation marks to indicate the perspective of many anthropologists of this time that the living peoples that they were studying were a "primitive" other or something of a throwback to early humanity. For example, Robert Lowie (1970:ix) once defined "primitive" thus: "[t]he word 'primitive' by its etymology suggests 'primeval,' but when the anthropologist speaks descriptively of 'primitive peoples' he means no more—at least, he has no right to mean more—than peoples of a relatively simple culture; or to be more specific, the illiterate peoples of the world."

23 Many early researchers of human skeletal anatomy were physicians by training, and the field did not really emerge as an anthropological subdiscipline until the collabora-

tions of Franz Boas (trained as a physicist) and Aleš Hrdlička (trained as a physician) in the final decade of the nineteenth century.

24 It is well documented today that Charles Darwin saw the application of his theories to interpretations of culture as improper and that late nineteenth-century and later notions of racism were anathema to Darwin's theories and thinking (Desmond and Moore 2009).

25 While these aspects of early anthropology in which colonial scientists pillaged Indigenous and other underprivileged groups' mortuary landscapes were often shameful, other aspects of anthropology were progressive for their time. Indeed, many of the same practitioners noted in this chapter as having mistreated human remains (e.g., Franz Boas and several of his students) were at the forefront of early to mid-twentieth-century efforts to combat racism in America (see, e.g., Gupta and Stoolman 2022; Bashow 2023). Thus, painting even the people discussed here as universally bad actors would be disingenuous.

26 Comment of Rep. Faleomavaega during the Joint Hearings before the Committee on Interior and Insular Affairs House of Representatives and the Subcommittee on Libraries and Memorials of the Committee on House Administration and the Subcommittee on Public Buildings and Grounds of the Committee on Public Works and Transportation, One Hundred First Congress, H.R. 2668, National American Indian Museum Act, p.226 (March 9, 1989). In fairness, this was apparently a recurring statement by Rep. Faleomavaega, who, in 2006, during the Joint Hearing before the Subcommittee on Africa, Global Human Rights and International Operations and the Subcommittee on Asia and the Pacific of the Committee on International Relations, One Hundred Ninth Congress, p. 178 (March 29, 2006), stated that "[t]he next time I catch an anthropologist coming to my islands, I am going to shoot them. We have had more problems [with] these anthropologists studying my people to death."

27 It is important to note that the United States was not the first nation to enact such sweeping legislation to protect Indigenous human remains. Australia passed similar legislation in 1984, and other countries have followed suit since (Seidemann 2004, 2020). Other nations, such as Sweden, have also worked toward repatriation of materials to their own Indigenous peoples (Harlin 2008).

28 It is crucial to note that NAGPRA provided such agency only to federally recognized Native American tribes, Native Hawaiian Organizations, and Alaska Native Corporations (Chapman et al. 2020). Although later state enactments have expanded the reach of human remains protection laws to state-recognized groups and others, this remains a shortcoming of NAGPRA.

29 See, generally, Meighan 1992, 1994. Perhaps Meighan's (1992, 1994) perception that NAGPRA would spell doom for skeletal studies—especially those conducted on Native American human remains—is partially justifiable because of the temporal proximity of his writings to the passage of NAGPRA. What is more surprising is the continued adherence to such a notion on the fringes of bioarchaeology more than 30 years on (see Weiss and Springer 2020, 2023). Simply, the end of this field of study has not come to pass, and practitioners such as Weiss and Springer (2020) need to move past the hurtful rhetoric of the early NAGPRA years in order for this field of inquiry to truly thrive.

30 The complexity of applying this law to culturally unaffiliated human remains was on display during what was colloquially known as the Kennewick Man litigation (Bonnichsen v. U.S., 357 F.3d 962 [9th Cir. 2004]); Bonnichsen v. U.S., 367 F.3d 864 (9th Cir. 2004); Bonnichsen v. U.S., 217 F.Supp. 2d 1116 (D.Or. 2002) in which northwest Native American groups fought with several anthropologists over the right to study or reinter 9,000-year-old human remains discovered in Washington State (Schneider and Barron 2014; Seidemann 2003). This litigation and the vagueness of NAGPRA regarding its application to unaffiliated remains was resolved in 2015 when the National Park Service promulgated regulations of questionable legal authority mandating repatriation of many such remains (Seidemann 2009).

31 The term "Native American" is one fraught with positive and negative connotations as well as being susceptible to innumerable definitions. In the context of the NAGPRA discussions in this book, "Native American" is used as a legal term to refer to federally recognized Indigenous groups (i.e., Native Americans, Native Hawaiians, and Alaska Native Corporations, as well as any juridical persons authorized to act for such peoples under the law).

32 Although not the subject of this book, the regulatory efforts by the National Park Service (NPS) over the past decade or more have, according to some (e.g., Seidemann 2009; cf., Tsosie 2012) expanded the scope of the plain language of NAGPRA. This risk of regulating in areas beyond the scope of enabling legislation is that such laws are at risk of constitutional challenges as being unlawful delegations of congressional authority, thus exposing all actions taken thereunder to reversal. In other words, if NPS's culturally unaffiliated remains and artifacts regulations are ever declared to be unconstitutional, the protections intended to exist for these items can be wiped away with the stroke of a judge's pen.

33 Because many of these items are simply left in institutional collections, NAGPRA and the NPS's regulations actually serve an unintended benefit to archaeologists by providing an accessible database of the locations of millions of artifacts and even (occasionally) human remains that are still available for study. No such universal catalogue existed until the passage of NAGPRA and the NPS regulations.

34 The term "possession" as it relates to human remains is critical for an understanding of all related laws. Under no legal system is there any acknowledged right of ownership in human remains with the exception of the individual whose remains they are. In other words, one owns their own bones, organs, and other tissues. However, anyone else, unless explicitly provided ownership pursuant to the donor's consent, can only ever "possess" human remains. Thus, NAGPRA, because it speaks of "ownership" of human remains, may be the only deviation from the notion of possession in any legal tradition, and this deviation is a stark one from centuries of existing law in common and civil law traditions. Moreover, because there is such a substantial break with precedent with the use of the term "ownership" in NAGPRA, it is debatable that even Congress intended something other than possession to apply under this law. Accordingly, NAGPRA's "ownership" is here referred to as the possession recognized for all other human remains. Although perhaps a strictly academic distinction, because precision is key to legal interpretations, erring on the side of precedent (as his done here) is akin to erring on the side of caution.

35 This estimate seems overly conservative, and it is certainly not an indication of the number of individual bones or bone fragments in such institutions, which should number in the millions.

36 As interpreted by the District of Oregon and later the U.S. Court of Appeals for the Ninth Circuit in the matter of *Bonnichsen v. United States* (known colloquially as the Kennewick Man case). Bonnichsen v. U.S., 357 F.3d 962 (9th Cir. 2004); Bonnichsen v. U.S., 367 F.3d 864 (9th Cir. 2004); Bonnichsen v. U.S., 217 F.Supp. 2d 1116 (D.Or. 2002). Although it is arguable that the NPS regulations have superseded this decision regarding what is and what is not culturally affiliated under NAGPRA, the *Bonnichsen* case stands as the only-existing critical analysis of the affiliation question under NAGPRA and also as a significant constitutional challenge to the viability of the NPS's culturally unidentifiable regulations (especially the "geographic affiliation" standard in those regulations) should suit ever be brought to test the legal viability of these rules.

37 The term "deathcare" has been defined by Kopp and Kemp (2007:151) thus: "The death care industry can be divided into five primary components: (1) funeral homes, (2) crematories, (3) cemeteries, (4) preneed sales of funeral plans, and (5) third-party sales of funeral goods" (citing General Accounting Office 2003).

38 Congress has made a recent attempt to make such cases more attractive to prosecutors by amending NAGPRA's penalties from first conviction misdemeanor to first conviction felony (McKeown 2023). States should take notice.

Chapter 4. The Cemetery Dedication and Archaeology

1 It is important to note that the name "St. Peter Street Cemetery" is not necessarily the actual moniker for the site given or used by New Orleans' colonial inhabitants. That name has been lost to time. The name today is merely a reference to the site's location at the intersection of St. Peter and Rampart streets.

2 This seemingly antiquated nature of New Orleans cemeteries continues in such places as Holt Cemetery, where a walk across the site is a study in human osteology (Seidemann and Seidemann 2005; Krummel 2013).

3 It is important to note that the focus of Demirakin's research was the use of expropriation power in Turkey to change the use of a cemetery to something else. It is disappointing that his research did not delve into the questions of what became of the human remains that may have needed to be moved as a result of such expropriations.

4 These experiences derived from the realities of applying the later-enacted cemetery protection laws discussed herein to sites after the discovery of forgotten cemeteries during Hurricane Katrina rebuilding efforts. As was discovered, all such legal concepts have work-arounds that undermine strong protections for cemeteries such as the Unmarked Burials Act's and the Historic Preservation Act's requirements for excavation only of human remains that might be disturbed by new construction rather than a requirement to protect all remains within the footprint of a project, regardless of whether they will actually be directly affected (Seidemann 2010b, 2010c; 2010d).

5 To be clear, the interactions with the St. Peter Street Cemetery site reuse were never anything but cordial, and no adverse legal action was necessary. The landowner's forethought and cooperation in this regard were refreshing.

6 Important exceptions to this reality have begun to emerge from the planning literature in Scandinavia, where scholars are actively advocating for the incorporation of existing cemeteries into city planning (e.g., Nordh and Evensen 2018; Grabalov and Nordh 2020).

7 As with the St. Peter Street Cemetery, the "Girod Street Cemetery" is the common moniker used by New Orleanians to refer to the Christ Church Cemetery once located on Girod Street in the Central Business District. The common, modern name is used here.

8 Although La. R.S. 8:307 is a part of the cemetery dedication, it merely contains procedural notice requirements for the removal of the dedication and is thus not reproduced here.

9 See, e.g., M.J. Farms, Ltd. v. ExxonMobil Corp., 2007–2371 (La. 7/1/08), 998 So.2d 16; Landgraf v. USI Film Products, 511 U.S. 244 (1994).

10 Exceptions to this reality include the prohibition of mineral exploration in cemeteries (now, La. R.S. 8:901), which was enacted in Louisiana in 1940 as a response to the facts elicited in the matter of Humphreys v. Bennett Oil Corp., 179 So. 222 (La. 1940) (discussed in the next chapter).

11 It is noteworthy that, in at least two jurisdictions—Rhode Island (Seidemann 2013:19–20) and Minnesota (National Trust for Historic Preservation 1990)—courts have suggested that it is questionable whether regulation of burial sites on private property is, in fact, a taking under the United States and state constitutions. Although presented with this issue in the matter of Knick v. Township of Scott, 139 S.Ct. 2162 (2019), the U.S. Supreme Court has yet to opine on the constitutionality of such laws (Seidemann 2018b).

12 Choppin v. LaBranche, 20 So. 681, 682 (La. 1896).

13 Humphreys v. Bennett Oil Corp., 197 So. 222, 228 (La. 1940).

14 Humphreys v. Bennett Oil Corp., 197 So. 222, 229 (La. 1940) (quoting Jackson 1936:206).

15 Humphreys v. Bennett Oil Corp., 197 So. 222, 229 (La. 1940) (quoting Jackson 1936:206).

16 As recently observed by one legal scholar (Stinson 2010:220–221): "Because of the rule-making power judges enjoy under principles of stare decisis, our judicial system depends on understanding what is and what is not a holding. Everyone agrees that subsequent courts are bound only by a prior case's holding. But too often lawyers argue for, and judges treat, extraneous statements made in a prior case—that is, *dicta*—as holding."

This observation highlights the inherent problem present in the *Humphreys* case to have non-controlling commentary regarding the ephemeral nature of the cemetery dedication in the published jurisprudence in Louisiana. Though that statement was not intended to be controlling and, indeed, it should not be, there is risk that the disappearing dedication may be picked up by a later court as part of the controlling holding of the case. One potential distinction in Louisiana is that, unlike Stinson's observation regarding *stare decisis,* this concept—which establishes the controlling nature of prior legal decisions in a common law jurisdiction—does not exist in Louisiana. Louisiana is governed by the concept of *jurisprudence constante* which, while similar to *stare decisis,* allows for judges to depart from prior rulings when the circumstances warrant (Maraist 2019).

17 City of New Orleans v. Christ Church Corp., 81 So.2d 855, 861 (La. 1955).

18 Touro Synagogue v. Goodwill Industries of New Orleans Area, Inc., 96 So.2d 29, 29 (La. 1957).

19 Anecdotal evidence exists that, before the advent of modern archaeological methods in the dedication removal process in the 1990s–2000s, much of this "respectful" removal was accomplished with laborers digging up remains under the loose supervision of funeral directors or clergy (e.g., Kretzler 2012). While such an approach may have been reasonably calculated to account for the proper moving of human remains in sturdy burial containers, experience has shown that it was not unusual for human remains to be missed and left behind during these relocation events when the burial containers had broken down and the remains had become mixed with the surrounding matrix. Although such a scenario was of concern in the situation in the *Touro Synagogue* matter, during post–Hurricane Katrina excavations at the site (Seidemann 2010b; Hahn et al. 2017), later analyses of the bone material recovered in those excavations demonstrated that no human remains were encountered (Halling, pers. comm. 2022).

20 Similar royal decrees were issued in the eighteenth century by Louis XVI of France for the Cimetière des Innocents, but efforts at that site were made to remove the remains to Paris's catacombs (Legacey 2019; Melville 2022).

21 Recent histories of English common law, though focusing on the development of that legal system from the Anglo-Saxon period onward, acknowledge the not-insignificant influence of Roman legal concepts on the common law (Hogerty 1992; Sandberg 2023; Watkin 2007).

22 For international purposes, it is important to note that the majority of the world has adopted some form of civil (rather than common) law system, making the link in these countries to Roman law direct.

23 Scarre's (1995:85) characterization of the stable government period as lasting for 80 years is a bit perplexing, as the emperors in this period spanned a 144-year range. However, limiting the time to just the closest constriction of emperors in this mold (Marcus Aurelius to Alexander Severus), the dates run for roughly 74 years.

24 Indeed, as recently as 2019, Justice Neil Gorsuch of the U.S. Supreme Court discusses Roman law in a published dissent in *Gamble v. United States,* 139 S.Ct. 1960, 1998 (2019) (Gorsuch, J., dissenting) (this specific case involved the interpretation of the jurisdiction of both federal and state legal systems in the United States' criminal law system). See also Minerva Surgical, Inc. v. Hologic, Inc., 141 S.Ct. 2298, 2319 (2021) (Barrett, J., dissenting) (a patent case in which certain procedural concepts are recognized as deriving from "'the Roman law and the Canonists.'").

25 By way of reference, hundreds of Louisiana cases directly reference Roman law precursors to the modern Louisiana Civil Code. See, e.g., Acurio v. Acurio, 2016–1395 (La. 5/3/17), 224 So.3d 935, 940, fn. 1 (Weimer, J., dissenting) (referencing Roman concepts for interpreting Louisiana's civil code).

26 Most civil law jurisdictions recognize custom as a source of law. See, e.g., La. C.C. art. 1.

27 There is no doubt that today these ancient concepts are not still wholly applicable to religious property. The law as it relates to that property has continued to evolve. However, much cemetery law relating to land use limitations has gone unchanged for centuries.

28 Further, the French Napoleonic Code also contains no cemetery-specific laws (though this is probably less important for the purposes of this review, as Louisiana was already an American territory by the time of the enactment of the Napoleonic Code).

29 Of course, just because such rights impingements are disfavored does not mean that they are illegal. Indeed, the United States and Louisiana constitutions make provision for such activities by requiring that property owners be provided "just compensation" if their rights are unreasonably restricted by regulation. U.S. Const., Amend. V, XIV; La. Const art. I, sec. 4.

30 See, e.g., Narragansett Improvement Co. v. Wheeler, 21 A.3d 430 (R.I. 2011) (a Rhode Island Supreme Court case noting that cemeteries are merely a condition of the property much like a hill or a stream).

31 Martínez-Fernández (1992:25) notes that the Spanish similarly restricted Jews and others with the observation that "Jews, Muslims, Protestants and new converts [to Catholicism] were barred from the Spanish domains when *limpieza de sangre* became a requisite for immigration."

32 Though these portions of St. Louis No. 1 Cemetery are known to have been put to non-cemetery uses without the removal of human remains, this cemetery is not contained in the structural violence discussions in this book. The reason for this is simple: At this time, not enough is known about the conversion of this property from a cemetery to other uses, and not enough is known about those buried in this portion of the cemetery to make any definitive conclusions regarding this property use conversion. A cursory search of archival records and anecdotal information regarding the nature of those interred (i.e., minorities and underprivileged people) suggest that this cemetery reuse was legally unsanctioned and likely represents yet another example of landscape structural violence much like the situation at Charity Hospital Cemetery No. 2. But additional research—archival, archaeological, and skeletal—is needed to confirm this supposition.

33 These constitutional protections are important because they are intended, at least in a de jure sense, to ensure that all people in the United States are treated equally. In a cemetery sense, these protections should extend not to the dead (who, being dead, can have no legal rights), but rather to the descendants of the dead whose rights of sepulchre and other associated mortuary rights should receive equal protection to those same rights of the white majority. As with all other de jure protections, their de facto application is often only as strong as activists and the courts are willing to make them. The de jure as opposed to de facto nature of these protections was recently evident when an African American sheriff's deputy was denied burial in a white Louisiana cemetery (Li 2021).

34 The U.S. Supreme Court has interpreted the Thirteenth Amendment, which explicitly abolishes chattel slavery in the United States, as implicitly authorizing "Congress . . .

to pass all laws necessary and proper for abolishing all badges and incidents of slavery." *The Civil Rights Cases*, 109 U.S. 3, 20 (1883). These "badges and incidents" are understood to incorporate actions or limitations that result in a deviation of minority rights from those of the majority (Rothstein 2017; Serafin 2022). Accordingly, the protections afforded to white cemeteries and descendants should equally be afforded to minority cemeteries and descendants. That the U.S. Supreme Court has indicated the Thirteenth Amendment "clothes Congress with the power to pass all laws necessary and proper" strongly suggests that this extension of the Thirteenth Amendment is not self-executing. See, e.g., Palmer v. Thompson, 403 U.S. 217, 227 (1971); Carter (2014). Rather, it requires positive action by Congress to level the playing field. Such leveling occurred in 1990 with the passage of NAGPRA. However, as discussed above, NAGPRA's scope is narrow. Moreover, the recent passage of the African American Burial Grounds Preservation Act falls grossly short of extending the level playing field to African American cemeteries (Seidemann 2023), much less to the cemeteries of other minority groups. In this regard, Congress needs to act.

Chapter 5. Archival and Archaeological Evidence of Historical Cemetery and Human Remains Treatment in Louisiana

1 The court filings only indicate the cemetery's location as Township 9 South, Range 2 West, Section 41, in Acadia Parish (figure 2.12). The cemetery does not appear on the 1935 United States Geological Survey quadrangle map for Branch, Louisiana, and research into well files at the Louisiana Department of Natural History has not revealed a specific location for this site aside from its location in the above-noted, irregularly shaped USGS section. Thus, the cemetery's exact location today is unknown.

2 Louisiana Supreme Court record (hereafter "S.Ct. Rec.") at 11–12. This case file is contained within the Louisiana Supreme Court records at the Louisiana State Archives in Baton Rouge.

3 S. Ct. Rec. at 13.

4 *Humphreys v. Bennett Oil Corp.* trial transcript (hereafter "*Humphreys* Tr.") at 15. This transcript is contained within the Louisiana Supreme Court records at the Louisiana State Archives in Baton Rouge.

5 *Humphreys* Tr. at 17.

6 *Humphreys* Tr. at 62. See also *Humphreys* Tr. at 66.

7 *Humphreys* Tr. at 63.

8 *Humphreys* Tr. at 69.

9 *Humphreys* Tr. at 73. *See also Humphreys v. Bennett Oil Corp.*, 197 So. 222, 228 (La. 1940).

10 *Humphreys* Tr. at 32.

11 *Humphreys* Tr. at 38.

12 *Humphreys* Tr. at 43.

13 *Humphreys* Tr. at 82–83.

14 Importantly, unlike some of the other sites discussed in this research (e.g., Charity Hospital Cemetery No. 1 and Locust Grove), there is no newspaper coverage of the Gates of Mercy Cemetery that provides any additional insight into this case.

15 See, e.g., Seidemann and Seidemann (2020) for a discussion of the logistical and legal problems associated with such a lackadaisical removal of remains.

16 *Touro Synagogue,* 96 So.2d at 34–35.

17 Trial transcript of *Christ Church Corp. v. City of New Orleans,* at 2 (hereinafter "*Girod* Tr."). This case file is contained within the Louisiana Supreme Court records at the Louisiana State Archives in Baton Rouge.

18 *Girod* Tr. at 7.

19 La. R.S. 8:671 et seq., and La. R.S. 25:931 et seq.

20 *Girod* Tr. at 7.

21 *Girod* Tr. at 8.

22 *Girod* Tr. at 8.

23 *Girod* Tr. at 8.

24 *Girod* Tr. at 8.

25 *Girod* Tr. at 9.

26 *Girod* Tr. at 12.

27 *Girod* Tr. at 12.

28 *Girod* Tr. at 13.

29 *Girod* Tr. at 19.

30 *Girod* Tr. at 22. This question was asked of Bisso by one of the city's attorneys, Charles E. Cabibi.

31 In this regard, Bisso was commenting that the necessary turns to avoid and leave intact Girod would create hazardous driving conditions in the area that would result in car crashes.

32 *Girod* Tr. at 72.

33 *Girod* Tr. at 73.

34 *Girod* Tr. at 73.

35 *Girod* Tr. at 74.

36 *Girod* Tr. at 73–74.

37 The additional fragments included one vertebra and four femoral shaft fragments.

38 This is a similar scenario to what played out in the late eighteenth century when King Charles IV decreed the closure and reuse of the St. Peter Street Cemetery (Gray 2017).

39 Act of Donation from George Garig to the Roman Catholic Church, dated June 9, 1819, and recorded as Entry 568 of Judges G Book at p. 546 and again in Donation Book C at p. 1 (the latter recordation dated April 19, 1827). The "superficial arpent" refers to an area measurement rather than a linear one (the latter being the original French use of the term). In early Louisiana, one arpent was the equivalent of 1.262 acres (Darton and Clark 1994:17).

40 It is important to note that this small excavation is not the entirety of the archaeological work undertaken at Highland. Rather, this unit was excavated at the end of a decade-long project at the site (Kleinpeter and Seidemann 2013; Seidemann and Kleinpeter 2013, 2014; Seidemann et al. 2016; Seidemann 2018c) to specifically examine the question of whether archaeological evidence of burials extending beyond the cemetery's visible boundaries could be identified.

Chapter 6. Isolated and Clandestine Burials

1 Although the Icelandic Constitution provides for the protection of "cultural assets," traditionally, cemeteries are not simply protected as important natural landforms, but rather as sacred sites. Icelandic Constitution, Chap. II, Art. 32 (adopted 2012).

2 Indeed, Seidemann and Halling (2022) have indicated that existing online sales of cemetery dirt may constitute the knowing or inadvertent sale of human remains. According to Davis (1985), such grave-related items and remains figure largely in various Vodun practices, which, along with various unspecified witchcraft activities, is often the stated purpose of these online sales (Seidemann and Halling 2022).

3 Hearing transcript dated June 3, 2022, The Descendants Project v. St. John the Baptist Parish, et al., Docket No. C-77305, Fortieth Judicial District Court, Division C, Edgard, Louisiana, pp. 45, 81–84.

4 Cases like this have not been limited to the United States. First Nations in Canada are also reckoning with the search for clandestine graves at residential schools—another opportunity for archaeologists to be active participants in social justice efforts (Montgomery and Supernant 2022).

5 While the *Columbia* astronauts have actual burial locations, there is little doubt that small pieces of them are still scattered across the crash area. This supposition is supported by the reality that, some 30 years after the *Challenger* explosion, fragments are still occasionally found and returned to NASA (Leinbach and Ward 2018).

6 The collection and commodification of such morbid mementos—whether from lynchings or just from human remains pilfered from other contexts—is robust online (Huxley and Finnegan 2004; Seidemann et al. 2009; Halling and Seidemann 2016b; others). Although not the subject of this book, the policing of such trade is essential to affording all disturbed remains a modicum of decent treatment in death. All U.S. jurisdictions prohibit this trade (Halling and Seidemann 2016b), but few enforce these restrictions. Such enforcement needs to be part of any larger reparations movement.

Chapter 7. Discussion and Conclusions

1 This proof is considered "virtual" because, as Kimmerle (2022) and others observe, remote sensing and oral histories are not infallible for the identification of lost graves. The evidence uncovered by Moates and O'Sullivan (2020a, 2020b) is compelling, but only ground truthing archaeological excavations can definitively prove the presence of an unmarked cemetery or burial.

2 See La. Const. art. I, sec. 4 for the Louisiana analogue to these federal constitutional mandates.

3 H.B. 1179, 116th Congress.

4 H.R. 51, 2018 Louisiana Regular Legislative Session.

5 Mack and Blakey (2004) provide a great example from the African Burial Ground of what narratives can be created even for unnamed individuals.

6 Indeed, Texas's statutory cemetery dedication, Tex. Health & Safety Code § 711.035, was not enacted until 1989.

7 See, e.g., Damon v. State, 52 S.W.2d 368, 370 (Tex.App. Sec. A 1932) (stating that, "[w]e think no particular instrument or ceremony is required to dedicate a tract of land to cemetery purposes. Its actual use as such is sufficient.").

8 Some portion of the paucity of substantial planning literature on the interaction of cemeteries and planning may be, as proposed by Koonce (2011:40), "a certain level of cultural aversion toward the discussion of burial and death. The unease this topic can evoke may be the culprit behind the lack of planning for these spaces."

9 This idea of forgotten cemeteries was interestingly quantified in a pilot study by Hannon (1990), in which he coined the term, "the forgetting rate," or the time it should take for an ordinary dead person to be forgotten by the living. This low forgetting rate even in this pilot study provides a probable suggestion for the high number of cemeteries lost over time.

REFERENCES CITED

Adame, Fernanda

2023 Dear Scientists: Stop Calling America the 'New World,' *Nature,* DOI: 10.1038/d41586-023-00992-4.

Ades, Stephanie Ann

1995 The Archaeological Resources Protection Act: A New Application in the Private Property Context, *Catholic University Law Review* 44:599–630.

Afrasiabi, Peter R.

1997 Property Rights in Ancient Human Skeletal Remains, *Southern California Law Review* 70:805–839.

Amanat, Mehrdad

2012 Set in Stone: Homeless Corpses and Desecrated Graves in Modern Iran, *International Journal of Middle East Studies* 44:257–283.

Ander, Lisa

1986 The Marketable Record Title Act: Chasing the Clouds Away in California, *Real Estate Law Journal* 14(4):354–359.

Anderson, Ed, and Greg Belanger

1985 Construction Crews Find Bones, Coffins Uptown, *Times-Picayune,* A-19–A-20 (Aug. 14, 1985).

Anderson, Keith A., and Joseph E. Gaugler

2006 The Grief Experiences of Certified Nursing Assistants: Personal Growth and Complicated Grief, *Omega: The Journal of Death and Dying* 54(4):301–318.

Anonymous

1930 Cemetery Filling Stations Proposed, *Times-Picayune,* 35 (Dec. 6, 1930).

1952 Records Explain Casket Mystery, *Times-Picayune,* 13 (Dec. 18, 1952).

1954a The Crumbling World of Girod Cemetery, *Dixie: Times-Picayune States Roto Magazine,* 6–7 (Aug. 29, 1954).

1954b Girod Cemetery Strip Is Sought: City Filed Expropriation Suit for Land, *Times-Picayune,* 1 (Nov. 12, 1954).

1968 A Growing Enterprise Decrease in Value? Cemeteries Do!, *Appraisal Journal* 36(2):285–287.

1969 Compulsory Removal of Cadaver Organs, *Columbia Law Review* 69:693–705.

2017 Damage to Historic Black Cemetery Spurs Complaints, Probe. *Associated Press* (located online at https://apnews.com/766a83cac89b4c16a6e21a462e95dbfd) (last accessed Sept. 12, 2024).

Ariès, Philippe

1981 *The Hour of Our Death.* Vintage Books, New York.

Armelagos, George J., and Dennis P. Van Gerven
2003 A Century of Skeletal Biology and Paleopathology: Contrasts, Contradictions, and Conflicts, *American Anthropologist* 105(1):53–64.
Arndt, Grant
2023 Joining the Ongoing Struggle: Vine Deloria, Nancy Lurie, and the Quest for a Decolonial Anthropology, *Journal of Anthropological Research* 79(4):468–491.
Arnold, Bettina, and Robert J. Jeske
2014 The Archaeology of Death: Mortuary Archaeology in the United States and Europe 1990–2013, *Annual Reviews of Anthropology* 43:325–346.
Aronson, Jay D.
2016 *Who Owns the Dead? The Science and Politics of Death at Ground Zero.* Harvard University Press, Cambridge, MA.
Barrett, Stanley R.
1997 *Anthropology: A Student's Guide to Theory and Method.* University of Toronto Press, Toronto.
Bashow, Ira
2023 There's More to Anthropology's Past Than Most of Us Know, *American Anthropologist* 125(1):177–180.
Bates, Warren
2020 Discrimination of the Deceased, *Journal of Race, Gender and Poverty* 11:101–119.
Baugher, Sherene, and Richard F. Veit
2014 *The Archaeology of American Cemeteries and Gravemarkers.* University of Florida Press, Gainesville.
Beavers, Richard C., Teresia R. Lamb, and John R. Greene
1993 Burial Archaeology and Osteology of Charity Hospital/Cypress Grove II Cemetery, New Orleans, Louisiana, Volume I: Archaeology and History. Archaeology and Cultural Research Program, Department of Anthropology, University of New Orleans. Unpublished report.
Bender, Thomas
1974 The "Rural" Cemetery Movement: Urban Travail and the Appeal of Nature, *New England Quarterly* 47(2):196–211.
Benedict, Ruth
1934 *Patterns of Culture.* Houghton Mifflin Company, Boston, MA.
Bennett, G., and P. J. Davies
2015 Urban Cemetery Planning and the Conflicting Role of Local and Regional Interests. *Land Use Policy* 42:450–459.
Ben-Sasson, H. H. (editor)
1976 *A History of the Jewish People.* Harvard University Press, Cambridge, MA.
Bernard, Hugh Y.
1966 *The Law of Death and Disposal of the Dead.* Oceana Publications, New York.
Bernstein, Bruce
1991 Repatriation and Collaboration: The Museum of New Mexico, *Museum Anthropology* 15(3):19–21.

Blakely, Robert, and Judith M. Harrington

1997 *Bones in the Basement: Postmortem Racism in Nineteenth-Century Medical Training*. Smithsonian Institution, Washington, D.C.

Blakey, Michael L.

1996 Foreword. In *Lay Down Body: Living History in African American Cemeteries*, authored by Roberta Hughes Wright and Wilbur B. Hughes III, pp. xiii–xv. Visible Ink Press, Detroit.

2010 African Burial Ground Project: Paradigm for Cooperation?, *Museum International*, 62(1–2): 61–68.

Boas, Franz

1909 *The Kwakiutl of Vancouver Island*. G. E. Stechert, New York.

2016 [1893] Ethnology at the Exposition. In *Coming of Age in Chicago: The 1893 World's Fair and the Coalescence of American Anthropology*, edited by Curtis M. Hinsley and David R. Wilcox, pp. 78–83. University of Nebraska Press, Lincoln.

Bohannan, Paul, and Mark Glazer

1988 *High Points in Anthropology*, 2nd ed. McGraw-Hill, New York.

Boutin, Alexis

2020 BIG Chairs and Ethics Subcommittee Statement on Recent Publication (email to members of Society for American Archaeology's Bioarchaeology Interest Group and Ethics Subcommittee, dated Dec. 20, 2020).

Boutin, Alexis T., Madison Long, Rudy A. Dinarte, and Erica R. Thompson

2017 Building a Better Bioarchaeology through Community Collaboration, *Bioarchaeology International* 1(3–4):191–204.

Bown, Stephen R.

2012 *The Last Viking: The Life of Roald Amundsen*. DaCapo Press, Boston.

Bowring, Jacky

2011 Containing Marginal Memories: The Melancholy Landscapes of Hart Island (New York), Cockatoo Island (Sydney), and Ripapa Island (Christchurch), *Memory Connection* 1(1): 252–270.

Branyon, Ian C. M.

1998 An Investigation into the Ethnographic and Historical Significance of Holt Cemetery. MA thesis, University of New Orleans.

Bray, Tamara

2001 American Archaeologists and Native Americans: A Relationship Under Construction. In *The Future of the Past: Archaeologists, Native Americans, and Repatriation*, edited by Tamara Bray, pp. 1–5. Garland Publishing, London.

Brewer, Catherine

2005 The Status of the Jews in Roman Legislation: The Reign of Justinian 527–565 CE, *European Judaism* 38(2):127–139.

Brown, Ian W.

2016 *Marking Graves in Tuscaloosa County, Alabama: Musings of a Teacher*. Borgo Publishing, Tuscaloosa, AL.

Brown, Tim

2013 The Making of Urban "Healtheries": The Transformation of Cemeteries and Burial Grounds in Late-Victorian East London, *Journal of Historical Geography* 42:12–23.

Buikstra, Jane E.

2006a A Historical Introduction. In *Bioarchaeology: The Contextual Analysis of Human Remains,* edited by Jane E. Buikstra and Lane A. Beck, pp. 7–25. Academic Press, Amsterdam.

2006b Repatriation and Bioarchaeology: Challenges and Opportunities. *Bioarchaeology: The Contextual Analysis of Human Remains,* edited by Jane E. Buikstra and Lane A. Beck, pp. 389–415. Academic Press, Amsterdam.

Bullard, Robert D.

2000 *Dumping in Dixie: Race, Class, and Environmental Quality,* 3rd ed. Westview Press, Boulder, CO.

Burnston, Sharon Ann

1997 The Invisible People: The Cemetery at Catoctin Furnace. In *In Remembrance: Archaeology and Death,* edited by David A. Poirier and Nicholas F. Bellantoni, pp. 93–103. Bergin and Garvey, Westport, CT.

Callahan, Constance M.

1993 Warp and Weft: Weaving a Blanket of Protection for Cultural Resources on Private Property, *Environmental Law* 23:1323–1351.

Canning, Louise, and Isabelle Szmigin

2010 Death and Disposal: The Universal, Environmental Dilemma, *Journal of Marketing Management* 26(11–12):1129–1142.

Cannon, Aubrey

2002 Spatial Narratives of Death, Memory, and Transcendence. In *The Space and Place of Death,* edited by Helaine Silverman and David B. Small, pp. 191–199. *Archaeological Papers of the American Anthropological Association* Number 11. American Anthropological Association, Arlington, VA.

Carlin, A. Roberta

2014 *Puzzle Pieces of the Past: Spanish Abbreviations 1500–1700.* Universal Publishers, Boca Raton, FL.

Carmack, Sharon D.

2002 *Your Guide to Cemetery Research.* Betterway Books, Cincinnati, OH.

Carrega, Christina

2020 $9.4 Billion Plastics Facility to Be Built on Slave Burial Grounds, Report Says, *ABC News* (available online at https://abcnews.go.com/US/94-billion-plastics-facility-built-slave-burial-grounds/story?id=69555811) (last accessed Nov. 25, 2023).

Carson, Rachel

1962 *Silent Spring.* Houghton Mifflin, Boston.

Chapman, Ellen, Libby Cook, and Ana Edwards

2020 Bones in Stasis: The Challenging History and Uncertain Future of the Virginia State Penitentiary Collection, *Journal for the Anthropology of North America* 23(1):12–31.

Clancy, Kate

2023 *Period: The Real Story of Menstruation.* Princeton University Press, Princeton, NJ.

Clever, Iris Isabelle

2020 The Lives and Afterlives of Skulls: The Development of Biometric Methods of Measuring Race (1880–1950). PhD dissertation, University of California Los Angeles.

Clinton, Carter K., and Fatimah L.C. Jackson

2020 Historical Overview, Current Research, and Emerging Bioethical Guidelines in Researching the New York African Burial Ground, *American Journal of Physical Anthropology,*175(2):339–349.

Coastal Environments, Inc.

1975 Historical Cemetery Restoration (unpublished report).

2020a Cartographic Regression Analysis of Certain Tracts of Land Located in T. 11 S. and T. 12 S., R. 15 E. (Southeastern Land District West of the Mississippi River), St. James Parish, Louisiana, Part 1: Acadia Plantation Cemetery (unpublished archaeological report).

2020b Cartographic Regression Analysis of Certain Tracts of Land Located in T. 11 S. and T. 12 S., R. 15 E. (Southeastern Land District West of the Mississippi River), St. James Parish, Louisiana, Part 2: Lauderdale and Elina Plantation Cemeteries (unpublished archaeological report).

Colbert, Brandy

2021 *Black Birds in the Sky: The Story and Legacy of the 1921 Tulsa Race Massacre.* Balzer + Bray, New York.

Collier, Ivy D.

2016 More Than a Bag of Bones: A History of Animal Burials. In *Mourning Animals: Rituals and Practices Surrounding Animal Death,* edited by Margo DeMello, pp. 3–9. Michigan State University Press, East Lansing.

Colwell, Chip

2017 *Plundered Skulls and Stolen Spirits: Inside the Fight to Reclaim Native America's Culture.* University of Chicago Press, Chicago.

Comas, Juan

1960 *Manual of Physical Anthropology.* Charles C. Thomas Publisher, Springfield, IL.

Cook, Della Collins

2006 The Old Physical Anthropology and the New World: A Look at the Accomplishments of an Antiquated Paradigm. In *Bioarchaeology: The Contextual Analysis of Human Remains,* edited by Jane E. Buikstra and Lane A. Beck, pp. 27–71. Academic Press, Amsterdam.

Coutts, Christopher, Carlton Basmajian, and Timothy Chapin

2011 Projecting Landscapes of Death, *Landscape and Urban Planning* 102:254–261.

Curl, James S.

2001 *The Victorian Celebration of Death.* History Press, Charleston, SC.

Curtin, Mary

2013 Cleaning House: Achieving Effective Consumer Protection Through TILA Reform, *Arizona State Law Journal* 45:1685–1718.

Dailey, R. C., and Dan Morse

1984 The Sowell Mound, A Weeden Island Period Burial Site in Bay County, Northwest Florida, *Florida Anthropologist* 37(4):165–171.

Damiata, Brian N., John M. Steinberg, Douglas J. Bolender, Guðný Zöega, and John W. Schoenfelder
2017 Subsurface Imaging a Viking-Age Churchyard Using GPR With TDR: Direct Comparison to the Archaeological Record from an Excavated Site in Northern Iceland. *Journal of Archaeological Science: Reports* 12:244–256.
Darton, Mike, and John Clark
1994 *The Macmillan Dictionary of Measurement.* John Wiley, New York.
Darwin, Charles
1859 *On the Origin of Species by Means of Natural Selection, or the Preservation of Favoured Races in the Struggle for Life.* John Murray, London.
Dasgupta, Rana
2015 *Capital: The Eruption of Delhi.* Penguin Books, London.
Davidson, James M.
2007 "Resurrection Men" in Dallas: The Illegal Use of Black Bodies as Medical Cadavers (1900–1907), *International Journal of Historical Archaeology* 11:193–220.
Davis, Wade
1985 *The Serpent and the Rainbow.* Warner Books, New York.
Dedek, Peter B.
2017 *The Cemeteries of New Orleans: A Cultural History.* Louisiana State University Press, Baton Rouge.
Deloria, Vine, Jr.
1969 *Custer Died for Your Sins: An Indian Manifesto.* Avon Books, New York.
Demirakin, N. Işik
2012 Expropriation as a Modernizing Tool in the Nineteenth-Century Ottoman Empire: The Case of Cemeteries in Beyoğlu, *International Journal of Turkish Studies* 18(1–2):1–15.
Desmond, Adrian, and James Moore
2009 *Darwin's Sacred Cause: How Hatred of Slavery Shaped Darwin's Views on Human Evolution.* Houghton Mifflin Harcourt, Boston.
deSousa, Ana N.
2015 Death in the City: What Happens When All Our Cemeteries are Full?, *The Guardian* (accessible online at https://www.theguardian.com/cities/2015/jan/21/death-in-the-city-what-happens-cemeteries-full-cost-dying, last accessed Nov. 1, 2020).
Dethlefsen, Edwin, and James F. Deetz
1966 Death's Heads, Cherubs, and Willow Trees: Experimental Archaeology in Colonial Cemeteries, *American Antiquity* 31(4):502–510.
DeVito, Carlo
2015 *Mrs. Lee's Rose Garden: The True Story of the Founding of Arlington.* Cider Mill Press, Kennebunkport, ME.
Dillehay, Thomas D.
2000 *The Settlement of the Americas: A New Prehistory.* Basic Books, New York.
Dongoske, Kurt E.
1996 The Native American Graves Protection and Repatriation Act: A New Begin-

ning, Not the End, for Osteological Analysis—A Hopi Perspective, *American Indian Quarterly* 20(2):287–296.

Doran, Glen H.
2002 *Windover: Multidisciplinary Investigations of an Early Archaic Florida Cemetery* University Press of Florida, Gainesville.

Douglass, Kristina, and Jago Cooper
2020 Archaeology, Environmental Justice, and Climate Change on Islands of the Caribbean and Southwestern Indian Ocean. *Proceedings of the National Academy of Sciences* 117(57):8254–8262.

Downer, Joseph A.
2015 Hallowed Ground, Sacred Place: The Slave Cemetery at George Washington's Mount Vernon and the Cultural Landscapes of the Enslaved. MA thesis, George Washington University.

Dunbar-Ortiz, Roxanne
2014 *An Indigenous Peoples' History of the United States.* Beacon Press, Boston.

Duncan, William N.
2004 Understanding Veneration and Violation in the Archaeological Record. In *Interacting with the Dead: Perspectives on Mortuary Archaeology for the New Millennium,* edited by Gordon F. M. Rakita, Jane E. Buikstra, Lane A. Beck, and Sloan R. Williams, pp. 207–227. University Press of Florida, Gainesville.

Dunk, Julie, and Julie Rugg
1994 *The Management of Old Cemetery Land: Now and the Future.* Shaw, Crayford, UK.

Dunnavant, Justin, Deland Justinvil, and Chip Colwell
2021 Craft an African American Graves Protection and Repatriation Act, *Nature* 593:337–340.

Dymond, David
1999 God's Disputed Acre, *Journal of Ecclesiastical History* 50(3):464–497.

Ellis, Carolyn
2003 Grave Tending: With Mom at the Cemetery, *Forum: Qualitative Social Research,* 4(2). https://doi.org/10.17169/fqs-4.2.701.

Erickson, Renee
2020 Phase I Archaeological Investigation of the Greenfield Development on Robert Brothers' Farm in St. John the Baptist Parish, Louisiana. Unpublished report by Gulf South Research Corporation, Baton Rouge, LA.

Evans, Jakob
2023 Rayne Man Accused of Stealing Bones from Cemetery and Leaving Them on Church Steps, *KPLC* (available online at: www.kplctv.com/2023/05/24/rayne-man-accused-stealing-bones-cemetery-leaving-them-church-steps/) (last accessed Nov. 25, 2023).

Evensen, Katinka H., Helena Nordh, and Margrete Skaar
2017 Everyday Use of Urban Cemeteries: A Norwegian Case Study, *Landscape and Urban Planning* 159:76–84.

Fairclough, Adam
1999 *Race and Democracy: The Civil Rights Struggle in Louisiana, 1915–1972.* University of Georgia Press, Athens.

Farmer, Paul

2004 An Anthropology of Structural Violence, *Current Anthropology* 45(3):305–325.

Farrell, John A.

2011 *Clarence Darrow: Attorney for the Damned.* Vintage Books, New York.

Farris, Neal

2003 Between Colonial and Indigenous Archaeologies: Legal and Extra-legal Ownership of the Archaeological Past in North America, *Canadian Journal of Archaeology/Journal Canadien d'Archéologie* 27:154–190.

Faust, Drew Gilpin

2008 *This Republic of Suffering: Death and the American Civil War.* Knopf, New York.

Feldman, Brian

2016 Cops Bust Tumblr Witch Over "Boneghazi," *New York Magazine* (available online at https://nymag.com/intelligencer/2016/03/cops-bust-tumblr-witch-over-boneghazi.html) (last accessed Nov. 25, 2023).

Ferguson, T. J.

1996 Native Americans and the Practice of Archaeology, *Annual Review of Anthropology* 25(1):63–79.

Foucault, Michel

1986 Of Other Spaces, *Diacritics* 16(1):22–27.

Fowler, Louise, and Natasha Powers

2012 *Doctors, Dissection and Resurrection Men: Excavations in the 19th-Century Burial Ground of the London Hospital, 2006.* Museum of London, London.

Francaviglia, Richard V.

1971 The Cemetery as an Evolving Cultural Landscape, *Annals of the American Association of Geographers* 61(3):501–509.

Franklin, Maria, Anna Agbe-Davies, Kimball Banks, Jodi A. Barnes, Thomas Cuthbertson, Sarah Herr, J. W. Joseph, Edward Morin, Burr Neely, Holly Norton, Tsim Schneider, and William White

2022 Recommendations for Raising the Visibility of Black Heritage Resources and Engaging with Black Stakeholders: Results from a Survey of State and Territorial Historic Preservation Offices and State Archaeologists. *The Digital Archaeological Record* (available online at https://core.tdar.org/document/470405/recommendations-for-raising-the-visibility-of-black-heritage-resources-and-engaging-with-black-stakeholders-results-from-a-survey-of-state-and-territorial-historic-preservation-offices-and-state-archaeologists) (last visited Sept. 26, 2022).

Frohne, Andrea E.

2015 *The African Burial Ground in New York City: Memory, Spirituality, and Space.* Syracuse University Press, Syracuse, NY.

Galtung, Johan

1969 Violence, Peace, and Peace Research, *Journal of Peace Research* 6(3):167–191.

1980 *The True Worlds: A Transnational Perspective.* Free Press, New York.

Garcia-Putnam, Alexander, Christine L. Halling, and Ryan M. Seidemann

2021 Stress, Health, and Demography at Charity Hospital Cemetery #2 (AD 1847–1929), *International Journal of Osteoarchaeology* 31(6):1192–1202.

2023 Postmortem Examination as Necroviolence at Charity Hospital Cemetery #2 (A.D. 1847–1929), *Historical Archaeology* 57(2):788–808.

Garner, Brian A. (editor)
2019 *Black's Law Dictionary,* 11th ed. Thompson Reuters, Toronto.

General Accounting Office
2003 *Death Care Industry—Regulation Varies across States and Industry Segments.* U.S. General Accounting Office, Washington, D.C.

Gosden, Chris
2006 Race and Racism in Archaeology: Introduction, *World Archaeology* 38(1):1–7.

Godzinski, Michael, Mary Manhein, Jeanne Marquez, Benjamin Maygarden, Rhonda L. Smith, Harriet Swift, Jill-Karen Yakubik, and Jessica Barton
2008 Phase I/II Archaeological Investigations at the Proposed Site of the Canal Boulevard Transit Terminal at Charity Hospital Cemetery No. 2 (16OR108), New Orleans, Orleans Parish, Louisiana. Unpublished archaeological site report. Earth Search, Inc., New Orleans.

Godzinski, Michael, Shawna A. Atkins, Donna Greer, Tegan Hanson, Aubra L. Lee, Marie Richards, and Rhonda L. Smith
2013 Phase I and II Cultural Resources Investigations of Blacks I and J (With Portions of Blocks E, F, G, and H) at the Iberville Housing Project, New Orleans, Orleans Parish, Louisiana. Unpublished archaeological report. Earth Search, Inc., New Orleans.

González-Tennant, Edward
2018 *The Rosewood Massacre: An Archaeology and History of Intersectional Violence.* University Press of Florida: Gainesville.

Gould, Stephen Jay
1981 *The Mismeasure of Man.* Norton, New York.

Grabalov, Pavel, and Helena Nordh
2020 "Philosophical Park": Cemeteries in the Scandinavian Urban Context, *Sociální Studia* 1:33–54.

Graham, Shawn, and Damien Huffer
2020 Reproducibility, Replicability, and Revisiting the Insta-Dead and the Human Remains Trade, *Internet Archaeology* 55, https://doi.org/10.11141/ia.55.11.

Gray, D. Ryan
2011 Incorrigible Vagabonds and Suspicious Spaces in Nineteenth-Century New Orleans, *Historical Archaeology* 45(3):55–73.
2017 Archaeological Excavations and Recovery of Human Remains from the St. Peter Street Cemetery (16OR92), Orleans Parish, Louisiana. Unpublished report. University of New Orleans, New Orleans.
2020 *Uprooted: Race, Public Housing, and the Archaeology of Four Lost New Orleans Neighborhoods.* University of Alabama Press, Tuscaloosa.

Greenfield, T. L., A. M. McMahon, T. C. O'Connell, H. Reade, C. Holmden, A. C. Fletcher, R. L. Zettler, and C. A. Petrie
2022 Were There Royal Herds? Understanding Herd Management and Mobility Using Isotopic Characterizations of Cattle Tooth Enamel from Early Dynastic Ur, *PLoS ONE* 17(6): e0265170. https://doi.org/10.1371/journal.pone.0265170.

Gupta, Akhil, and Jessie Stoolman
2022 Decolonizing US Anthropology, *American Anthropologist* 124:778–799.
Hahn, Sara A., Michael Carpenter, Thurston H.G. Hahn III, Philip Jungeblut, Anne Marie, Maher Blank, Joanne Ryan
2017 Former Gates of Mercy Cemetery (ירעש ימחר תיב תורבקה) Site (16OR707) Archaeological Monitoring, Phase I Limited Survey and Phase II Testing at the Allie Mae Williams Multi-Service Center, New Orleans, Orleans Parish, Louisiana, Report No. 22–5301. Unpublished report. Coastal Environments, Inc., Baton Rouge.
Hahn, Thurston H.G. and Andrea McCarthy
2012 Archaeological Monitoring of the Demolition of Thomy Lafon Elementary School, Locust Grove Cemetery/Lafon School Site (16OR565), Orleans Parish, Louisiana. Unpublished report. Coastal Environments, Inc., Baton Rouge.
Halcrow, Siân, Amber Aranui, Stephanie Halmhofer, Annalisa Heppner, Norma Johnson, Kristina Killgrove, and Gwen Robbins Schug
2021 Moving Beyond Weiss and Springer's Repatriation and Erasing the Past: Indigenous Values, Relationships, and Research, *International Journal of Cultural Property* 28(2):211–220.
Haley, Bryan S.
2003 Geophysical Survey of Highland Cemetery, Baton Rouge, Louisiana. Unpublished report. Center for Archaeological Research, University of Mississippi, Oxford.
Halling, Christine L., and Ryan M. Seidemann
2016a Descriptive Bioarchaeological Analysis of Human Remains Seized from Devon Machuca a.k.a. Facebook User "Ender Darling." In Louisiana Department of Justice Report 39-106. Louisiana Department of Justice, Baton Rouge.
2016b They Sell Skulls Online?! A Review of Internet Sales of Human Skulls on eBay and the Laws in Place to Restrict Sales. *Journal of Forensic Sciences* 61:1322–1326.
2017 Structural Violence in New Orleans: Skeletal Evidence from Charity Hospital's Cemeteries 1847–1929. In *The Bioarchaeology of Dissection and Autopsy in the United States*, edited by K. C. Nystrom, pp.165–184. Springer, New York.
Hammil, Jan, and Larry J. Zimmerman (editors)
1983 Perspectives from Lakota Spiritual Men and Elders. Unpublished meeting transcript. Forty-first Plains Conference, Rapid City, SD.
Hanna, Margaret G.
1999 A Time to Choose: "Us" Versus "Them," or "All of Us Together," *Plains Anthropologist* 44(170):43–52.
Hannon, Bruce
1990 The Forgetting Rate: Evidence from a Country Cemetery, *Landscape Journal* 9(1):16–21.
Harjo, Suzan Shown
2004 American Indian Religious Freedom Act After Twenty-Five Years: An Introduction, *Wicazo Sa Review* 19(2):129–136.
Harlin, Eeva-Kristiina
2008 Repatriation as Knowledge Sharing—Returning the Sámi Cultural Heritage. In

UTIMUT: Past Heritage-Future Partnerships: Discussions on Repatriation in the 21st Century, edited by Mille Gabriel and Jens Dahl, pp. 134–147. Eks-Skolens Trykkeri, Copenhagen, Denmark.

Harper, Kenn
2000 *Give Me My Father's Body: The Life of Minik, the New York Eskimo.* Steerforth Press, South Royalton, VT.

Harrison, Simon
2014 *Dark Trophies: Hunting and the Enemy Body in Modern War.* Berghahn Books, New York.

Harrod, Ryan P., Jennifer L. Thompson, and Debra L. Martin
2012 Hard Labor and Hostile Encounters: What Human Remains Reveal about Institutionalized Violence and Chinese Immigrants Living in Carlin, Nevada (1885–1923), *Historical Archaeology* 46(4):85–111.

Harvey, Thomas
2006 Sacred Spaces, Common Places: The Cemetery in the Contemporary American City, *Geographical Review* 96(2):295–312.

Hawkins, Drew
2023 Place, Erased: The Fight for the Remains of a Louisiana Town, *WWNO* (located online at www.wwno.org/news/2023-11-01/place-erased-the-fight-for-the-remains-of-a-louisiana-town) (last accessed Dec. 15, 2023).

Henderson, A. Gwynn
2015 Remembering Slack Farm. In *Archaeology for the People: Joukowsky Institute Perspectives,* edited by John F. Cherry and Felipe Rojas, pp. 53–67. Oxbow Books, Oxford.

Herzfeld, Schmuel
2020 Protecting the Souls in an African Cemetery, *Forward* (located online at: https://forward.com/scribe/450762/protecting-the-souls-in-an-african-cemetery/) (last accessed Aug. 9, 2020).

Hinsley, Curtis M.
2016 Anthropology as Education and Entertainment: Frederic Ward Putnam at the World's Fair. In *Coming of Age in Chicago: The 1893 World's Fair and the Coalescence of American Anthropology,* edited by Curtis M. Hinsley and David R. Wilcox, pp. 1–77. University of Nebraska Press, Lincoln.

Hobbs, June Hadden
2005 The Cowboy Cemetery of Kenton, Oklahoma, *Markers* 22:34–69.

Hochschild, Arlie Russell
2016 *Strangers in Their Own Land: Anger and Mourning on the American Right—A Journey to the Heart of Our Political Divide.* New Press, New York.

Hoffer, Mark
2020 Cemetery Desecrated by Driver "Doing Doughnuts" among Tombstones, NC Cops Say, *Raleigh News and Observer* (located online at www.newsobserver.com/news/local/article241361861.html) (last accessed Mar. 27, 2020).

Hogan, N. S., D. B. Greenfield, and L. A. Schmidt
2001 Development and Validation of the Hogan Grief Reaction Checklist, *Death Studies* 25:1–32.

Hogan, Nancy S., and Lee A. Schmidt
2002 Testing the Grief to Personal Growth Model Using Structural Equation Modeling, *Death Studies* 26:615–634.
Hogerty, John J., II
1992 Reflections at the Close of Three Years of Law School: A Student's Perspective on the Value and Importance of Teaching Roman Law in Modern American Law Schools, *Tulane Law Review* 66:1889–1897.
Hong, Mai-Linh K.
2017 "Get Your Asphalt Off My Ancestors!": Reclaiming Richmond's African Burial Ground, *Law, Culture and the Humanities* 13(1):81–103.
Horn, Stacy
2018 *Damnation Island: Poor, Sick, Mad and Criminal in 19th Century New York.* Algonquin Books, Chapel Hill, NC.
Horwitz, Tony
2011 *Midnight Rising: John Brown and the Raid That Sparked the Civil War.* Henry Holt, New York.
Hotard, Corey David
2003 Bombarding the City of the Dead: Who Has a Right to the Past? MA thesis, Louisiana State University, Baton Rouge.
Hrdlička, Aleš
1908 *Physiological and Medical Observations among the Indians of Southwestern United States and Northern Mexico.* Bureau of American Ethnology Number 34. Smithsonian Institution, Washington, D.C.
1943 *Alaska Diary, 1926–1931.* Jaques Cattel Press, Lancaster, PA.
Huber, Leonard V., and Guy F. Bernard
1961 *To Glorious Immortality: The Rise and Fall of the Girod Street Cemetery, New Orleans' First Protestant Cemetery, 1822–1957.* Alblen Books, New Orleans.
Huffer, D., and D. Chappell
2014 The Mainly Nameless and Faceless Dead: An Exploratory Study of the Illicit Traffic in Archaeological and Ethnographic Human Remains, *Crime, Law and Social Change* 62:131–153.
Huffer, D., D. Chappell, N. Charlton, and B. F. Spatola
2019 Bones of Contention: The Online Trade in Archaeological, Ethnographic and Anatomical Human Remains on Social Media Platforms. In *The Palgrave Handbook on Art Crime,* edited by S. Hufnagel and D. Chappell, pp. 527–556. Macmillan UK, London.
Huffer, D., and S. Graham
2018 Fleshing Out the Bones: Studying the Human Remains Trade with Tensorflow and Inception, *Journal of Computer Applications in Archaeology* 1:55–63.
Humfress, Caroline
2005 Law and Legal Practice in the Age of Justinian. In *The Cambridge Companion to the Age of Justinian,* edited by Michael Maas, pp. 161–184. Cambridge University Press, Cambridge.
Huxley, Angela K., and Michael Finnegan
2004 Human Remains Sold to the Highest Bidder! A Snapshot of the Buying and Sell-

ing of Human Skeletal Remains on eBay, an Internet Auction Site, *Journal of Forensic Sciences* 49:17–20.

Ifill, Sherrilyn A.

2018 *On the Courthouse Lawn: Confronting the Legacy of Lynching in the 21st Century.* Beacon Press, Boston.

Irwin, Geoffrey

1994 *The Prehistoric Exploration and Colonisation of the Pacific.* Cambridge University Press, Cambridge.

Iserson, Kenneth V.

1993 *Death to Dust: What Happens to Dead Bodies?* Galen Press, Tucson, AZ.

Jackson, Percival E.

1936 *The Law of Cadavers and of Burials and Burial Places.* Prentice Hall, New York.

Jacobs, Janet

2004 From the Profane to the Sacred: Ritual and Mourning at Sites of Terror and Violence, *Journal for the Scientific Study of Religion* 43(3):311–315.

Jarus, Owen

2020 Looted Skulls and Human Remains Are Being Sold in Black Markets on Facebook, *Live Science* (located online at www.livescience.com/human-bone-trade-facebook.html) (last accessed July 3, 2020).

Jenkins, Morgan

2020 Black Cemetery Loss Is a National Crisis, *ZORA* (located online at https://zora.medium.com/black-cemetery-loss-is-a-national-crisis-875adf6b7448) (last accessed Aug. 9, 2020).

Jenner, Mark

2005 Death, Decomposition and Dechristianisation? Public Health and Church Burial in Eighteenth-Century England, *English Historical Review* 120(487):615–632.

Johnson, Steven

2006 *The Ghost Map: The Story of London's Most Terrifying Epidemic—and How It Changed Science, Cities, and the Modern World.* Riverhead Books, New York.

Joiner, Mary Catherine, and Ryan M. Seidemann

2019a Rising from the Dead: A Jurisprudential Review of Recent Cemetery and Human Remains Cases, *Ohio Northern University Law Review* 45:1–68.

2019b What Lies Beneath: A Jurisprudential Review of Recent Cemetery and Human Remains Cases. *Drake University Law Review* 67:375–412.

Jones, D. Gareth, and Robyn J. Harris

1998 Archeological Human Remains: Scientific, Cultural, and Ethical Considerations, Current Anthropology 39:253–264.

Jones, Diane

2011 The City of the Dead: The Place of Cultural Identity and Environmental Sustainability in the African American Cemetery, *Landscape Journal* 30:2–11.

Jones, Terry L.

2019 Activists Want $9.4B Formosa Project Stopped Due to Slave Cemetery at St. James Site. *The Advocate* (located online at www.theadvocate.com/baton_rouge/news/activists-want-9-4b-formosa-project-stopped-due-to-slave-cemetery-at-st-james-site/article_5b6b4acc-20ed-11ea-a1d8-839c5ace48ea.html#:~:text

=Activists%20are%20calling%20for%20the,is%20believed%20slaves%20were %20buried) (last accessed Jan. 15, 2022).

Josephy, Alvin M., Jr.

1971 *Red Power: The American Indians' Fight for Freedom.* American Heritage Press, Winter Park, FL.

Jumonville, Florence

2016 *Nameless Graves: Indigent Cemeteries of New Orleans.* Save Our Cemeteries, Inc., New Orleans.

Kakaliouras, Ann M.

2014 When Remains Are "Lost": Thoughts on Collections, Repatriation, and Research in American Physical Anthropology, *Curator: The Museum Journal* 57(2):213–223.

2021 Review of *Repatriation and Erasing the Past,* by Elizabeth Weiss and James W. Springer, *American Antiquity* 86(3):646–647.

Kay, Dianne H.

1998 Cemetery Relocation: Emerging Urban Land Development Issue. *Journal of Urban Planning and Development* 124(1):1–10.

Kearley, Timothy G.

2007 Justice Fred Blume and the Translation of Justinian's Code, *Law Library Journal* 99(3): 525–554.

Keegan, William F.

1992 *The People Who Discovered Columbus: The Prehistory of the Bahamas.* University Press of Florida, Gainesville.

Keith, LeeAnna

2008 *The Colfax Massacre: The Untold Story of Black Power, White Terror, and the Death of Reconstruction.* Oxford University Press, Oxford.

Kennedy, Randall

2008 *Sellout: The Politics of Racial Betrayal.* Pantheon Books, New York.

Killion, Thomas W.

2007 Opening Archaeology: Repatriation's Impact on Contemporary Research and Practice. In *Opening Archaeology: Repatriation's Impact on Contemporary Research and Practice,* edited by Thomas W. Killion, pp. 3–26. School for Advanced Research Press, Santa Fe, NM.

Kimmerle, Erin

2022 *We Carry Their Bones: The Search for Justice at the Dozier School for Boys.* William Morrow, New York.

King, Gilbert

2013 *Devil in the Grove: Thurgood Marshall, the Groveland Boys, and the Dawn of a New America.* Harper Perennial, New York.

King, Thomas F.

2012 *Cultural Resource Laws and Practice,* 4th ed. Altamira Press, Lanham, MD.

Klaufus, Christien

2014 Deathscapes in Latin America's Metropolises: Urban Land Use, Funerary Transformations, and Daily Inconveniences, *European Review of Latin American and Caribbean Studies* 96:99–111.

2016 "The Dead Are Killing the Living": Spatial Justice, Funerary Services, and Cemetery Land Use in Urban Colombia. *Habitat International* 54:74–79.

Klaus, H.

2013 The Bioarchaeology of Structural Violence: A Theoretical Model and Case Study. In *The Bioarchaeology of Violence,* edited by D. Martin, R. Harrod, and V. Perez, 29–62. University of Florida Press, Gainesville.

Kleinpeter, Kenneth P., and Ryan M. Seidemann

2013 The Anatomy of a Debris Pile: Nine Months' Worth of Excavations at Historic Highland Cemetery (16EBR190). Presentation at the Louisiana Archaeological Society's 39th Annual Meeting, Lafayette, LA.

Kline, Andrew

2007 Who Are the Culturally Unidentifiable? United States Department of Interior unpublished report, Washington, D.C.

Klopotek, Brian

2011 *Recognition Odysseys: Indigeneity, Race, and Federal Tribal Recognition Policy in Three Louisiana Communities.* Duke University Press, Durham, NC.

Kniffen, Fred

1967 Necrogeography in United States, *Geographical Review* 57(3):426–427.

Kolbuszewski, J.

1995 Cemeteries as a Text of Culture. In *Cemetery Art,* edited by O. Czerner and I. Juszkiewicz, 17–40. ICOMOS, Wroclaw.

Kong, Lily

2012 No Place, New Places: Death and Its Rituals in Urban Asia, *Urban Studies* 49(2):415–433.

Koonce, Collin

2011 Cemeteries in the Urban Plan: Opportunities and Constraints. Master of Environmental Planning and Design thesis. University of Georgia, Athens.

Kopp, Steven W., and Elyria Kemp

2007 The Death Care Industry: A Review of Regulatory and Consumer Issues, *Journal of Consumer Affairs* 41(1):150–173.

Krauss, Deborah J.

1992 The Changing Influence of Roman Law: Ideals and Reality in Nineteenth Century America, *Digest* 2:79–108.

Kretzler, Ian E.

2012 For the Past, For the Future: NAGPRA, Repatriation, and the Native American-Archaeologist Relationship. Bachelor's honors thesis, Whitman College.

Kroeber, Alfred L.

1927 Disposal of the Dead, *American Anthropologist* 29(3):308–315.

Krummel, Jordan Andrea

2013 Holt Cemetery: An Anthropological Analysis of an Urban Potter's Field. MA thesis, Tulane University.

Lamb, D. S.

1917 *A History of the United States Army Medical Museum 1862 to 1917.* U.S. Army Medical Museum, Washington, D.C.

Landry, Mark H.

2009 Letter to Attorney General James D. "Buddy" Caldwell in the Attorney General Opinion Collections of the Civil Division, Louisiana Department of Justice, Baton Rouge.

Lannan, Robert W.

1998 Anthropology and Restless Spirits: The Native American Graves Protection and Repatriation Act, and the Unresolved Issues of Prehistoric Human Remains, *Harvard Environmental Law Review* 22:369–439.

Lans, Aja M.

2020 Embodied Discrimination and "Mutilated Historicity": Archiving Black Women's Bodies in the Huntington Collection. In *The Bioarchaeology of Structural Violence: A Theoretical Framework for Industrial Era Inequality*, edited by Lori A. Tremblay and Sarah Reedy, pp. 31–52. Springer, Cham, Switzerland.

Larson, Edward J.

2006 *Summer for the Gods: The Scopes Trial and America's Continuing Debate over Science and Religion.* Basic Books, New York.

Leader, George M., Kimberlee Sue Moran, Jared Beatrice, Anna Dhody, and Richard F. Veit

2022 Eighteenth- and Nineteenth-Century Funerary Hardware and Material Culture from the Historic Cemetery (ca. 1702–1859) of the First Baptist Church of Philadelphia, *Historical Archaeology* 56(1):72–90.

Legacey, Erin-Marie

2019 *Making Space for the Dead: Catacombs, Cemeteries, and the Reimagining of Paris, 1780–1830.* Cornell University Press, Ithaca, NY.

Leinbach, Michael, and Johnathan H. Ward

2018 *Bringing Columbia Home: The Untold Story of a Lost Space Shuttle and Her Crew.* Arcade Publishing, New York.

Lemke, Ashley

2020 "Missing Cemeteries" and Structural Racism: Historical Maps and Endangered African/African American and Hispanic Mortuary Customs in Texas, *Historical Archaeology* 54:605–623.

Leshem, Noam

2015 "Over Our Dead Bodies": Placing Necropolitical Activism, *Political Geography* 45:34–44.

Lévi-Strauss, Claude

1968 *The Scope of Anthropology.* Translated by Sherry Ortner Paul and Robert A. Paul. Jonathan Cape, London.

Lewis, Herbert S.

2023 Does a Decolonized Anthropology Require Reinterpreting the Past? *American Anthropologist* 125(1):181–183.

Li, David K.

2021 Louisiana Cemetery Refused to Accept Remains of Sheriff's Deputy Because He Was Black, *NBC News* (available online at www.nbcnews.com/news/us-news/louisiana-cemetery-refused-accept-remains-sheriff-s-deputy-because-he-n1256203) (last accessed Dec. 15, 2023).

Little, Barbara

1997 Expressing Ideology without a Voice, or Obfuscation and the Enlightenment, *International Journal of Historical Archaeology* 1(3):225–241.

Littleton, Judith H., and Bruno Frolich

2012 Postmortem Violence? Identifying and Interpreting Postmortem Disturbance in Mongolia, *Landscapes of Violence* 2(2): Article 7.

Loring, Stephen

1995 Repatriation as a Guiding Principle for the Arctic Studies Center, *AnthroNotes* 17:13–16.

Lowie, Robert

1970 *Primitive Religion.* Liveright, New York.

Lynge, Aqqaluk

2008 Sharing the Hunt: Repatriation as a Human Right. In *UTIMUT: Past Heritage-Future Partnerships: Discussions on Repatriation in the 21st Century,* edited by Mille Gabriel and Jens Dahl, pp. 134–147. Eks-Skolens Trykkeri, Copenhagen, Denmark.

Mack, Mark E., and Michael L. Blakey

2004 The New York African Burial Ground Project: Past Biases, Current Dilemmas, and Future Research Opportunities, *Historical Archaeology* 38(1):10–17.

MacMillan, Ken

2003 Common and Civil Law? Taking Possession of the English Empire in America, 1575–1630, *Canadian Journal of History* 38:409–423.

Madden, M. Stuart

2013 Paths of Western Law after Justinian, *Widener Law Journal* 22:757–828.

Madigan, Tim

2003 *The Burning: Massacre, Destruction, and the Tulsa Race Riot of 1921.* Thomas Dunne Books, New York.

Mahoney, Anne Lucia

2014 Nominating Sweet Olive Cemetery: Baton Rouge's Oldest African American Cemetery and the Preservation Process of Urban Historic Cemeteries in Southeast Louisiana. MA thesis, University of Louisiana, Lafayette.

Malinowski, Bronislaw

1922 *Argonauts of the Western Pacific.* Routledge and Kegan Paul, London.

Maples, James N., and Elizabeth A. East

2013 Destroying Mountains, Destroying Cemeteries: Historic Mountain Cemeteries in the Coalfields of Boone, Kanawha, and Raleigh Counties, West Virginia, *Journal of Appalachian Studies* 19(1–2): 7–26.

Maraist, Frank L.

2019 *Louisiana Civil Law Treatise,* Vol. 1A: *Civil Procedure.* West Publishing, Eagen, MN.

Marquis, Donald M.

1978 *In Search of Buddy Bolden: First Man of Jazz.* Louisiana State University Press, Baton Rouge.

Marsh, Tanya D., and Daniel Gibson

2015 *Cemetery Law: The Common Law of Burying Grounds in the United States.* God's Acre Publishing, Winston-Salem, NC.

Marsh, Tanya D., and Ryan M. Seidemann

2018 Brief of Cemetery Law Scholars as *Amici Curiae* in Support of Respondents filed before the United States Supreme Court in the matter of *Knick v. Township of Scott, Pennsylvania,* 17–647, 139 S. Ct. 2162 (2019).

Martínez-Fernández, Luis

1992 "Don't Die Here": The Death and Burial of Protestants in the Hispanic Caribbean, 1840–1885, *Americas* 49(1): 23–47.

Masters, Sylvia

2020 Family Speaks Out After Relative's Grave Vandalized in Louisiana, *KLFY* (located online at www.brproud.com/louisiana-news/family-speaks-out-after-relatives-grave-vandalized) (last accessed Feb. 5, 2020).

Maturana, Antonio Calvo

2014 "Is It Useful to Deceive the People?" The Debate on Public Information in Spain at the End of the Ancien Régime (1780–1808), *Journal of Modern History* 86(1):1–46.

McConnaughey, Janet

2020 Some Areas Protected as Formosa's Louisiana Work Continues, *Washington Post,* July 24, 2020.

McCrea, Heather L.

2007 On Sacred Ground: The Church and Burial Rights in Nineteenth-Century Yucatán, Mexico, *Mexican Studies/Estudios Mexicanos* 23(1):33–62.

McGill, Kevin

2018 As Shell Preserves Louisiana Slave Burial Ground, Question Persists: Where are the Rest? *The Advocate* (Baton Rouge, LA) (located online at www.theadvocate.com/baton_rouge/news/article_5a1ab0fa-6fdb-11e8-b6d6-932aad7138e2.html) (last accessed Jan. 16, 2021).

McKeown, C. Timothy

2008 Considering Repatriation Legislation as an Option: The National Museum of the American Indian Act (NMAIA) & The Native American Graves Protection and Repatriation Act (NAGPRA). In *UTIMUT: Past Heritage-Future Partnerships: Discussions on Repatriation in the 21st Century,* edited by Mille Gabriel and Jens Dahl, pp. 134–147. Eks-Skolens Trykkeri, Copenhagen, Denmark.

2012 *In the Smaller Scope of Conscience: The Struggle for National Repatriation Legislation, 1986–1990.* University of Arizona Press, Tucson.

2023 Repatriation Update. Presentation at the 23rd Annual National Association of Tribal Historic Preservation Officers Conference, Cherokee, NC.

McManamon, Francis P.

2001 The Reality of Repatriation: Reaching Out to Native Americans. In *Implementing the Native American Graves Protection and Repatriation Act,* edited by Roxana Adams, 2. American Association of Museums, Washington, D.C.

McWhirter, Cameron

2011 *Red Summer: The Summer of 1919 and the Awakening of Black America.* St. Martin's Griffin, New York.

Mead, Margaret

1928 *Coming of Age in Samoa.* William Morrow, New York.

1960 Introduction. In *The Golden Age of American Anthropology*, edited by Margaret Mead and Ruth L. Bunzel, pp. 1–13. George Braziller, New York.

Meighan, Clement W.

1992 Some Scholars' Views on Reburial, *American Antiquity* 54(4):704–710.

1994 Burying American Archaeology, *Archaeology* 47:64, 66.

Melville, Greg

2022 *Over My Dead Body: Unearthing the Hidden History of America's Cemeteries*. Abrams Press, New York.

Mengis, Warren A.

1990 The Public Records Doctrine Revisited. Paper presented at the 37th Annual Institute on Mineral Law, Baton Rouge, LA.

Mihesuah, Devon A.

1996 American Indians, Anthropologists, Pothunters, and Repatriation: Ethical, Religious, and Political Differences, *American Indian Quarterly* 20(2):229–237.

Milanich, Jerald T.

2000 Prolific Pioneer or Mound Mauler? *Archaeology* 53(4):56–58.

Miles, Tiya

2015 *Tales from the Haunted South: Dark Tourism and Memories of Slavery from the Civil War Era*. North Carolina University Press, Chapel Hill, NC.

Miller, D. S., and J. D. Rivera

2006 Hallowed Ground, Place, and Culture: The Cemetery and Creation of Place, *Space and Culture* 9(4):334–350.

Milner, George R., and Keith P. Jacobi

2006 A New Deal for Human Osteology. In *Bioarchaeology: The Contextual Analysis of Human Remains*, edited by Jane E. Buikstra and Lane A. Beck, pp. 113–129. Academic Press, Amsterdam.

Mitchell, David J.

2020 Formosa Can't Build St. James Plant for Up to 7 Months, Can do Some Work that Avoids Graves, *The Advocate* (located online at www.theadvocate.com/baton_rouge/news/environment/article_e6c7abb6-cd3a-11ea-8f2e-a377364adab4.html) (last accessed July 24, 2020).

Mitford, Jessica

1963 *The American Way of Death*. Hutchinson, London.

MLH.

1952 Historic Cemeteries. Letter to the Editor. *Times-Picayune*, 12 (Mar. 20, 1952).

Moates, Jeffrey T., and Rebecca C. O'Sullivan

2020a Preliminary Report for Ground Penetrating Radar (GPR) Survey of Frank Crum Leasing Company Property in Clearwater, FL. Unpublished report for the NAACP Clearwater/Upper Pinellas Branch No. 5096.

2020b Preliminary Report for Additional Phase of Ground Penetrating Radar (GPR) Survey of Frank Crum Leasing Company Property in Clearwater, FL. Unpublished report for the NAACP Clearwater/Upper Pinellas Branch No. 5096.

Moen, Marianne

2020 Familiarity Breeds Remembrance: On the Reiterative Power of Cemeteries, *World Archaeology* 52(1):35–48.

Monroe, Dan L.

1993 Repatriation: A New Dawn, *Museums Journal* 93(3):29–31.

Montgomery, Lindsay M., and Kisha Supernant

2022 Archaeology in 2021: Repatriation, Reclamation, and Reckoning with Historical Trauma. *American Anthropologist* 124:800–812.

Moore, Alanha

2018 Using Digital Mapping Techniques to Rapidly Document Vulnerable Historical Landscapes in Coastal Louisiana: Holt Cemetery Case Study. MA thesis, University of New Orleans.

Morazán, Ronald Rafael

1972 Letters, Petitions, and Decrees of the Cabildo of New Orleans, 1800–1803: Edited and Translated. PhD dissertation, Louisiana State University.

Morgan, Lewis Henry

1871 *Systems of Consanguinity and Affinity of the Human Family.* Smithsonian Institution, Washington, D.C.

Morton, Samuel G.

2009 [1839] *Crania Americana: A Comparative View of Skulls of Various Aboriginal Nations of North and South America.* Gustav's Library, Davenport, IA.

Moyle, J. B. (translator)

1913 *Institutes of Justinian.* Clarendon Press, Oxford.

Muller, Jennifer L., Jennifer F. Byrnes, and David A. Ingleman

2020 The Erie County Poorhouse (1828–1926) as a Heterotopia: A Bioarchaeological Perspective. In *The Bioarchaeology of Structural Violence: A Theoretical Framework for Industrial Era Inequality,* edited by Lori A. Tremblay and Sarah Reedy, pp. 111–138. Springer, Cham, Switzerland.

Murphy, Ann M.

2007 Please Don't Bury Me Down in That Cold Cold Ground: The Need for Uniform Laws on the Disposition of Human Remains, *Elder Law Journal* 15:381–471.

Murray, Robert K., and Roger W. Brucker

1982 *Trapped! The Story of Floyd Collins.* University of Kentucky Press, Lexington.

Mustian, Jim

2016 Self-Styled Witch Faces Charges over Human Bones Collected from New Orleans Cemetery, *Times-Picayune* (located online at www.nola.com/news/courts/article_ab01739b-ef85-536d-b39d-e3c2e9e31268.html) (last accessed Aug. 16, 2020).

Muyard, Frank

2016 Taiwan Archaeology and Indigenous Peoples: Cross-Perspectives on Indigenous Archaeology and Interactions between Archaeologists and Indigenous Communities in Taiwan. In *Archaeology, History and Indigenous Peoples: New Perspectives on the Ethnic Relations of Taiwan,* edited by Li-Wan Hung, pp. 195–262. Shung Ye Museum of Formosan Aborigines, Taipei, Taiwan.

Nance, Cindy A.

1999 Out of Sight, Out of Mind: A GIS Study of Changes in Cemetery Locations in Southeastern Louisiana from an Archaeological and Geographic Perspective, 1930–1997. PhD dissertation, Louisiana State University, Baton Rouge.

National Trust for Historic Preservation

1990 Minnesota Court Dismisses Inverse Condemnation Challenge to State Human Remains Statute, *Preservation Law Reporter* 9(12):1158–1160.

Nordh, H., and K. H. Evensen

2018 Qualities and Functions Ascribed to Urban Cemeteries across the Capital Municipalities of Scandinavia, *Urban Forestry and Urban Greening* 33:80–91.

Nystrom, Kenneth C.

2014 The Bioarchaeology of Structural Violence and Dissection in the 19th-Century United States, *American Anthropologist* 116(4):765–779.

Nystrom, Kenneth C. (editor)

2017 *The Bioarchaeology of Dissection and Autopsy in the United States.* Springer, New York.

Ogolla, Christopher

2022 Emotional Distress Recovery for Mishandling of Human Remains: A Fifty State Survey, *Drexel Law Review* 14:297–403.

O'Gorman, Jodie A., Jennifer D. Bengtson, and Amy R. Michael

2020 Ancient History and New Beginnings: Necrogeography and Migration in the North American Midcontinent, *World Archaeology* 52(1):16–34.

Owsley, D. W., Mann, R. W., and Lanphear, K. M.

1990 Osteological Examination of Human Remains from the Charity Hospital/Cypress Grove II Cemetery, New Orleans, Louisiana (Final report of investigations—volume 2). Unpublished report. Department of Anthropology, National Museum of Natural History, Smithsonian Institution, Washington, D.C.

Owsley, Douglas W., and Richard L. Jantz

1994 An Integrative Approach to Great Plains Skeletal Biology. In *Skeletal Biology in the Great Plains: Migration, Warfare, Health, and Subsistence,* edited by Douglas W. Owsley and Richard L. Jantz, pp. 3–8. Smithsonian Institution Press, Washington, D.C.

Pacia, Richard A., and Raymond A. Pacia

2001 Roman Contributions to American Civil Jurisprudence, *Rhode Island Bar Journal* 49(5):5–40.

Paredes, J. Anthony

1997 The Influence of Government Policies and Academic Theories on the Practice of Applied Anthropology in the United States: Some Personal Observations, *Human Organization,* 56(4):484–489.

Parsons, Christopher M.

2021 *A Not-So-New-World: Empire and Environment in French Colonial North America.* University of Pennsylvania Press, Philadelphia.

Parsons, Kenneth A.

2007 Structural Violence and Power, *Peace Review: A Journal of Social Justice,* 19:173–181.

Pelley, Scott

2022 "This Is Not an Isolated Story": Forgotten Black Cemeteries Uncovered in Florida, *60 Minutes* (aired Nov. 27, 2022) (available online at www.cbsnews.com/

news/black-cemeteries-florida-60-minutes-2022-11-27/) (last accessed Jan. 10, 2023).

2023 Uncovering Black Cemeteries Paved over in Florida, *60 Minutes* (aired July 30, 2023) (available online at www.cbsnews.com/video/black-cemeteries-florida-60-minutes-video-2023-07-30/) (last accessed Nov. 24, 2023).

Person, Katarzyna

2021 *Warsaw Ghetto Police: The Jewish Order Service during the Nazi Occupation.* Cornell University Press, Ithaca, NY.

Petrella, Christopher

2019 Gentrification Is Erasing Black Cemeteries and, With it, Black History, *Guardian* (available online at www.theguardian.com/commentisfree/2019/apr/27/gentrification-is-erasing-black-cemeteries-and-with-it-black-history) (las accessed Jan. 15, 2023).

Pigati, Jeffrey S., Kathleen B. Springer, Jeffrey S. Honke, David Wahl, Marie R. Champagne, Susan R. H. Zimmerman, Harrison J. Gray, Vincent L. Santucci, Daniel Odess, and Matthew R. Bennett

2023 Independent Age Estimates Resolve the Controversy of Ancient Human Footprints at White Sands, *Science* 382(6666):73–75.

Pingitore, Claire, Christine L. Halling, and Ryan M. Seidemann

2023 Untangling the Convoluted Ownership History of Sweet Olive Cemetery in Baton Rouge, Louisiana, *Le Raconteur: The Journal of Le Comité des Archives de la Louisiane* 43(3):189–196.

Pitts, Mike

2015 *Digging for Richard III: The Search for the Lost King.* Thames and Hudson, New York.

Poirier, David A., and Nicholas F. Bellantoni

1997 In Partnership: Descendants, Friends-of-the-Dead, and Archaeologists. In *In Remembrance: Archaeology and Death,* edited by David A. Poirier and Nicholas F. Bellantoni, pp. 231–236. Bergin and Garvey: Westport, CT.

Poole, Robert M.

2010 *On Hallowed Ground: The Story of Arlington National Cemetery.* Bloomsbury, London.

Pope, John

1985 Progress Mislaid Many Meant to Rest in Peace, *Times-Picayune,* A-25, A-33 (Aug. 18, 1985).

Price, H. Marcus

1988 Bones of Contention: Reburial of Human Remains under RS Mo. 194.400–410. *Missouri Archaeological Society Quarterly* 5(1):4–6, 11, 18.

Preservation Maryland

2019 African American Burial Ground Network Act Introduced in Congress, *Preservation Maryland* (located online at https://preservationmaryland.org/african-american-burial-ground-network-act-introduced-in-congress/) (last accessed Jan. 16, 2021).

Pritsolas, Joshua, and Gillian Acheson

2017 The Evolution of a Small Midwestern Cemetery: Using GIS to Explore Cultural Landscape, *Material Culture* 49(1):49–77.

Pullar, Gordon L.

2008 Repatriation, Cultural Revitalization and Indigenous Healing in Alaska. In *UTIMUT: Past Heritage-Future Partnerships: Discussions on Repatriation in the 21st Century,* edited by Mille Gabriel and Jens Dahl, pp. 134–147. Eks-Skolens Trykkeri, Copenhagen, Denmark.

Quammen, David

2006 *The Reluctant Mr. Darwin: An Intimate Portrait of Charles Darwin and the Making of His Theory of Evolution.* Atlas Books, New York.

Quetone, Joe A.

1987 Chapter 872, Florida Statutes 1987 ("Offenses Concerning Dead Bodies and Graves"): A Native American's Perspective, *Florida Anthropologist* 40(4):328–329.

Quigley, Catherine

2001 *Skulls and Skeletons: Human Bone Collections and Accumulations.* McFarland Publishing, Jefferson, NC.

Rainville, Lynn

2009 Protecting Our Shared Heritage in African American Cemeteries, *Journal of Field Archaeology* 34:196–206.

Razek, Raja, and Elizabeth Wolfe

2022 More Unmarked Graves Discovered in Search for Tulsa Massacre Victims, *CNN* (available online at www.cnn.com/2022/11/01/us/tulsa-massacre-burials-excavation-reaj/index.html) (last accessed Jan. 15, 2023).

Reever, Logan

2018a APSO and Louisiana Cemetery Board Launch Investigations into Eunice Grave Movement, *KLFY* (located online at www.klfy.com/local/apso-and-louisiana-cemetery-board-launch-investigations-into-eunice-grave-movement/) (last accessed Nov. 23, 2020).

2018b Eunice Mother Who Was Searching for Infant Son's Remains Removed from Grave Dies Suddenly, *KLFY* (located online at www.klfy.com/local/eunice-mother-who-was-searching-for-infant-sons-remains-removed-from-grave-dies-suddenly/) (last accessed Nov. 23, 2020).

Richards, Patricia B., Eric E. Burant, Brooke L. Drew, Emily M. Epstein, Catherine R. Jones, Nicholas W., Richards, and Thomas J. Zych

2016 Nine for Mortal Men Doomed to Die: The Archaeology and Osteology of the 2013 Milwaukee County Poor Farm Cemetery Project (Froedtert Tract-47 MI 0527) University of Wisconsin-Milwaukee Cultural Resource Management Report of Investigations 381.

Richardson, Ruth

1988 *Death, Dissection and the Destitute: The Politics of the Corpse in Pre-Victorian Britain.* Routledge, London.

Rickert, Aprile

2017 Excavations Ongoing near Clarksville Cemetery; Investigation Necessary for Road Project. *News and Tribune* (Jeffersonville, IN) (located online at www.newsandtribune.com/news/excavations-ongoing-near-clarksvillecemetery/article_0454e358-560e-11e7-89db-0352b5e7e823.html) (last accessed June 22, 2017).

Riding In, James
2000 Repatriation: A Pawnee's Perspective. In *Repatriation Reader: Who Owns American Indian Remains?*, edited by Devon A. Mihesuah, pp. 238–250. University of Nebraska Press, Lincoln.
Riding In, James, Cal Seciwa, Suzan Shown Harjo, and Walter Echo-Hawk
2004 Protecting Native American Human Remains, Burial Grounds, and Sacred Places: Panel Discussion, *Wicazo Sa Review* 19(2):169–183.
Riley, Linda P., Lynda L. LaMontagne, Joseph T. Hepworth, and Barbara A. Murphy
2007 Parental Grief Responses and Personal Growth following the Death of a Child, *Death Studies* 31:277–299.
Rivera, José Ignacio
1989 The Reburial of Our Ancestors: A Moral, Ethical, and Constitutional Dilemma for California, *News from Native California* 3(6):12–13.
Rojas-Perez, Isaias
2015 Unearthing Ongoing Pasts: Forensic Anthropology, State Making, and Justice Making in Postwar Peru. In *Disturbing Bodies: Perspectives on Forensic Anthropology,* edited by Zoë Crossland and Rosemary A. Joyce, pp. 41–62. SAR Press, Santa Fe, NM.
Rothstein, Richard
2017 *The Color of Law: A Forgotten History of How Our Government Segregated America.* Everlight Publishing, New York.
Rugg, Julie
2000 Defining the Place of Burial: What Makes a Cemetery a Cemetery? *Mortality* 5(3):259–275.
2022 Social Justice and Cemetery Systems, *Death Studies* 46(4):861–874.
Russell, Larry
2003 Stopping by a Cemetery on a Snowy Morning. *Journal of Loss and Trauma,* 8:221–227.
Sandberg, Russell
2023 *A Historical Introduction to English Law: Genesis of the Common Law.* Cambridge University Press, Cambridge.
Sanders, William
2020 Confederate Section of Cemetery Damaged, *Arkansas Democrat Gazette* (located online at www.arkansasonline.com/news/2020/jul/27/confederate-section-of-cemetery-damaged) (last accessed July 31, 2020).
Scarre, Chris
1995 *Chronicle of the Roman Emperors: The Reign-By-Reign Record of the Rulers of Imperial Rome.* London: Thames and Hudson.
Scheper-Hughes, Nancy
1992 *Death without Weeping: The Violence of Everyday Life in Brazil.* University of California Press, Berkeley.
Schexnayder, Jessica H., and Mary H. Manhein
2017 *Fragile Grounds: Louisiana's Endangered Cemeteries.* University Press of Mississippi, Jackson, MS.

Schneider, Alan L., and Paula A. Barran
2014 The Precedent-Setting Case of Kennewick Man. In *Kennewick Man: The Scientific Investigation of An Ancient American Skeleton,* edited by Douglas W. Owsley and Richard L. Jantz, pp. 90–107. Texas A&M Press, College Station.

Scott, Samuel Parsons (translator) and Robert I. Burns (editor)
2001 *Las Siete Partidas,* Vol. 1: *The Medieval Church: The World of Clerics and Laymen.* University of Pennsylvania Press, Philadelphia.

Seidemann, Ericka L.
1999 Analysis of the Nonmetric Traits of the Skull in the Poole-Rose Ossuary, Ontario, Canada. MA thesis, Louisiana State University.

Seidemann, Ryan M.
1999 Descriptive Analysis of Maya Skeletal Remains from Fighting Conch Mound, Wild Cane Cay, Belize. MA thesis, Louisiana State University.
2003 Time for a Change? The Kennewick Man Case and Its Implications for the Future of the Native American Graves Protection and Repatriation Act, *West Virginia Law Review* 106(1):150–176.
2004 Bones of Contention: A Comparative Examination of Law Governing Human Remains from Archaeological Contexts in Formerly Colonial Countries, *Louisiana Law Review* 64(3):545–588.
2007 Archaeology as an Environmental Protection Tool, *SAA Archaeological Record* 7(5):44–45.
2009 Altered Meanings: The Department of the Interior's Rewriting of the Native American Graves Protection and Repatriation Act to Regulate Unaffiliated Human Remains, *Temple Journal of Science, Technology, and Environmental Law* 28:1–47.
2010a NAGPRA at 20: What Have the States Done to Expand Human Remains Protections?, *Museum Anthropology* 33(2):199–209.
2010b Louisiana Attorney General Opinion No. 10-0018.
2010c Louisiana Attorney General Opinion No. 10-259.
2010d Louisiana Attorney General Opinion No. 10-0234.
2010e Louisiana Attorney General Opinion No. 10-0258.
2012 Twenty-Plus Years from NAGPRA: What Have the States Done?—A Comparative Review of Louisiana, Texas, Arkansas, and Oklahoma Burial Site Protection Laws. Paper presented at the 54th Annual Caddo Conference, Natchitoches, LA.
2013 How Do We Deal with All the Bodies? A Review of Recent Cemetery and Human Remains Legal Issues, *University of Baltimore Journal of Land and Development* 3:1–70.
2014a Do Not Disturb: A Practical Guide for What Not to Do around Cemeteries and Human Remains for the Louisiana Energy and Land Use Practitioner, *LSU Journal of Energy Law and Resources* 2(2):239–280.
2014b Hell on the Border: Revisionist History in Oak Cemetery, Fort Smith, Arkansas, *Markers* 29:54–77.
2014c Louisiana Attorney General Opinion No. 14-0101.
2017 The Influence of the Law on the Postmortem Narratives of Known and Unknown Human Remains. In *Studies in Forensic Biohistory: Anthropological Perspectives,*

edited by Christopher M. Stojanowski and William N. Duncan, pp. 124–142. Cambridge University Press, Cambridge.

2018a Requiescat in Pace: The Cemetery Dedication and Its Implications for Land Use in Louisiana and Beyond, *William & Mary Environmental Law & Policy Review* 42:895–922.

2018b The Sanctity of the Dead: Cemetery Protection Laws Are Not Takings of Private Property, *Southern University Law Review* 46:53–79.

2018c Shallow Material Culture Findings from Highland Cemetery (16EBR190), Baton Rouge, LA, *Louisiana Archaeology* 45:75–97.

2020 "Colonizing" the Dead: Former Colonial Nations' Treatment of Indigenous Peoples' Human Remains, *Baylor Law Review* 72(2):271–293.

2023 A Collective Sigh from Congress: The African American Burial Grounds Preservation Program, *SAA Archaeological Record* 23(2):6–8.

Seidemann, Ryan M., and Christine L. Halling

2019 Landscape Structural Violence: A View from New Orleans' Cemeteries, *American Antiquity* 84(4):669–683.

2020 Whose Job Is It Anyway? Recovering Louisiana's Dead after a Disaster, *Southern University Law Review* 48(1):1–37.

2022 Dirt for Sale—Desecration, Site Disturbance, or Insignificant Gimmick? The Archaeological and Legal Implications of "Cemetery Dirt" Sale Offerings on eBay. Paper presented at the 87th Society for American Archaeology Annual Meeting, Chicago.

2023 Disturbed Rest: The Destruction and Commemoration of An African-American Cemetery in Haughton, LA—A Collaboration of Archaeology, Ethnology, Law Enforcement, and Community. Paper presented at the 88th Society for American Archaeology Annual Meeting, Portland, OR.

Seidemann, Ryan M., and William T. Hawkins

2019 Acquisition and Disposition Problems and Experiences Policing the Online Marketplace for Human Remains. In *Forensic Archaeology: A Multidisciplinary Approach,* edited by K.S. Moran and C. Gold, pp. 299–312. Springer, New York.

Seidemann, Ryan M., and Kenneth P. Kleinpeter

2013 Truthing Remote Sensing: An Interim Report on Excavations at Historic Highland Cemetery in Baton Rouge (16EBR190). Presentation at the 15th Annual South Central Historical Archaeology Conference, Baton Rouge, LA.

2014 Restorative Excavations and Ground Truthing: Remote Sensing on the Cheap in Historic Highland Cemetery (16EBR190). Paper presented at the Society for American Archaeology Conference, Austin, TX.

Seidemann, Ryan M., and Rachel L. Moss

2009 Places Worth Saving: A Legal Guide to the Protection of Historic Cemeteries in Louisiana and Recommendations for Additional Protection, *Loyola Law Review* 55:449–516.

Seidemann, Ryan M., and Ericka L. Seidemann

2005 Where Art, Junk, and Death Blur: Holt Cemetery, New Orleans. *American Cemetery* Apr.:18–21, 32–33.

2020 A Grave Discovery: Iceland's Dual Burial Places of Agnes Magnúsdóttir and Friđrik Sigurđsson, *AGS Quarterly* 43(4):22–26.

Seidemann, Ryan M., Christine L. Halling, and Kenneth P. Kleinpeter

2016 An Intact Iron Casket from Highland Cemetery (16EBR190) in Baton Rouge, Louisiana. Paper presented at the Joint Annual Meetings of the Louisiana Archaeological Society and the Mississippi Archaeological Association, Natchez, MS.

Seidemann, Ryan M., Christopher M. Stojanowski, and Fredrick J. Rich

2009 The Identification of a Human Skull Recovered from an eBay Sale, *Journal of Forensic Sciences* 54(6):1247–1253.

Serafin, Nicholas

2022 Redefining the Badges of Slavery, *University of Richmond Law Review* 56:1291–1338.

Servello, A. Frank, Mark J. Richard, and Buck Rigg

2003 Historical Investigations and Monitoring of Undertakings in the Stonewall Cemetery Area, Barksdale Air Force Base, Bossier Parish, Louisiana. Unpublished report prepared for Barksdale Air Force Base by Archaeological Resource Consultants, Inc., Natchitoches, LA.

Shaffer, Mark

2004 Arizona University Faces $25 Million Lawsuit for Alleged Blood-Sample Misuse, *Indian Country Today* (March 10, 2004).

Shahzad, Maryam

2020 Residents Protest Development on Historic Black Cemetery in Bethesda, *Montgomery Community Media* (located online at www.mymcmedia.org/residents-protest-development-on-historic-black-cemetery-in-bethesda/#:~:text=Protesters%20gathered%20off%20of%20River,an%20unmarked%20historic%20Black%20cemetery.&text=%E2%80%9CIt%20is%20indecent%2C%20it%20is,apart%20an%20ancient%20African%20cemetery.%E2%80%9D) (last accessed Aug. 16, 2020).

Sharer, Robert J., and Wendy Ashmore

1993 *Archaeology: Discovering Our Past.* Mayfield Publishing Company: California City, CA.

Shea, Christopher

2000 The Return of Ishi's Brain, *Lingua Franca* 10(1):46–56.

Sheppard-Simms, Emma A.

2016 Islands of the Abject: Absence, Trauma, and Memory in the Cemetery Island, *Landscapes of Violence* 4(1): Article 2.

Shultz, Suzanne M.

2005 *Body Snatching: The Robbing of Graves for the Education of Physicians in Early Nineteenth Century America.* McFarland, Jefferson, NC.

Silverman, Helaine

2002 Introduction: The Space and Place of Death. In *The Space and Place of Death,* edited by Helaine Silverman and David B. Small, pp. 1–11. *Archaeological Papers of the American Anthropological Association* Number 11. American Anthropological Association, Arlington, VA.

Simerman, John

2016 "Witch" pleads guilty to theft of bones *** Marijuana also found during search. *Baton Rouge Advocate*, B1 (Sept. 10, 2016).

Simpson, Moira G.

2008 Indigenous Heritage and Repatriation—A Stimulus for Cultural Renewal. In *UTIMUT: Past Heritage-Future Partnerships: Discussions on Repatriation in the 21st Century*, edited by Mille Gabriel and Jens Dahl, pp. 134–147. Eks-Skolens Trykkeri, Copenhagen, Denmark.

Simon, Brona G.

2006 Collaboration between Archaeologists and Native Americans in Massachusetts: Preservation, Archaeology, and Native American Concerns in Balance. In *Cross-Cultural Collaboration: Native Peoples and Archaeology in the Northeastern United States*, edited by Jordan E. Kerber, pp. 44–58. University of Nebraska Press, Lincoln.

Skloot, Rebecca

2011 *The Immortal Life of Henrietta Lacks*. Crown Publishing, New York.

Sloane, David Charles

1991 *The Last Great Necessity: Cemeteries in American History*. Johns Hopkins University Press, Baltimore.

2018 *Is the Cemetery Dead?* University of Chicago Press, Chicago.

Smith, Jeffrey

2017 *The Rural Cemetery Movement: Places of Paradox in Nineteenth-Century America*. Lexington Books, Lanham, MD.

Smith, Jonathan

2009 Hidden and Sacred: African American Cemeteries in Eastern North Carolina. MA thesis, East Carolina University, Greenville, NC.

Smith, Rhonda L., and Donna K. Stone

2014 Exploratory Excavations at the Proposed Cemeteries Transit Center, Canal Boulevard and City Park Avenue, Addendum to Phase I/II Archaeological Investigations at the Proposed Site of the Canal Boulevard Transit Terminal at Charity Hospital Cemetery No. 2 (16OR108), New Orleans, Orleans Parish, Louisiana. Earth Search, Inc., New Orleans.

Snortland, J. Singe

1994 Northern Plains Woodland Mortuary Practices. In, *Skeletal Biology in the Great Plains: Migration, Warfare, Health, and Subsistence*, edited by Douglas W. Owsley and Richard L. Jantz, pp. 51–72. Smithsonian Institution Press, Washington, D.C.

Soanes, Catherine, and Angus Stevenson (editors)

2006 *Concise Oxford English Dictionary*, 11th ed. Oxford University Press, Oxford.

Somers, Brandon M.

2021 Addendum 1: New Additions to the Phase I Archaeological Investigation of the Greenfield Development on Robert Brothers' Farm in St. John the Baptist Parish, Louisiana. Unpublished report by Gulf South Research Corporation, Baton Rouge, LA.

Spatola, Brian F., and Kristen E. Pearlstein

2023 The Role of the US Army Surgeons and Their Contributions to the Army Medical Museum in the Post Civil-War Era (1865–1890). In *Archaeology and Bioarchaeology of Anatomical Dissection a Nineteenth-Century Army Hospital in San Francisco,* edited by P. Willey, Peter Gavette, Eric J. Bartelink, and Colleen F. Milligan, pp. 45–63. University Press of Florida, Gainesville.

Spott, Elizabeth K.

2010 An Overview of Variation in Archaeologically Observed Mortuary Practices: A Case Study Examining Grave Placement, Headstone Type and Epitaph Content in Two Slave Cemeteries, *Field Notes: A Journal of Collegiate Anthropology* 2(1):98–107.

Springate, Megan E.

2015 *Coffin Hardware in Nineteenth-Century America.* Left Coast Press, Walnut Creek, CA.

Stein, Peter

1999 *Roman Law in European History.* Cambridge University Press, Cambridge.

Stewart, David J.

2007 Gravestones and Monuments in the Maritime Cultural Landscape: Research Potential and Preliminary Interpretations, *International Journal of Nautical Archaeology* 36(1):112–124.

Stinson, Judith M.

2010 Why Dicta Becomes Holding and Why It Matters, *Brooklyn Law Review* 76:219–264.

Stone, Pamela K.

2020 Female Beauty, Bodies, Binding, and the Bioarchaeology of Structural Violence in the Industrial Era through the Lens of Critical White Feminism. In *The Bioarchaeology of Structural Violence: A Theoretical Framework for Industrial Era Inequality,* edited by Lori A. Tremblay and Sarah Reedy, pp. 13–30. Springer, Cham, Switzerland.

Strangstad, Lynn

1995 *A Graveyard Preservation Primer.* American Association for State and Local History, Nashville, TN.

Stutz, Liv Nilsson

2013 Claims to the Past: A Critical Review of the Arguments Driving Repatriation of Cultural Heritage and Their Role in Contemporary Identity Politics, *Journal of Intervention and Statebuilding* 7(2):170–195.

Tesar, Louis D.

1986 Grave Robbing: Are the Guilty Innocent?, *Florida Anthropologist* 39(4):299.

Thom, Evelyn M.

2005 [1974] Highland Cemetery Preserved! Unpublished manuscript originally compiled in 1974 and updated in 2005.

Thomas, David Hurst

2000 *Skull Wars: Kennewick Man, Archaeology, and the Battle for Native American Identity.* Basic Books, New York.

Thomas, Larissa, Gary Joiner, and William Stanyard
2010 *Old Gravel Point Cemetery: The ETC Tiger Pipeline Project: Restoring a Historic Burial Place in DeSoto Parish, Louisiana.* Houston: Energy Transfer.
Thomas, Stephen B., and Sandra Crouse Quinn
1991 The Tuskegee Syphilis Study, 1932 to 1972: Implications for HIV Education and AIDS Risk Education Programs in the Black Community, *American Journal of Public Health* 81(11):1498–1505.
Tom, J. Dwight
2016 Easement Come, Easement Go—The Cemetery Access Easement: The Exception to the Right to Exclude Whose Time Has Come to Facilitate the Preservation of Nineteenth-Century Texas Family Cemeteries, *Environs: Environmental Law and Policy Journal* 39:173–202.
Toner, Mike
2020 As NAGPRA Turns Thirty, *American Archaeology* 24(3):40–46.
Tremblay, Lori A., and Sarah Reedy
2020 Introduction. In *The Bioarchaeology of Structural Violence: A Theoretical Framework for Industrial Era Inequality,* edited by Lori A. Tremblay and Sarah Reedy, pp. 1–9. Springer, Cham, Switzerland.
Trope, Jack F.
2013 The Case for NAGPRA. In, *Accomplishing NAGPRA: Perspectives on the Intent, Impact, and Future of the Native American Graves Protection and Repatriation Act,* edited by Sangita Chari and Jaime M. N. Lavallee, pp.19–54. Oregon State University Press, Corvallis.
Trouillot, Michel-Rolph
2015 *Silencing the Past: Power and the Production of History.* Beacon Press, Boston.
Tsosie, Krystal S., Joseph M. Yracheta, Jessica Kolopenuk, and Rick W. A. Smith
2020 Indigenous Data Sovereignties and Data Sharing in Biological Anthropology, *American Journal of Physical Anthropology.* 174(2):183–186.
Tsosie, Rebecca
2004 Introduction. In Protecting Native American Human Remains, Burial Grounds, and Sacred Places: Panel Discussion, by James Riding In, Cal Seciwa, Suzan Shown Harjo, Walter R. Echo-Hawk, and Rebecca Tsosie, *Wicazo Sa Review* 19(2):169–183.
2012 NAGPRA and the Problem of "Culturally Unidentifiable" Remains. *Arizona State Law Journal* 44:809–905.
Turnbull, Paul
1991 Ramsay's Regime: The Australian Museum and the Procurement of Aboriginal Bodies, c. 1874–1900, *Aboriginal History* 15:108–121.
Ubelaker, Douglas H.
1994 *Human Skeletal Remains: Excavation, Analysis, Interpretation,* 2nd ed. Taraxacum, Washington, D.C.
Ubelaker, Douglas H., and Lauryn Guttenplan Grant
1989 Human Skeletal Remains: Preservation or Reburial?, *Yearbook of Physical Anthropology* 32:249–287.

Upton, Dell

2008 *Another City: Urban Life and Urban Spaces in the New American Republic.* Yale University Press, New Haven, CT.

Vanderstraeten, Raf

2014 Burying and Remembering the Dead, *Memory Studies* 7(4):457–471.

Van Sickle, C. E.

1928 The Headings of Rescripts of the Severi in the Justinian Code, *Classical Philology* 23(3):270–277.

Vatomsky, Sonya

2018 The Mysterious Murder Case That's Captivated Iceland for Nearly 200 Years. *Mental Floss* (available online at http://mentalfloss.com/article/524143/mysterious-murder-case-thats-captivated-iceland-nearly-200-years) (last visited Aug. 16, 2019).

Veit, Richard F., and Alasdair M. Brooks

2011 Religious Sites in Historical Archaeology: An Introduction. In *Perspectives from Historical Archaeology Number 4: Mortuary and Religious Sites,* edited by Richard F. Veit and Alasdair M. Brooks, pp.1–19. Society for Historical Archaeology, Germantown, MD.

Walls, Samuel

2011 "Lest We Forget": The Spatial Dynamics of the Church and Churchyard as Commemorative Spaces for the War Dead in the Twentieth Century, *Mortality* 16(2):131–144.

Watkin, Thomas Glyn

2007 *The Legal History of Wales.* University of Wales Press, Cardiff.

Watkins, Joe

2008 Who's Right and What's Left on the Middle Ground? Repatriation as Political Action. In *UTIMUT: Past Heritage-Future Partnerships: Discussions on Repatriation in the 21st Century,* edited by Mille Gabriel and Jens Dahl, pp. 134–147. Eks-Skolens Trykkeri, Copenhagen, Denmark.

2020 SAA Celebrates 30 Years of NAGPRA, Begins Revision of Statement on the Treatment of Human Remains (open email to SAA membership dated Nov. 9, 2020).

Weinstein, Richard A., David B. Kelley, and Joe W. Saunders (editors)

2004 *The Louisiana and Arkansas Expeditions of Clarence Bloomfield Moore.* Classics in Southeastern Archaeology. University of Alabama Press, Tuscaloosa, AL.

Weiss, Elizabeth

2008 *Reburying the Past: The Effects of Repatriation and Reburial on Scientific Inquiry.* Nova Science Publishers, New York.

Weiss, Elizabeth, and James W. Springer

2020 *Repatriation and Erasing the Past.* University of Florida Press, Gainesville.

2023 Bone Wars: How Activists Are Targeting Teaching, *Skeptic Magazine* 28(3):30–35.

Wellons, Sovi-Mya, Ryan M. Seidemann, and Christine L. Halling

2024 Tourist Trinket, Religious Object, Human Remains, or Something Else: Kapalas in the Online Market. Paper presented at the 79th Society for American Archaeology annual meeting, New Orleans, LA.

West, Sharon Crook, and Joseph P. McKerns

2009 Death and Communists: The Funeral Industry's Attack on Jessica Mitford's *The American Way of Death, American Journalism* 26(1):31–53.

Wheeler, Ryan J.

2013 Florida's Unmarked Human Burial Law: A Retrospective 1987–2010, *Florida Anthropologist* 66(3):75–88.

White, Samuel Stockton

2014 The Anzick Site: Cultural Balance and the Treatment of Ancient Human Remains (Toward a Collaborative Standard). MA thesis, University of Montana, Missoula.

Whitehead, Neil

2010 Demon Landscapes: Sacrificial Architecture and Monumental Death, *Landscapes of Violence* 1(1): Article 2.

Wilkerson, Isabel

2010 *The Warmth of Other Suns: The Epic Story of America's Great Migration.* Vintage, New York.

2020 *Caste: The Origins of Our Discontents.* Random House, New York.

Wilkie, Laurie A.

2005 Inessential Archaeologies: Problems of Exclusion in Americanist Archaeological Thought, *World Archaeology* 37(3):337–351.

Williams, John A.

1994 Disease Profiles of Archaic and Woodland Populations in the Northern Plains. In *Skeletal Biology in the Great Plains: Migration, Warfare, Health, and Subsistence,* edited by Douglas W. Owsley and Richard L. Jantz, pp. 91–108. Smithsonian Institution Press, Washington, D.C.

Williams, Paul

2007 *Memorial Museums: The Global Rush to Commemorate Atrocities.* Berg, Oxford.

Willoughby, Christopher D. E.

2022 *Masters of Health: Racial Science and Slavery in U.S. Medical Schools.* University of North Carolina Press, Chapel Hill.

Woodthorpe, Kate

2011 Sustaining the Contemporary Cemetery: Implementing Policy alongside Conflicting Perspectives and Purpose, *Mortality* 16(3): 259–276.

Worpole, Ken

2003 *Last Landscapes: The Architecture of the Cemetery in the West.* Reaktion Books, London.

Wright, Alice P.

2015 Private Property, Public Archaeology: Resident Communities as Stakeholders in American Archaeology, *World Archaeology* 47(2):212–224.

Wright, Roberta Hughes, and Wilbur B. Hughes III

1996 *Lay Down Body: Living History in African American Cemeteries.* Visible Ink Press, Detroit.

Wyndham, Marivic, and Peter Read
2011 The Cemetery, the State and the Exiles: A Study of Cementerio Colón, Havana, and Woodlawn Cemetery, Miami, *PORTAL: Journal of Multidisciplinary International Studies* 8(1):1–19.

Yanner, Keith M., and Steven J. Ybarrola
2003 "He Didn't Have No Cross": Tombs and Graves as Racial Boundary Tactics on a Louisiana Barrier Island. *Oral History Review* 30(2):1–28.

Yiannopoulos, A. N.
1992 The 20th John M. Tucker, Jr. Lecture in Civil Law: Two Critical Years in the Life of the Louisiana Civil Code: 1870 and 1913, *Louisiana Law Review* 53:5–33.

Zimmerman, Larry J.
2007 Plains Indians and Resistance to "Public" Heritage Commemoration of Their Pasts. In *Cultural Heritage and Human Rights,* edited by H. Silverman and D. F. Ruggles, pp. 144–158. Springer, New York.
2014 Repatriation Acts: Before NAGPRA, in *Encyclopedia of Global Archaeology,* edited by Claire Smith, pp. 6298–6303. Springer-Verlag: New York.

Zöega, Guðný
2016 Life on the Edge of the Arctic: The Bioarchaeology of the Keldudalur Cemetery in Skagafjörður, Iceland, *International Journal of Osteoarchaeology* 26:574–584.

Zuckerman, Molly K.
2021 Gender in Bioarchaeology. In *Theoretical Approaches in Bioarchaeology,* edited by Colleen M. Cheverko, Julia R. Prince-Buitenhuys, and Mark Hubbe, pp. 28–44. Routledge, London.

Þorgrímsdóttir, Sigrún Huld
2005 Agnes og Friðrik fyrirog eftir dauðann, *Menningarblað/Lesbók* (available online at www.mbl.is/greinasafn/grein/1018633/ [access requires authentication]) (last visited July 27, 2019).

INDEX

Page numbers followed by *f* and *t* indicate figures and tables.

Ryan M. Seidemann is a former Louisiana assistant attorney general and is now the general counsel for The Water Institute in Baton Rouge. He also holds appointments as adjunct professor of law at the Southern University Law Center in Baton Rouge, adjunct professor in the anthropology and sociology and the planning and urban studies departments at the University of New Orleans, and and faculty associate in the School of Human Evolution and Social Change at Arizona State University. Seidemann is the founding chairman of the Louisiana Cemetery Response Task Force (2018–2024), the executive director of the North American Death Care Regulators Association, and on the board of trustees of the Association for Gravestone Studies.

www.ingramcontent.com/pod-product-compliance
Lightning Source LLC
Chambersburg PA
CBHW051400160826
49871CB00062B/130
9781683405108